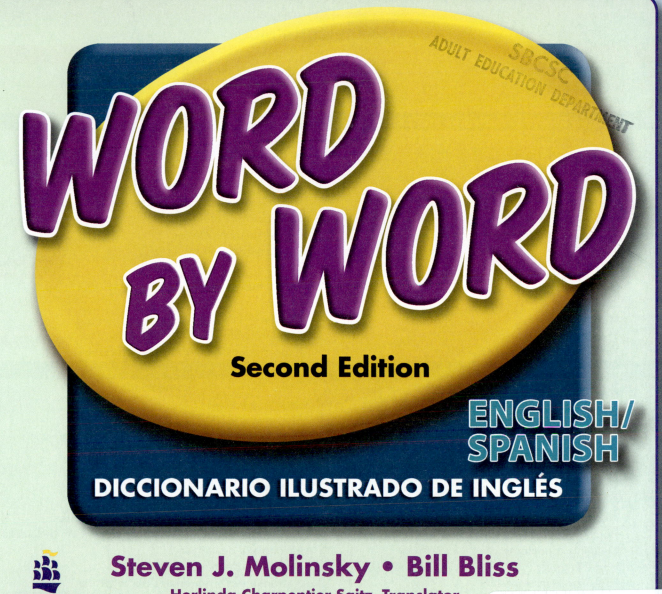

WORD BY WORD

Second Edition

ENGLISH/SPANISH

DICCIONARIO ILUSTRADO DE INGLÉS

Steven J. Molinsky • Bill Bliss

Herlinda Charpentier Saitz, Translator

Illustrated by
Richard E. Hill

PEARSON
Longman

D0226387

Word by Word Picture Dictionary,
English/Spanish second edition

Pearson Education, 10 Bank Street, White Plains, NY 10606

Editorial director: Pam Fishman
Vice president, director of design and
production: Rhea Banker
Director of electronic production: Aliza Greenblatt
Director of manufacturing: Patrice Fraccio
Senior manufacturing manager: Edith Pullman
Marketing manager: Oliva Fernandez
Editorial assistant: Katherine Keyes
Senior digital layout specialist: Wendy Wolf

Text design: Wendy Wolf
Cover design: Tracey Munz Cataldo
Realia creation: Warren Fischbach, Paula Williams
Illustrations: Richard E. Hill
Contributing artists: Steven Young, Charles Cawley,
Willard Gage, Marlon Violette
Reviewers: Marta E. Luján, The University of Texas at Austin;
Carmen Schlig, Georgia State University;
Project management by TransPac Education Services,
Victoria, BC, Canada with assistance from Yu Jian Yo,
Studio G, Robert Zacharias, & Susa Oñate

ISBN 0-13-191626-2
Longman on the Web
Longman.com offers online resources for teachers and
students. Access our Companion Websites, our online
catalog, and our local offices around the world.

Visit us at longman.com.

Printed in the United States of America
1 2 3 4 5 6 7 8 9 10 – RRD – 11 10 09 08 07 06

CONTENTS

ÍNDICE/CONTENIDO

Unit / Theme	Communication Skills	Writing & Discussion
1 Personal Information and Family	• Asking for & giving personal information • Identifying information on a form • Spelling name aloud • Identifying family members • Introducing others	• Telling about yourself • Telling about family members • Drawing a family tree
2 Common Everyday Activities and Language	• Identifying classroom objects & locations • Identifying classroom actions • Giving & following simple classroom commands • Identifying everyday & leisure activities • Inquiring by phone about a person's activities • Asking about a person's plan for future activities • Social communication: Greeting people, Leave taking, Introducing yourself & others, Getting someone's attention, Expressing gratitude, Saying you don't understand, Calling someone on the telephone • Describing the weather • Interpreting temperatures on a thermometer (Fahrenheit & Centigrade) • Describing the weather forecast for tomorrow	• Describing a classroom • Making a list of daily activities • Describing daily routine • Making a list of planned activities • Describing favorite leisure activities • Describing the weather
3 Numbers/ Time/ Money/ Calendar	• Using cardinal & ordinal numbers • Giving information about age, number of family members, residence • Telling time • Indicating time of events • Asking for information about arrival & departure times • Identifying coins & currency – names & values • Making & asking for change • Identifying days of the week • Identifying months of the year • Asking about the year, month, day, date • Asking about the date of a birthday, anniversary, appointment • Giving date of birth	• Describing numbers of students in a class • Identifying a country's population • Describing daily schedule with times • Telling about time management • Telling about the use of time in different cultures or countries • Describing the cost of purchases • Describing coins & currency of other countries • Describing weekday & weekend activities • Telling about favorite day of the week & month of the year
4 Home	• Identifying types of housing & communities • Requesting a taxi • Calling 911 for an ambulance • Identifying rooms of a home • Identifying furniture • Complimenting • Asking for information in a store • Locating items in a store • Asking about items on sale • Asking the location of items at home • Telling about past weekend activities • Identifying locations in an apartment building • Identifying ways to look for housing: classified ads, listings, vacancy signs • Renting an apartment • Describing household problems • Securing home repair services • Making a suggestion • Identifying household cleaning items, home supplies, & tools • Asking to borrow an item • Describing current home activities & plans for future activities	• Describing types of housing where people live • Describing rooms & furniture in a residence • Telling about baby products & early child-rearing practices in different countries • Telling about personal experiences with repairing things • Describing an apartment building • Describing household cleaning chores
5 Community	• Identifying places in the community • Exchanging greetings • Asking & giving the location of places in the community • Identifying government buildings, services, & other places in a city/town center • Identifying modes of transportation in a city/town center	• Describing places in a neighborhood • Making a list of places, people, & actions observed at an intersection

Unit / Theme	Communication Skills	Writing & Discussion
6 Describing	• Describing people by age • Describing people by physical characteristics • Describing a suspect or missing person to a police officer • Describing people & things using adjectives • Describing physical states & emotions • Expressing concern about another person's physical state or emotion	• Describing physical characteristics of yourself & family members • Describing physical characteristics of a favorite actor or actress or other famous person • Describing things at home & in the community • Telling about personal experiences with different emotions
7 Food	• Identifying food items (fruits, vegetables, meat, poultry, seafood, dairy products, juices, beverages, deli, frozen foods, snack foods, groceries) • Identifying non-food items purchased in a supermarket (e.g., household supplies, baby products, pet food) • Determining food needs to make a shopping list • Asking the location of items in a supermarket • Identifying supermarket sections • Requesting items at a service counter in a supermarket • Identifying supermarket checkout area personnel & items • Identifying food containers & quantities • Identifying units of measure • Asking for & giving recipe instructions • Complimenting someone on a recipe • Offering to help with food preparation • Identifying food preparation actions • Identifying kitchen utensils & cookware • Asking to borrow an item • Comprehending product advertising • Ordering fast food items, coffee shop items, & sandwiches • Indicating a shortage of supplies to a co-worker or supervisor • Taking customers' orders at a food service counter • Identifying restaurant objects, personnel, & actions • Making & following requests at work • Identifying & correctly positioning silverware & plates in a table setting • Inquiring in person about restaurant job openings • Ordering from a restaurant menu • Taking customers' orders as a waiter or waitress in a restaurant	• Describing favorite & least favorite foods • Describing foods in different countries • Making a shopping list • Describing places to shop for food • Telling about differences between supermarkets & food stores in different countries • Making a list of items in kitchen cabinets & the refrigerator • Describing recycling practices • Describing a favorite recipe using units of measure • Telling about use of kitchen utensils & cookware • Telling about experience with different types of restaurants • Describing restaurants and menus in different countries • Describing favorite foods ordered in restaurants
8 Colors and Clothing	• Identifying colors • Complimenting someone on clothing • Identifying clothing items, including outerwear, sleepwear, underwear, exercise clothing, footwear, jewelry, & accessories • Talking about appropriate clothing for different weather conditions • Expressing clothing needs to a store salesperson • Locating clothing items • Inquiring about ownership of found clothing items • Indicating loss of a clothing item • Asking about sale prices in a clothing store • Reporting theft of a clothing item to the police • Stating preferences during clothing shopping • Expressing problems with clothing & the need for alterations • Identifying laundry objects & activities • Locating laundry products in a store	• Describing the flags of different countries • Telling about emotions associated with different colors • Telling about clothing & colors you like to wear • Describing clothing worn at different occasions (e.g., going to schools, parties, weddings) • Telling about clothing worn in different weather conditions • Telling about clothing worn during exercise activities • Telling about footwear worn during different activities • Describing the color, material, size, & pattern of favorite clothing items • Comparing clothing fashions now & a long time ago • Telling about who does laundry at home

Unit / Theme	Communication Skills	Writing & Discussion
9 Shopping	• Identifying departments & services in a department store • Asking the location of items in a department store • Asking to buy, return, exchange, try on, & pay for department store items • Asking about regular & sales prices, discounts, & sales tax • Interpreting a sales receipt • Offering assistance to customers as a salesperson • Expressing needs to a salesperson in a store • Identifying electronics products, including video & audio equipment, telephones, cameras, & computers • Identifying components of a computer & common computer software • Complimenting someone about an item & inquiring where it was purchased • Asking a salesperson for advice about different brands of a product • Identifying common toys & other items in a toy store • Asking for advice about an appropriate gift for a child	• Describing a department store • Telling about stores that have sales • Telling about an item purchased on sale • Comparing different types & brands of video & audio equipment • Describing telephones & cameras • Describing personal use of a computer • Sharing opinions about how computers have changed the world • Telling about popular toys in different countries • Telling about favorite childhood toys
10 Community Services	• Requesting bank services & transactions (e.g., deposit, withdrawal, cashing a check, obtaining traveler's checks, opening an account, applying for a loan, exchanging currency) • Identifying bank personnel • Identifying bank forms • Asking about acceptable forms of payment (cash, check, credit card, money order, traveler's check) • Identifying household bills (rent, utilities, etc.) • Identifying family finance documents & actions • Following instructions to use an ATM machine • Requesting post office services & transactions • Identifying types of mail & mail services • Identifying different ways to buy stamps • Requesting non-mail services available at the post office (money order, selective service registration, passport application) • Identifying & locating library sections, services, & personnel • Asking how to find a book in the library • Identifying community institutions, services, and personnel (police, fire, city government, public works, recreation, sanitation, religious institutions) • Identifying types of emergency vehicles • Reporting a crime • Identifying community mishaps (gas leak, water main break, etc.) • Expressing concern about community problems	• Describing use of bank services • Telling about household bills & amounts paid • Telling about the person responsible for household finances • Describing use of ATM machines • Describing use of postal services • Comparing postal systems in different countries • Telling about experience using a library • Telling about the location of community institutions • Describing experiences using community institutions • Telling about crime in the community • Describing experience with a crime or emergency
11 Health	• Identifying parts of the body & key internal organs • Describing ailments, symptoms, & injuries • Asking about the health of another person • Identifying items in a first-aid kit • Describing medical emergencies • Identifying emergency medical procedures (CPR, rescue breathing, Heimlich maneuver) • Calling 911 to report a medical emergency • Identifying major illnesses • Talking with a friend or co-worker about illness in one's family • Following instructions during a medical examination • Identifying medical personnel, equipment, & supplies in medical & dental offices • Understanding medical & dental personnel's description of procedures during treatment • Understanding a doctor's medical advice and instructions • Identifying over-the-counter medications • Understanding dosage instructions on medicine labels • Identifying medical specialists • Indicating the date & time of a medical appointment • Identifying hospital departments & personnel • Identifying equipment in a hospital room • Identifying actions & items related to personal hygiene • Locating personal care products in a store • Identifying actions & items related to baby care	• Describing self • Telling about a personal experience with an illness or injury • Describing remedies or treatments for common problems (cold, stomachache, insect bite, hiccups) • Describing experience with a medical emergency • Describing a medical examination • Describing experience with a medical or dental procedure • Telling about medical advice received • Telling about over-the-counter medications used • Comparing use of medications in different countries • Describing experience with a medical specialist • Describing a hospital stay • Making a list of personal care items needed for a trip • Comparing baby products in different countries

Unit / Theme	Communication Skills	Writing & Discussion

12 **School, Subjects, and Activities**	• Identifying types of educational institutions
	• Giving information about previous education during a job interview
	• Identifying school locations & personnel
	• Identifying school subjects
	• Identifying extracurricular activities
	• Sharing after-school plans
	• MATH:
	  • Asking & answering basic questions during a math class
	  • Using fractions to indicate sale prices
	  • Using percents to indicate test scores & probability in weather forecasts
	  • Identifying high school math subjects
	  • Using measurement terms to indicate height, width, depth, length, distance
	  • Interpreting metric measurements
	  • Identifying types of lines, geometric shapes, & solid figures
	• ENGLISH LANGUAGE ARTS:
	  • Identifying types of sentences
	  • Identifying parts of speech
	  • Identifying punctuation marks
	  • Providing feedback during peer-editing
	  • Identifying steps of the writing process
	  • Identifying types of literature
	  • Identifying forms of writing
	• GEOGRAPHY:
	  • Identifying geographical features & bodies of water
	  • Identifying natural environments (desert, jungle, rainforest, etc.)
	• SCIENCE:
	  • Identifying science classroom/laboratory equipment
	  • Asking about equipment needed to do a science procedure
	  • Identifying steps of the scientific method
	  • Identifying key terms to describe the universe, solar system, & space exploration
		• Telling about different types of schools in the community
		• Telling about schools attended, where, when, & subjects studied
		• Describing a school
		• Comparing schools in different countries
		• Telling about favorite school subject
		• Telling about extracurricular activities
		• Comparing extracurricular activities in different countries
		• Describing math education
		• Telling about something bought on sale
		• Researching & sharing information about population statistics using percents
		• Describing favorite books & authors
		• Describing newspapers & magazines read
		• Telling about use of different types of written communication
		• Describing the geography of your country
		• Describing geographical features experienced
		• Describing experience with scientific equipment
		• Describing science education
		• Brainstorming a science experiment & describing each step of the scientific method
		• Drawing & naming a constellation
		• Expressing an opinion about the importance of space exploration

13 **Work**	• Identifying occupations • Stating work experience (including length of time in an occupation) during a job interview • Talking about occupation during social conversation • Expressing job aspirations • Identifying job skills & work activities • Indicating job skills during an interview (including length of time) • Identifying types of job advertisements (help wanted signs, job notices, classified ads) • Interpreting abbreviations in job advertisements • Identifying each step in a job-search process • Identifying workplace locations, furniture, equipment, & personnel • Identifying common office tasks • Asking the location of a co-worker • Engaging in small-talk with co-workers • Identifying common office supplies • Making requests at work • Repeating to confirm understanding of a request or instruction • Identifying factory locations, equipment, & personnel • Asking the location of workplace departments & personnel to orient oneself as a new employee • Asking about the location & activities of a co-worker • Identifying construction site machinery, equipment, and building materials • Asking a co-worker for a workplace item • Warning a co-worker of a safety hazard • Asking whether there is a sufficient supply of workplace materials • Identifying job safety equipment • Interpreting warning signs at work • Reminding someone to use safety equipment • Asking the location of emergency equipment at work	• Career exploration: sharing ideas about occupations that are interesting, difficult • Describing occupation & occupations of family members • Describing job skills • Describing a familiar job (skill requirements, qualifications, hours, salary) • Telling about how people found their jobs • Telling about experience with a job search or job interview • Describing a familiar workplace • Telling about office & school supplies used • Describing a nearby factory & working conditions there • Comparing products produced by factories in different countries • Describing building materials used in ones dwelling • Describing a nearby construction site • Telling about experience with safety equipment • Describing the use of safety equipment in the community

Unit / Theme	Communication Skills	Writing & Discussion
14 **Transportation and Travel**	• Identifying modes of local & inter-city public transportation • Expressing intended mode of travel • Asking about a location to obtain transportation (bus stop, bus station, train station, subway station) • Locating ticket counters, information booths, fare card machines, & information signage in transportation stations • Identifying types of vehicles • Indicating to a car salesperson need for a type of vehicle • Describing a car accident • Identifying parts of a car & maintenance items • Indicating a problem with a car • Requesting service or assistance at a service station • Identifying types of highway lanes & markings, road structures (tunnels, bridges, etc.), traffic signage, & local intersection road markings • Reporting the location of an accident • Giving & following driving directions (using prepositions of motion) • Interpreting traffic signs • Warning a driver about an upcoming sign • Interpreting compass directions • Asking for driving directions • Following instructions during a driver's test • Repeating to confirm instructions • Identifying airport locations & personnel (check-in, security, gate, baggage claim, Customs & Immigration) • Asking for location of places & personnel at an airport • Indicating loss of travel documents or other items • Identifying airplane sections, seating areas, emergency equipment, & flight personnel • Identifying steps in the process of airplane travel (actions in the security area, at the gate, boarding, & being seated) • Following instructions of airport security personnel, gate attendants, & flight crew • Identifying sections of a hotel & personnel • Asking for location of places & personnel in a hotel	• Describing mode of travel to different places in the community • Describing local public transportation • Comparing transportation in different countries • Telling about common types of vehicles in different countries • Expressing opinion about favorite type of vehicle & manufacturer • Expressing opinion about most important features to look for when making a car purchase • Describing experience with car repairs • Describing a local highway • Describing a local intersection • Telling about dangerous traffic areas where many accidents occur • Describing your route from home to school • Describing how to get to different places from home and school • Describing local traffic signs • Comparing traffic signs in different countries • Describing a familiar airport • Telling about an experience with Customs & Immigration • Describing an air travel experience • Using imagination: being an airport security officer giving passengers instructions; being a flight attendant giving passengers instructions before take-off • Describing a familiar hotel • Expressing opinion about hotel jobs that are most interesting, most difficult
15 **Recreation and Entertainment**	• Identifying common hobbies, crafts, & games & related materials/equipment • Describing favorite leisure activities • Purchasing craft supplies, equipment, & other products in a store • Asking for & offering a suggestion for a leisure activity • Identifying places to go for outdoor recreation, entertainment, culture, etc. • Describing past weekend activities • Describing activities planned for a future day off or weekend • Identifying features & equipment in a park & playground • Asking the location of a park feature or equipment • Warning a child to be careful on playground equipment • Identifying features of a beach, common beach items, & personnel • Identifying indoor & outdoor recreation activities & sports, & related equipment & supplies • Asking if someone remembered an item when preparing for an activity • Identifying team sports & terms for players, playing fields, & equipment • Commenting on a player's performance during a game • Indicating that you can't find an item • Asking the location of sports equipment in a store • Reminding someone of items needed for a sports activity • Identifying types of winter/water sports, recreation, & equipment • Engaging in small talk about favorite sports & recreation activities • Using the telephone to inquire whether a store sells a product • Making & responding to an invitation • Following a teacher or coach's instructions during sports practice, P.E. class, & an exercise class • Identifying types of entertainment & cultural events, & the performers • Commenting on a performance • Identifying genres of music, plays, movies, & TV programs • Expressing likes about types of entertainment • Identifying musical instruments • Complimenting someone on musical ability	• Describing a favorite hobby, craft, or game • Comparing popular games in different countries, and how to play them • Describing favorite places to go & activities there • Describing a local park & playground • Describing a favorite beach & items used there • Describing an outdoor recreation experience • Describing favorite individual sports & recreation activities • Describing favorite team sports & famous players • Comparing popular sports in different countries • Describing experience with winter or water sports & recreation • Expressing opinions about Winter Olympics sports (most exciting, most dangerous) • Describing exercise habits & routines • Using imagination: being an exercise instructor leading a class • Telling about favorite types of entertainment • Comparing types of entertainment popular in different countries • Telling about favorite performers • Telling about favorite types of music, movies, & TV programs • Describing experience with a musical instrument • Comparing typical musical instruments in different countries

Unit / Theme	Communication Skills	Writing & Discussion
16 **Nature**	• Identifying places & people on a farm • Identifying farm animals & crops • Identifying animals & pets • Identifying birds & insects • Identifying fish, sea animals, amphibians, & reptiles • Asking about the presence of wildlife in an area • Identifying trees, plants, & flowers • Identifying key parts of a tree and flower • Asking for information about trees & flowers • Warning someone about poisonous vegetation in an area • Identifying sources of energy • Describing the kind of energy used to heat homes & for cooking • Expressing an opinion about good future sources of energy • Identifying behaviors that promote conservation (recycling, conserving energy, conserving water, carpooling) • Expressing concern about environmental problems • Identifying different kinds of natural disasters	• Comparing farms in different countries • Telling about local animals, animals in a zoo, & common local birds & insects • Comparing common pets in different countries • Using imagination: what animal you would like to be, & why • Telling a popular folk tale or children's story about animals, birds, or insects • Describing fish, sea animals, & reptiles in different countries • Identifying endangered species • Expressing opinions about wildlife – most interesting, beautiful, dangerous • Describing local trees & flowers, & favorites • Comparing different cultures' use of flowers at weddings, funerals, holidays, & hospitals • Expressing an opinion about an environmental problem • Telling about how people prepare for natural disasters
17 **U.S. Civics**	• Producing correct form of identification when requested (driver's license, social security card, student I.D. card, employee I.D. badge, permanent resident card, passport, visa, work permit, birth certificate, proof of residence) • Identifying the three branches of U.S. government (legislative, executive, judicial) & their functions • Identifying senators, representatives, the president, vice-president, cabinet, Supreme Court justices, & the chief justice, & the branches of government in which they work • Identifying the key buildings in each branch of government (Capitol Building, White House, Supreme Court Building) • Identifying the Constitution as "the supreme law of the land" • Identifying the Bill of Rights • Naming freedoms guaranteed by the 1st Amendment • Identifying key amendments to the Constitution • Identifying key events in United States history • Answering history questions about events and the dates they occurred • Identifying key holidays & dates they occur • Identifying legal system & court procedures (arrest, booking, obtaining legal representation, appearing in court, standing trial, acquittal, conviction, sentencing, prison, release) • Identifying people in the criminal justice system • Engaging in small talk about a TV crime show's characters & plot • Identifying rights & responsibilities of U.S. citizens • Identifying steps in applying for citizenship	• Telling about forms of identification & when needed • Describing how people in a community "exercise their 1st Amendment rights" • Brainstorming ideas for a new amendment to the Constitution • Expressing an opinion about the most important event in United States history • Telling about important events in the history of different countries • Describing U.S. holidays you celebrate • Describing holidays celebrated in different countries • Describing the legal system in different countries • Telling about an episode of a TV crime show • Expressing an opinion about the most important rights & responsibilities of people in their communities • Expressing an opinion about the rights of citizens vs. non-citizens

Welcome to the second edition of the WORD BY WORD Picture Dictionary! This text presents more than 4,000 vocabulary words through vibrant illustrations and simple accessible lesson pages that are designed for clarity and ease-of-use with learners at all levels. Our goal is to prepare students for success using English in everyday life, in the community, in school, and at work.

WORD BY WORD organizes the vocabulary into 17 thematic units, providing a careful research-based sequence of lessons that integrates students' development of grammar and vocabulary skills through topics that begin with the immediate world of the student and progress to the world at large. Early lessons on the family, the home, and daily activities lead to lessons on the community, school, workplace, shopping, recreation, and other topics. The text offers extensive coverage of important lifeskill competencies and the vocabulary of school subjects and extracurricular activities, and it is designed to meet the objectives of current national, state, and local standards-based curricula you can find in the Scope & Sequence on the previous pages.

Since each lesson in *Word by Word* is self-contained, it can be used either sequentially or in any desired order. For users' convenience, the lessons are listed in two ways: sequentially in the Table of Contents, and alphabetically in the Thematic Index. These resources, combined with the Glossary in the appendix, allow students and teachers to quickly and easily locate all words and topics in the Picture Dictionary.

The *Word by Word* Picture Dictionary is the centerpiece of the complete *Word by Word* Vocabulary Development Program, which offers a wide selection of print and media support materials for instruction at all levels.

A unique choice of workbooks at Beginning and Intermediate levels offers flexible options to meet students' needs. Vocabulary Workbooks feature motivating vocabulary, grammar, and listening practice, and standards-based Lifeskills Workbooks provide competency-based activities and reading tied to national, state, and local curriculum frameworks. A Literacy Workbook is also available.

The Teacher's Guide and Lesson Planner with CD-ROM includes lesson-planning suggestions, community tasks, Internet weblinks, and reproducible masters to save teachers hours of lesson preparation time. An Activity Handbook with step-by-step teaching strategies for key vocabulary development activities is included in the Teacher's Guide.

The Audio Program includes all words and conversations for interactive practice and —as bonus material—an expanded selection of WordSongs for entertaining musical practice with the vocabulary.

Additional ancillary materials include Color Transparencies, Vocabulary Game Cards, and a Testing Program. Bilingual Editions are also available.

Teaching Strategies

Word by Word presents vocabulary words in context. Model conversations depict situations in which people use the words in meaningful communication. These models become the basis for students to engage in dynamic, interactive practice. In addition, writing and discussion questions in each lesson encourage students to relate the vocabulary and themes to their own lives as they share experiences, thoughts, opinions, and information about themselves, their cultures, and their countries. In this way, students get to know each other "word by word."

In using *Word by Word*, we encourage you to develop approaches and strategies that are compatible with your own teaching style and the needs and abilities of your students. You may find it helpful to incorporate some of the following techniques for presenting and practicing the vocabulary in each lesson.

1. **Preview the Vocabulary:** Activate students' prior knowledge of the vocabulary by brainstorming with students the words in the lesson they already know and writing them on the board, or by having students look at the transparency or the illustration in *Word by Word* and identify the words they are familiar with.

2. **Present the Vocabulary:** Using the transparency or the illustration in the Picture Dictionary, point to the picture of each word, say the word, and have the class repeat it chorally and individually. (You can also play the word list on the Audio Program.) Check students' understanding and pronunciation of the vocabulary.

3. **Vocabulary Practice:** Have students practice the vocabulary as a class, in pairs, or in small groups. Say or write a word, and have students point to the item or tell the number. Or, point to an item or give the number, and have students say the word.

4. **Model Conversation Practice:** Some lessons have model conversations that use the first word in the vocabulary list. Other models are in the form of skeletal dialogs, in which vocabulary words can be inserted. (In many skeletal dialogs, bracketed numbers indicate which words can be used for practicing the conversation. If no bracketed numbers appear, all the words in the lesson can be used.)

The following steps are recommended for Model Conversation Practice:

a. Preview: Have students look at the model illustration and discuss who they think the speakers are and where the conversation takes place.

b. The teacher presents the model or plays the audio one or more times and checks students' understanding of the situation and the vocabulary.

c. Students repeat each line of the conversation chorally and individually.

d. Students practice the model in pairs.

e. A pair of students presents a conversation based on the model, but using a different word from the vocabulary list.

f. In pairs, students practice several conversations based on the model, using different words on the page.

g. Pairs present their conversations to the class.

5. **Additional Conversation Practice:** Many lessons provide two additional skeletal dialogs for further conversation practice with the vocabulary. (These can be found in the yellow-shaded area at the bottom of the page.) Have students practice and present these conversations using any words they wish. Before they practice the additional conversations, you may want to have students listen to the sample additional conversations on the Audio Program.

6. **Spelling Practice:** Have students practice spelling the words as a class, in pairs, or in small groups. Say a word, and have students spell it aloud or write it. Or, using the transparency, point to an item and have students write the word.

7. **Themes for Discussion, Composition, Journals, and Portfolios:** Each lesson of *Word by Word* provides one or more questions for discussion and composition. (These can be found in a blue-shaded area at the bottom of the page.) Have students respond to the questions as a class, in pairs, or in small groups. Or, have students write their responses at home, share their written work with other students, and discuss as a class, in pairs, or in small groups.

Students may enjoy keeping a journal of their written work. If time permits, you may want to write a response in each student's journal, sharing your own opinions and experiences as well as reacting to what the student has written. If you are keeping portfolios of students' work, these compositions serve as excellent examples of students' progress in learning English.

8. **Communication Activities:** The *Word by Word* Teacher's Guide and Lesson Planner with CD-ROM provides a wealth of games, tasks, brainstorming, discussion, movement, drawing, miming, role-playing, and other activities designed to take advantage of students' different learning styles and particular abilities and strengths. For each lesson, choose one or more of these activities to reinforce students' vocabulary learning in a way that is stimulating, creative, and enjoyable.

WORD BY WORD aims to offer students a communicative, meaningful, and lively way of practicing English vocabulary. In conveying to you the substance of our program, we hope that we have also conveyed the spirit: that learning vocabulary can be genuinely interactive . . . relevant to our students' lives . . . responsive to students' differing strengths and learning styles . . . and fun!

Steven J. Molinsky

Bill Bliss

INFORMACIÓN PERSONAL

Gloria P. Sánchez
95 Garden St. Apt. 3G
Los Angeles, CA 90036

14 · 323 695-1864

15 From: gloria97@ail.com
To:
Subject:

SOCIAL SECURITY
16 · 227-93-6185
Gloria P. Sánchez

MAY
12
1988

ENTERING
CENTERVILLE
POPULATION
64?

Registration Form

Name	Gloria	P.	Sánchez
	First	Middle Initial	Last

Address	95	Garden Street	3G
	Number	Street	Apartment Number
	Los Angeles	CA	90036
	City	State	Zip Code

Telephone __323-524-3278__   Cell Phone __323-695-1864__

E-Mail Address __gloria97@ail.com__   SSN __227-93-6185__ Sex M__ F **X**

Date of Birth __5/12/88__   Place of Birth __Centerville, Texas__

nombre completo	**1** name	código/zona postal	**11** zip code
nombre de pila	**2** first name	código/prefijo telefónico/clave telefónica	**12** area code
inicial del segundo nombre	**3** middle initial	número de teléfono	**13** telephone number/phone number
apellidos (paterno y materno)	**4** last name/family name/surname	número de teléfono celular/móvil	**14** cell phone number
domicilio	**5** address	dirección de correo electrónico	**15** e-mail address
número de la casa	**6** street number	número de seguro social	**16** social security number
calle	**7** street	sexo	**17** sex
número del apartamento	**8** apartment number	fecha de nacimiento	**18** date of birth
ciudad	**9** city	lugar de nacimiento	**19** place of birth
estado/provincia/departamento	**10** state		

A. What's your **name**?
B. Gloria P. Sánchez.

A. What's your _____?
B. ....
A. Did you say ....?
B. Yes. That's right.

A. What's your last name?
B. ....
A. How do you spell that?
B. ....

Tell about yourself:
  My name is ....
  My address is ....
  My telephone number is ....

Now interview a friend.

esposo **1** husband	**hijos children**	**abuelos grandparents**
esposa **2** wife	hija **5** daughter	abuela **10** grandmother
	hijo **6** son	abuelo **11** grandfather
padres parents	bebé/nene(a) **7** baby	
padre/papá **3** father		**nietos grandchildren**
madre/mamá **4** mother	**hermanos(as) siblings**	nieta **12** granddaughter
	hermana **8** sister	nieto **13** grandson
	hermano **9** brother	

A. Who is he?
B. He's my **husband**.
A. What's his name?
B. His name is *Jack*.

A. Who is she?
B. She's my **wife**.
A. What's her name?
B. Her name is *Nancy*.

A. I'd like to introduce my _____.
B. Nice to meet you.
C. Nice to meet you, too.

A. What's your _____'s name?
B. His/Her name is ....

Who are the people in your family?
What are their names?

Tell about photos of family members.

LA FAMILIA (PARIENTES) II

tío	**1**	uncle		suegra	**6**	mother-in-law
tía	**2**	aunt		suegro	**7**	father-in-law
sobrina	**3**	niece		yerno	**8**	son-in-law
sobrino	**4**	nephew		nuera	**9**	daughter-in-law
primo/prima	**5**	cousin		cuñado	**10**	brother-in-law
				cuñada	**11**	sister-in-law

1. Jack is Alan's ____.
2. Nancy is Alan's ____.
3. Jennifer is Frank and Linda's ____.
4. Timmy is Frank and Linda's ____.
5. Alan is Jennifer and Timmy's ____.
6. Helen is Jack's ____.
7. Walter is Jack's ____.
8. Jack is Helen and Walter's ____.
9. Linda is Helen and Walter's ____.
10. Frank is Jack's ____.
11. Linda is Jack's ____.

A. Who is he/she?
B. He's/She's my _____.
A. What's his/her name?
B. His/Her name is _____.

A. Let me introduce my _____.
B. I'm glad to meet you.
C. Nice meeting you, too.

Tell about your relatives:
What are their names?
Where do they live?

Draw your family tree and tell about it.

EL SALÓN/LA SALA DE CLASES/EL AULA

maestro(a)	**1** teacher	reloj	**11** clock
asistente/auxiliar	**2** teacher's aide	mapa	**12** map
alumno(a)/estudiante	**3** student	cartelera/tablero/tablilla/mural/de anuncios	**13** bulletin board
pupitre/escritorio	**4** desk	sistema de altavoz/altoparlante	**14** P.A. system/loudspeaker
silla/banco	**5** seat/chair	pizarra/pizarrón/tablero para marcadores	**15** whiteboard/board
mesa	**6** table	globo terráqueo/del mundo	**16** globe
computadora/ordenador	**7** computer	librera/librero/librería/ estante para libros	**17** bookcase/bookshelf
retroproyector/proyector de transparencias	**8** overhead projector		
pantalla	**9** screen	escritorio de la maestra/del maestro	**18** teacher's desk
pizarra/pizarrón/tablero	**10** chalkboard/board	papelera/cesto/canasta de papeles	**19** wastebasket

Spanish	#	English
bolígrafo / pluma (estilográfica) / lapicero	**20**	pen
lápiz / lapicero	**21**	pencil
borrador / goma de borrar	**22**	eraser
sacapuntas	**23**	pencil sharpener
libro / texto	**24**	book / textbook
cuaderno / manual de ejercicios / de actividades	**25**	workbook
cuaderno / carpeta con espiral	**26**	spiral notebook
carpeta / portafolios	**27**	binder / notebook
papel para carpetas / para portafolios	**28**	notebook paper
papel cuadriculado	**29**	graph paper

Spanish	#	English
regla	**30**	ruler
calculadora	**31**	calculator
tiza / gis / pizarrín	**32**	chalk
borrador	**33**	eraser
marcador	**34**	marker
tachuela / chinche / chincheta	**35**	thumbtack
teclado	**36**	keyboard
pantalla / monitor	**37**	monitor
ratón	**38**	mouse
impresora	**39**	printer

A. Where's the **teacher**?
B. The **teacher** is *next to* the **board**.

A. Where's the **globe**?
B. The **globe** is *on* the **bookcase**.

A. Is there a/an _____ in your classroom?*
B. Yes. There's a/an _____
   next to/on the _____.

A. Is there a/an _____ in your classroom?*
B. No, there isn't.

Describe your classroom.
(There's a/an ....)

*With 28, 29, 32 use: Is there _____ in your classroom?

ACCIONES EN EL SALÓN/LA SALA DE CLASES/EL AULA

Diga(n) su nombre.	**1** Say your name.	Levante(n)/Alce(n) la mano.	**16** Raise your hand.
Repita(n) su nombre.	**2** Repeat your name.	Haga(n) una pregunta./ Pregunte(n).	**17** Ask a question.
Deletree(n) su nombre.	**3** Spell your name.	Escuche(n) la pregunta.	**18** Listen to the question.
Escriba(n) su nombre.	**4** Print your name.	Conteste(n) la pregunta.	**19** Answer the question.
Firme(n).	**5** Sign your name.	Escuche(n) la respuesta.	**20** Listen to the answer.
Levánte(n)se.	**6** Stand up.	Haga(n) su tarea/sus deberes.	**21** Do your homework.
Vaya(n) a la pizarra/ al pizarrón/al tablero.	**7** Go to the board.	Traiga(n) su tarea/ sus deberes.	**22** Bring in your homework.
Escriba(n) en la pizarra/ el pizarrón/el tablero.	**8** Write on the board.	Revise(n) las respuestas/ las contestaciones.	**23** Go over the answers.
Borre(n) la pizarra/el pizarrón/ el tablero.	**9** Erase the board.	Corrija(n) sus errores.	**24** Correct your mistakes.
Siénte(n)se/Tome(n) asiento.	**10** Sit down./Take your seat.	Entregue(n) su tarea.	**25** Hand in your homework.
Abra(n) el libro.	**11** Open your book.	Comparta(n) un libro.	**26** Share a book.
Lea(n) la página diez.	**12** Read page ten.	Discuta(n) la pregunta.	**27** Discuss the question.
Estudie(n) la página diez.	**13** Study page ten.	Ayúdense.	**28** Help each other.
Cierre(n) el libro.	**14** Close your book.	Trabajen juntos(as).	**29** Work together.
Guarde(n) el libro.	**15** Put away your book.	Comparta(n) con la clase.	**30** Share with the class.

Consulte(n) el diccionario. **31** Look in the dictionary.
Busque(n) una palabra. **32** Look up a word.
Pronuncie(n) la palabra. **33** Pronounce the word.
Lea(n) la definición. **34** Read the definition.
Copie(n) la palabra. **35** Copy the word.
Trabaje(n) individualmente. **36** Work alone./ Do your own work.

Trabajen en parejas/pares. **37** Work with a partner.
Divídanse en equipos/ **38** Break up into small groups pequeños. groups.
Trabaje(n) en grupos/equipos. **39** Work in a group.
Trabajen con toda la clase. **40** Work as a class.
Baje(n) las persianas. **41** Lower the shades.
Apague(n) las luces. **42** Turn off the lights.
Mire(n) la pantalla. **43** Look at the screen.
Tome(n) notas. **44** Take notes.
Prenda(n)/Ponga(n)/ **45** Turn on the lights.
Encienda(n)/las luces.

Saque(n) un papel. **46** Take out a piece of paper.
Pase(n) los exámenes/las **47** Pass out the tests.
pruebas.

Conteste(n) las preguntas. **48** Answer the questions.
Revise(n) sus respuestas/ **49** Check your answers.
sus contestaciones.
Entregue(n) los exámenes/las **50** Collect the tests.
pruebas.
Escoja(n)/Elija(n) la respuesta **51** Choose the correct
correcta. answer.
Encierre(n) en un círculo **52** Circle the correct answer.
la respuesta correcta.
Llene(n) el espacio. **53** Fill in the blank.
Rellene(n) el círculo. **54** Mark the answer sheet./ Bubble the answer.
Relacione(n)/Paree(n) **55** Match the words.
las palabras.
Subraye(n) la palabra. **56** Underline the word.
Tache(n) la palabra. **57** Cross out the word.

Ordene(n)/acomode(n) **58** Unscramble the word.
las letras de la palabra.
Ordene(n)/acomode(n) **59** Put the words in order.
las palabras.
Escriba(n) en una hoja aparte. **60** Write on a separate sheet of paper.

You're the teacher! Give instructions to your students!

PREPOSICIONES

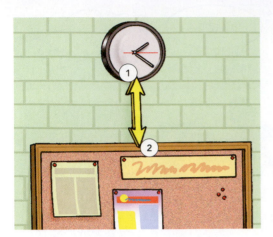

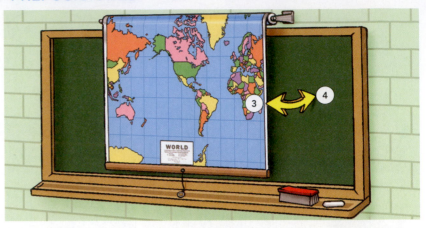

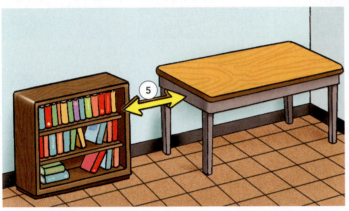

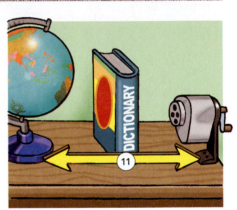

arriba	**1**	above
abajo	**2**	below
enfrente/ delante (de)	**3**	in front of
detrás (de)	**4**	behind

junto a	**5**	next to
sobre	**6**	on
bajo/debajo (de)	**7**	under
a la izquierda de	**8**	to the left of
a la derecha de	**9**	to the right of

en/dentro (de)	**10**	in
entre	**11**	between

[1–10]
A. Where's the *clock*?
B. The *clock* is **above** the *bulletin board*.

[11]
A. Where's the *dictionary*?
B. The *dictionary* is **between** the *globe* and the *pencil sharpener*.

Tell about the classroom on page 4. Use the prepositions in this lesson.

Tell about your classroom.

HÁBITOS Y QUEHACERES DOMÉSTICOS I

me levanto	**1**	get up
me baño/me ducho	**2**	take a shower
me lavo/*me* cepillo los dientes	**3**	brush *my** teeth
me afeito/me rasuro	**4**	shave
me visto	**5**	get dressed
me lavo la cara	**6**	wash *my** face
me maquillo/me pinto	**7**	put on makeup
me cepillo el pelo/cabello	**8**	brush *my** hair
me peino el pelo/cabello	**9**	comb *my** hair
hago/tiendo la cama	**10**	make the bed

me desvisto	**11**	get undressed
me baño/me meto en la tina	**12**	take a bath
me acuesto	**13**	go to bed
me duermo	**14**	sleep
hago/preparo el desayuno	**15**	make breakfast
hago/preparo el almuerzo	**16**	make lunch
hago/preparo la cena	**17**	cook/make dinner
desayuno	**18**	eat/have breakfast
almuerzo	**19**	eat/have lunch
ceno	**20**	eat/have dinner

* my, his, her, our, your, their

A. What do you do every day?
B. I **get up**, I **take a shower**, and I **brush my teeth**.

A. What does he do every day?
B. He _____s, he _____s,
and he _____s.

A. What does she do every day?
B. She _____s, she _____s,
and she_____s.

What do you do every day? Make a list.

Interview some friends and tell about
their everyday activities.

HÁBITOS Y QUEHACERES DOMÉSTICOS II

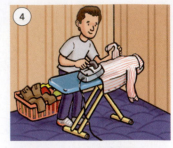

limpiar el apartamento/ departamento/la casa	**1**	clean the apartment/ clean the house	estudiar	**8** study
lavar los platos/trastos	**2**	wash the dishes	ir al trabajo	**9** go to work
lavar la ropa	**3**	do the laundry	ir a la escuela/al colegio	**10** go to school
alisar con la plancha/planchar	**4**	iron	manejar/conducir para ir al trabajo	**11** drive to work
darle de comer al bebé/ a la bebé/al nene/a la nena	**5**	feed the baby	tomar el autobús/bus/ camión para ir a la escuela	**12** take the bus to school
darle de comer al gato	**6**	feed the cat	trabajar	**13** work
pasear al perro	**7**	walk the dog	salir del trabajo	**14** leave work
			ir a la tienda	**15** go to the store
			llegar a casa	**16** come home/get home

A. Hello. What are you doing?
B. I'm **clean**ing the **apartment**.

A. Hello, ... This is ....
    What are you doing?
B. I'm _____ing. How about you?
A. I'm _____ing.

A. Are you going to _____ soon?
B. Yes. I'm going to _____ in a
    little while.

What are you going to do tomorrow?
Make a list of everything you are
going to do.

ACTIVIDADES RECREATIVAS

ver la televisión/tele	**1** watch TV	tocar la guitarra	**9** play the guitar
oír/escuchar el/la radio	**2** listen to the radio	tocar el piano	**10** practice the piano
oír/escuchar música	**3** listen to music	hacer ejercicio	**11** exercise
leer un libro	**4** read a book	nadar	**12** swim
leer el periódico/diario	**5** read the newspaper	sembrar/plantar flores	**13** plant flowers
jugar	**6** play	usar la computadora/el ordenador	**14** use the computer
jugar barajas/a los naipes/las cartas	**7** play cards	escribir cartas	**15** write a letter
jugar baloncesto/básquetbol	**8** play basketball	descansar/relajarse	**16** relax

A. Hi. What are you doing?
B. I'm **watch**ing **TV**.

A. Hi, ... Are you
_____ing?

B. No, I'm not. I'm _____ing.

A. What's your (husband/wife/son/ daughter/. . .) doing?

B. He's/She's _____ing.

What leisure activities do you like to do?

What do your family members and friends like to do?

CONVERSACIONES DIARIAS

Greeting People   **Saludos**

Leave Taking   **Despedidas**

Hola.	**1** Hello. / Hi.	¿Qué hay de nuevo?/	**7** What's new?/
Buenos días.	**2** Good morning.	¿Qué te cuentas?	What's new with you?
Buenas tardes.	**3** Good afternoon.	Nada./No mucho.	**8** Not much. / Not too much.
Buenas noches./Buenas tardes.	**4** Good evening.	Adiós.	**9** Good-bye. / Bye.
¿Cómo está(s)?/¿Cómo te va?/	**5** How are you?/	Buenas noches.	**10** Good night.
¿Cómo le va?	How are you doing?	Hasta luego./	**11** See you later. /
Bien./Bien, gracias.	**6** Fine. / Fine, thanks. / Okay.	Hasta pronto.	See you soon.

Introducing Yourself and Others   Presentaciones

Getting Someone's Attention
Expresiones para llamar la atención

Expressing Gratitude
Expresiones de agradecimiento

Saying You Don't Understand
Expresiones de duda

Calling Someone on the Telephone
En el teléfono

Hola. Me llamo	**12**	Hello. My name is ..../ Hi. I'm	¿Cómo?/No entiendo./ Disculpe(a). No entiendo.	**20** I don't understand. / Sorry. I don't understand.
Mucho gusto.	**13**	Nice to meet you.	¿Repita(e), por favor?	**21** Can you please repeat that?/ Can you please say that again?
El gusto es mío.	**14**	Nice to meet you, too.		
Te/Le presento a	**15**	I'd like to introduce ..../ This is	Hola. Habla .... ¿Podría/Puedo hablar con ....?/	**22** Hello. This is .... May I please speak to ....?
Permiso./Disculpe(a).	**16**	Excuse me.	¿Está ....?	
¿Puedo hacerle(te) una pregunta?	**17**	May I ask a question?	Sí, un momento, por favor.	**23** Yes. Hold on a moment.
Gracias.	**18**	Thank you. / Thanks.	Lo siento. .... no está aquí en este momento/	**24** I'm sorry. .... isn't here right now.
De nada./No hay de qué.	**19**	You're welcome.	Lo siento. .... no se encuentra en este momento.	

Practice conversations with other students. Use all the expressions on pages 12 and 13.

EL ESTADO DEL TIEMPO

    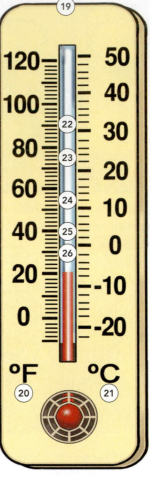

El estado del tiempo	Weather		
está soleado	1 sunny	relámpagos/truenos/rayos	14 lightning
está nublado/nuboso	2 cloudy	tormenta de rayos/de truenos	15 thunderstorm
está despejado/claro	3 clear	tormenta de nieve	16 snowstorm
hay bruma/calina	4 hazy	tolvanera/polvareda	17 dust storm
hay niebla/neblina	5 foggy	ola de calor	18 heat wave
está contaminado	6 smoggy		
hace viento/está ventoso/sopla viento	7 windy	La temperatura	Temperature
está húmedo/pegajoso/bochornoso	8 humid/muggy	termómetro	19 thermometer
llueve	9 raining	Fahrenheit	20 Fahrenheit
llovizna	10 drizzling	Centígrados/Celsius	21 Centigrade/Celsius
cae nieve/nieva	11 snowing	hace calor	22 hot
graniza	12 hailing	es (un día/un clima) caluroso/cálido	23 warm
cellisquea/cae aguanieve/una helada	13 sleeting	hace fresco	24 cool
		hace frío	25 cold
		está helado	26 freezing

[1–13]
A. What's the weather like?
B. It's _____.

[14–18]
A. What's the weather forecast?
B. There's going to be __[14]__/ a __[15–18]__.

[20–26]
A. How's the weather?
B. It's __[22–26]__.
A. What's the temperature?
B. It's . . . degrees __[20–21]__.

What's the weather like today? What's the temperature?   What's the weather forecast for tomorrow?

LOS NÚMEROS

Cardinal Numbers   Los números cardinales

0 zero	**11** eleven	**21** twenty-one	**101** one hundred (and) one
1 one	**12** twelve	**22** twenty-two	**102** one hundred (and) two
2 two	**13** thirteen	**30** thirty	**1,000** one thousand
3 three	**14** fourteen	**40** forty	**10,000** ten thousand
4 four	**15** fifteen	**50** fifty	**100,000** one hundred thousand
5 five	**16** sixteen	**60** sixty	**1,000,000** one million
6 six	**17** seventeen	**70** seventy	**1,000,000,000** one billion
7 seven	**18** eighteen	**80** eighty	
8 eight	**19** nineteen	**90** ninety	
9 nine	**20** twenty	**100** one hundred	
10 ten			

A. How old are you?
B. I'm _____ years old.

A. How many people are there in your family?
B. _____.

Ordinal Numbers   Los números ordinales (1°, 1ª; 2°, 2ª; etc.)

1st first	**11th** eleventh	**21st** twenty-first	**101st** one hundred (and) first
2nd second	**12th** twelfth	**22nd** twenty-second	**102nd** one hundred (and) second
3rd third	**13th** thirteenth	**30th** thirtieth	**1,000th** one thousandth
4th fourth	**14th** fourteenth	**40th** fortieth	**10,000th** ten thousandth
5th fifth	**15th** fifteenth	**50th** fiftieth	**100,000th** one hundred thousandth
6th sixth	**16th** sixteenth	**60th** sixtieth	**1,000,000th** one millionth
7th seventh	**17th** seventeenth	**70th** seventieth	**1,000,000,000th** one billionth
8th eighth	**18th** eighteenth	**80th** eightieth	
9th ninth	**19th** nineteenth	**90th** ninetieth	
10th tenth	**20th** twentieth	**100th** one hundredth	

A. What floor do you live on?
B. I live on the _____ floor.

A. Is this your first trip to our country?
B. No. It's my _____ trip.

How many students are there in your class?

How many people are there in your country?

What were the names of your teachers in elementary school? (My *first*-grade teacher was Ms./Mrs./Mr. . . .)

LA HORA

two o'clock

two fifteen/
a quarter after two

two thirty/
half past two

two forty-five
a quarter to three

two oh five

two twenty/
twenty after two

two forty/
twenty to three

two fifty-five
five to three

A. What time is it?
B. It's _____.

A. What time does the movie begin?
B. At _____.

two A.M.

two P.M.

noon/
twelve noon

midnight/
twelve midnight

A. When does the train leave?
B. At _____.

A. What time will we arrive?
B. At _____.

Tell about your daily schedule:
   What do you do? When?
   (I get up at _____. I ....)

Do you usually have enough time to do things, or do you "run out of time"? Tell about it.

Tell about the use of time in different cultures or countries you know:
   Do people arrive on time for work? appointments? parties?
   Do trains and buses operate exactly on schedule?
   Do movies and sports events begin on time?
   Do workplaces use time clocks or timesheets to record employees' work hours?

EL DINERO

Coins
Moneda suelta/Suelto/Sencillo

	Name	Value		Written as:
1	penny	one cent	1¢	$ .01
2	nickel	five cents	5¢	$ .05
3	dime	ten cents	10¢	$ .10
4	quarter	twenty-five cents	25¢	$ .25
5	half dollar	fifty cents	50¢	$ .50
6	silver dollar	one dollar		$1.00

A. How much is a **penny** worth?
B. A **penny** is worth **one cent**.

A. *Soda* costs *ninety-five cents*. Do you have enough change?
B. Yes. I have a/two/three _____(s) and . . . .

Currency   **Papel moneda**

	Name	We sometimes say:	Value	Written as:
7	(one-) dollar bill	a one	one dollar	$ 1.00
8	five-dollar bill	a five	five dollars	$ 5.00
9	ten-dollar bill	a ten	ten dollars	$ 10.00
10	twenty-dollar bill	a twenty	twenty dollars	$ 20.00
11	fifty-dollar bill	a fifty	fifty dollars	$ 50.00
12	(one-) hundred dollar bill	a hundred	one hundred dollars	$100.00

A. I'm going to the supermarket. Do you have any cash?
B. I have a **twenty-dollar bill**.
A. **Twenty dollars** is enough. Thanks.

A. Can you change a **five-dollar bill**/**a five**?
B. Yes. I have **five one-dollar bills**/ **five ones.**

Written as:	We say:
$1.30	a dollar and thirty cents
	a dollar thirty
$2.50	two dollars and fifty cents
	two fifty
$56.49	fifty-six dollars and forty-nine cents
	fifty-six forty-nine

Tell about some things you usually buy. What do they cost?

Name and describe the coins and currency in your country. What are they worth in U.S. dollars?

EL CALENDARIO

2012 JANUARY

SUN	MON	TUE	WED	THU	FRI	SAT
1	2	3	4	5	6	7
8	9	10	11	12	13	14
15	16	17	18	19	20	21
22	23	24	25	26	27	28
29	30	31				

13 JAN 14 FEB 15 MAR 16 APR
17 MAY 18 JUN 19 JUL 20 AUG
21 SEP 22 OCT 23 NOV 24 DEC

25 **1/3/12** JAN 3 2012

26 27 HAPPY 25th

28 APPOINTMENT
Charles Wong, M.D.
Date: February 21
Time: 3:00 PM

año	**1**	year	**Los meses del año**	**Months of the Year**	3 de enero de 2012/	**25** January 3, 2012
mes	**2**	month	enero	**13** January	el tres de enero de	January third,
semana	**3**	week	febrero	**14** February	dos mil doce	two thousand
día	**4**	day	marzo	**15** March		twelve
fin de semana	**5**	weekend	abril	**16** April	cumpleaños	**26** birthday
			mayo	**17** May	aniversario	**27** anniversary
Los días de la semana		**Days of the Week**	junio	**18** June	cita	**28** appointment
domingo	**6**	Sunday	julio	**19** July		
lunes	**7**	Monday	agosto	**20** August		
martes	**8**	Tuesday	septiembre	**21** September		
miércoles	**9**	Wednesday	octubre	**22** October		
jueves	**10**	Thursday	noviembre	**23** November		
viernes	**11**	Friday	diciembre	**24** December		
sábado	**12**	Saturday				

A. What year is it?
B. It's _____.

[13–24]
A. What month is it?
B. It's _____.

[6–12]
A. What day is it?
B. It's _____.

A. What's today's date?
B. It's _____.

[26–28]
A. When is your _____?
B. It's on _____.

Which days of the week do you go to work/school?
(I go to work/school on _____.)

What do you do on the weekend?

What is your date of birth?
(I was born on ..... *month day, year* .....)

What's your favorite day of the week? Why?

What's your favorite month of the year? Why?

EXPRESIONES DE TIEMPO Y LAS ESTACIONES

		ayer	**1**	yesterday
		hoy	**2**	today
		mañana	**3**	tomorrow
		por la mañana	**4**	morning
		por la tarde	**5**	afternoon
		por la tardecita/nochecita/al	**6**	evening
		atardecer/al anochecer		
		por la noche	**7**	night
		ayer por la mañana	**8**	yesterday morning
		ayer por la tarde	**9**	yesterday afternoon
		ayer por la tardecita/nochecita/al	**10**	yesterday evening
		atardecer/al anochecer		
		anoche	**11**	last night
		esta mañana	**12**	this morning
		esta tarde	**13**	this afternoon
		por la tardecita/nochecita/	**14**	this evening
		al atardecer/al anochecer		
		esta noche	**15**	tonight

mañana por la mañana	**16**	tomorrow morning
mañana por la tarde	**17**	tomorrow afternoon
mañana por la tardecita/nochecita/	**18**	tomorrow evening
al atardecer/al anochecer		
mañana por la noche	**19**	tomorrow night
la semana pasada	**20**	last week
esta semana	**21**	this week
la próxima semana/	**22**	next week
la semana entrante		
una vez a la semana	**23**	once a week
dos veces a la semana	**24**	twice a week
tres veces a la semana	**25**	three times a week
todos los días/a diario	**26**	every day

Las estaciones Seasons

primavera	**27**	spring
verano	**28**	summer
otoño	**29**	fall/autumn
invierno	**30**	winter

What did you do yesterday morning/afternoon/evening? What did you do last night?

What did you do last week?

How many times a week do you have English class?/go to the supermarket?/exercise?

What are you going to do tomorrow morning/afternoon/evening/night?

What are your plans for next week?

What's your favorite season? Why?

TIPOS DE VIVIENDA Y COMUNIDADES

edificio de apartamentos/ departamentos	**1** apartment building	refugio/asilo para desvalidos/ albergue para desamparados	**9**	shelter
casa	**2** house	hacienda/granja/finca	**10**	farm
dúplex	**3** duplex/two-family house	rancho	**11**	ranch
casas (de 2 o 3 plantas) en hileras	**4** townhouse/townhome	casa flotante	**12**	houseboat
condominio/condo/piso	**5** condominium/condo	la ciudad	**13**	the city
dormitorio/residencia estudiantil	**6** dormitory/dorm	los suburbios/las afueras	**14**	the suburbs
casa prefabricada/móvil/rodante	**7** mobile home	el campo	**15**	the country
asilo/casa de ancianos/de reposo	**8** nursing home	un pueblo/un poblado/una villa	**16**	a town/village

A. Where do you live?

B. I live
{ in a/an _____[1–9]_____.
  on a _____[10–12]_____.
  in _____[13–16]_____.

[1–12]

A. Town Taxi Company.

B. Hello. Please send a taxi to
.....*(address)*.....

A. Is that a house or an apartment building?

B. It's a/an _____.

A. All right. We'll be there right away.

[1–12]

A. This is the Emergency Operator.

B. Please send an ambulance to
.....*(address)*.....

A. Is that a private home?

B. It's a/an _____.

A. What's your name and telephone number?

B. ....

Tell about people you know and where they live.

Discuss:
  Who lives in dormitories?
  Who lives in nursing homes?
  Who lives in shelters?
  Why?

LA SALA

librero/librería/estante para libros	**1** bookcase	mueble/unidad de pared	**15** wall unit
foto/fotografía/retrato	**2** picture / photograph	bocina/altoparlante/altavoz	**16** speaker
cuadro/pintura	**3** painting	estéreo/equipo estereofónico	**17** stereo system
manto de la chimenea/del hogar	**4** mantel	revistero	**18** magazine holder
hogar/chimenea	**5** fireplace	cojín	**19** (throw) pillow
pantalla/rejilla de la chimenea	**6** fireplace screen	sofá	**20** sofa / couch
DVD/reproductor de video digital	**7** DVD player	mata/planta	**21** plant
televisor/TV/televisión/tele	**8** television / TV	mesa de centro	**22** coffee table
videocasetera/videograbadora	**9** VCR / video cassette recorder	alfombra/alfombrilla/tapete	**23** rug
pared/muro/tapia	**10** wall	lámpara	**24** lamp
cielo raso/techo	**11** ceiling	pantalla	**25** lampshade
cortinas	**12** drapes	mesita/esquinera/mesilla	**26** end table
ventana	**13** window	piso	**27** floor
confidente/canapé/sofá	**14** loveseat	lámpara de pie	**28** floor lamp
		sillón/silla de brazos/butaca	**29** armchair

A. Where are you?
B. I'm in the living room.
A. What are you doing?
B. I'm dusting* the **bookcase**.

* dusting/cleaning

A. You have a very nice living room!
B. Thank you.
A. Your _____ is/are beautiful!
B. Thank you for saying so.

A. Uh-oh! I just spilled coffee on your _____!
B. That's okay. Don't worry about it.

Tell about your living room.
(In my living room there's ....)

mesa de comedor	**1**	(dining room) table	vajilla/vajilla de porcelana/loza	**12**	china	pimentero	**22**	pepper shaker

mesa de comedor **1** (dining room) table
silla de comedor **2** (dining room) chair
aparador **3** buffet
bandeja/charola **4** tray
tetera **5** teapot
cafetera **6** coffee pot
azucarera **7** sugar bowl
jarrita para la leche/crema **8** creamer
jarro(a) **9** pitcher
lámpara de araña/ **10** chandelier
de techo/candil de techo
armario/alacena/ **11** china cabinet
vitrina/chinero

vajilla/vajilla de **12** china
porcelana/loza
ensaladera **13** salad bowl
sopera/ **14** serving bowl
fuente honda
bandeja **15** serving dish
florero/jarrón **16** vase
candela/vela **17** candle
candelero **18** candlestick
bandeja **19** platter
mantequillera **20** butter dish
salero **21** salt shaker

pimentero **22** pepper shaker
mantel **23** tablecloth
servilleta **24** napkin
tenedor/trinche **25** fork
plato **26** plate
cuchillo **27** knife
cuchara **28** spoon
plato hondo/tazón **29** bowl
taza **30** mug
vaso **31** glass
taza **32** cup
plato pequeño/ **33** saucer
platito/platillo

A. This **dining room table** is very nice.
B. Thank you. It was a gift from my *grandmother*.*

*grandmother/grandfather/aunt/uncle/. . .

[In a store]
A. May I help you?
B. Yes, please. Do you have _____s?*
A. Yes. _____s* are right over there.
B. Thank you.

*With 12, use the singular.

[At home]
A. Look at this old _____ I just bought!
B. Where did you buy it?
A. At a yard sale. How do you like it?
B. It's VERY unusual!

Tell about your dining room.
(In my dining room there's
..............)

LA RECÁMARA/EL DORMITORIO

cama	**1**	bed	persianas	**14**	blinds
cabecera	**2**	headboard	cortinas	**15**	curtains
almohada	**3**	pillow	lámpara	**16**	lamp
funda	**4**	pillowcase	despertador	**17**	alarm clock
sábana ceñida	**5**	fitted sheet	radio reloj despertador	**18**	clock radio
sábana	**6**	(flat) sheet	mesita/mesa de noche/buró	**19**	night table/nightstand
manta/frazada/cobija/frisa	**7**	blanket	espejo	**20**	mirror
manta/cobija/frisa eléctrica	**8**	electric blanket	joyero/alhajero	**21**	jewelry box
volante/rodapié/pollera	**9**	dust ruffle	cómoda/tocador	**22**	dresser/bureau
colcha/cubrecama/sobrecama	**10**	bedspread	colchón	**23**	mattress
edredón/cobertor relleno	**11**	comforter/quilt	colchón de muelles	**24**	box spring
alfombra	**12**	carpet	marco/armadura	**25**	bed frame
chifonier/ropero/gavetero	**13**	chest (of drawers)			

A. Ooh! Look at that big bug!
B. Where?
A. It's on the **bed**!
B. I'll get it.

[In a store]

A. Excuse me. I'm looking for a/an _____.*

B. We have some very nice _____s, and they're all on sale this week!

A. Oh, good!

* With 14 & 15, use: Excuse me. I'm looking for _____.

[In a bedroom]

A. Oh, no! I just lost my contact lens!

B. Where?

A. I think it's on the _____.

B. I'll help you look.

Tell about your bedroom.
(In my bedroom there's ....)

LA COCINA

refrigerador(a)/nevera	1	refrigerator
congelador	2	freezer
cubo/bote de basura/	3	garbage pail
basurero/tinaco/zafacón		
batidora eléctrica/	4	(electric)
mezcladora eléctrica		mixer
estante/armario/	5	cabinet
gabinete		
colgador para	6	paper towel
papel toalla		holder
envases/tarrones/	7	canister
recipientes para		
harina, azúcar, té o sal		
mostrador	8	(kitchen)
		counter
jabón para el lavaplatos/	9	dishwasher
lavavajillas		detergent
líquido de fregar/	10	dishwashing
lavar los platos		liquid

grifo/llave/pluma	11	faucet
fregadero/fregador	12	(kitchen) sink
lavaplatos/lavavajillas	13	dishwasher
triturador de	14	(garbage)
desperdicios		disposal
trapo/paño/toalla de	15	dish towel
cocina/limpión		
escurridor de	16	dish rack/
platos		dish drainer
especiero/repisa	17	spice rack
para especias/		
condimentos		
abrelatas eléctrico	18	(electric) can
		opener
licuadora eléctrica	19	blender
hornito/horno	20	toaster oven
pastelero/tostador		
horno microondas	21	microwave (oven)
agarrador de ollas	22	potholder

tacho/hervidor	23	tea kettle
estufa/cocina	24	stove/range
quemador/fogón	25	burner
horno	26	oven
tostador/tostadora	27	toaster
cafetera	28	coffeemaker
compresor de	29	trash
basura		compactor
tablita/tabla para	30	cutting
picar/picador		board
libro de recetas	31	cookbook
de cocina		
molinillo/procesador	32	food
de alimentos		processor
silla	33	kitchen chair
mesa	34	kitchen table
individual/	35	placemat
mantelito		
individual		

A. I think we need a new **refrigerator**.
B. I think you're right.

[In a store]

A. Excuse me. Are your _____s
   still on sale?

B. Yes, they are. They're twenty percent off.

[In a kitchen]

A. When did you get this/these
   new _____(s)?

B. I got it/them last week.

Tell about your kitchen.
(In my kitchen there's ....)

osito	**1**	teddy bear	corral	**16** playpen
intercomunicador/monitor de bebé	**2**	baby monitor/intercom	sonajero(a)/sonaja/	**17** rattle
ropero/gavetero	**3**	chest (of drawers)	maraquita	
cuna	**4**	crib	andadera/pollera/andador	**18** walker
orillero/paragolpes	**5**	crib bumper/bumper pad	cuna/cuna mecedora	**19** cradle
móvil	**6**	mobile	carriola/cochecito	**20** stroller
camilla/mesa para cambiar pañales	**7**	changing table	coche/carricoche	**21** baby carriage
mameluco/pelele/	**8**	stretch suit	asiento para automóvil	**22** car seat/safety seat
pijamita de una pieza/mono			portabebé/sillita infantil	**23** baby carrier
colchoneta/almohadilla para	**9**	changing pad	plato térmico para bebés	**24** food warmer
la mesa de cambiar pañales			sillita elevadora	**25** booster seat
cubo/bote/zafacón para pañales	**10**	diaper pail	portabebé/sillita infantil	**26** baby seat
lamparita/lucecita de noche	**11**	night light	trona/silla alta	**27** high chair
baúl para juguetes	**12**	toy chest	moisés/cuna portátil	**28** portable crib
peluche	**13**	stuffed animal	bacinilla/bacenilla/bacín/bacinica	**29** potty
muñeca	**14**	doll	portabebé/canguro	**30** baby frontpack
columpio	**15**	swing	portabebé	**31** baby backpack

A. Thank you for the **teddy bear**. It's a very nice gift.
B. You're welcome. Tell me, when are you due?
A. In a few more weeks.

A. That's a very nice _____.
    Where did you get it?

B. It was a gift from ....

A. Do you have everything you need
    before the baby comes?

B. Almost everything. We're still
    looking for a/an _____ and a/an
    _____.

Tell about your country:
    What things do people buy for a new baby?
    Does a new baby sleep in a separate room,
    as in the United States?

EL BAÑO

cesto/canasta	**1**	wastebasket	ventilador	**17**	fan	asiento del	**27**	toilet
gabinete/mueble	**2**	vanity	toalla grande	**18**	bath towel	excusado/		seat
jabón	**3**	soap	toalla para las manos	**19**	hand towel	redondela		
jabonera	**4**	soap dish	toallita para la cara	**20**	washcloth/	regadera/	**28**	shower
dispensador	**5**	soap dispenser			facecloth	ducha/baño		
de jabón			barra para la toalla/	**21**	towel rack	regadera/ducha	**29**	shower head
lavabo/lavamanos	**6**	(bathroom) sink	colgador de toallas/			cortina de baño	**30**	shower
llave/pluma/grifo	**7**	faucet	toallero					curtain
botiquín/gabinete	**8**	medicine cabinet	bomba	**22**	plunger	tina/bañera	**31**	bathtub/
espejo	**9**	mirror	destapacaños/					tub
vaso	**10**	cup	desatascador			parche	**32**	rubber
cepillo de dientes	**11**	toothbrush	cepillo	**23**	toilet brush	antirresbalón/		mat
portacepillos	**12**	toothbrush holder	papel higiénico/	**24**	toilet paper	alfombrilla/		
cepillo de dientes	**13**	electric	sanitario			estera de goma		
eléctrico		toothbrush	desodorante/	**25**	air freshener	desagüe/escurridor	**33**	drain
secadora	**14**	hair dryer	desodorizador/			esponja	**34**	sponge
de cabello/pelo			aromatizante			alfombra/	**35**	bath mat
repisa/tablilla	**15**	shelf	ambiental			alfombrilla/tapete		
canasta/cesto para	**16**	hamper	excusado/retrete/	**26**	toilet	de baño		
la ropa sucia			inodoro			báscula/balanza	**36**	scale

A. Where's the **hair dryer**?
B. It's *on* the **vanity**.

A. Where's the **soap**?
B. It's *in* the **soap dish**.

A. Where's the **plunger**?
B. It's *next to* the **toilet brush**.

A. [Knock. Knock.] Did I leave my glasses in there?
B. Yes. They're on/in/next to the _____.

A. *Bobby*? You didn't clean up the bathroom! There's toothpaste on the _____, and there's powder all over the _____!
B. Sorry. I'll clean it up right away.

Tell about your bathroom. (In my bathroom there's ....)

EL EXTERIOR/FUERA DE LA CASA

		El patio delantero		Front Yard
		farol	**1**	lamppost
		buzón/casilla/casillero postal	**2**	mailbox
		entrada	**3**	front walk
		escalinatas	**4**	front steps
		porche/portal/soportal	**5**	(front) porch
		contrapuerta	**6**	storm door
		puerta principal	**7**	front door
		timbre	**8**	doorbell
		luz de la entrada	**9**	(front) light
		ventana	**10**	window
		malla/tela metálica/mosquitero	**11**	(window) screen
		contraventana/postigo	**12**	shutter
		tejado/techo	**13**	roof
		garaje/estacionamiento/cochera	**14**	garage
		puerta del garaje/estacionamiento/de la cochera	**15**	garage door
		entrada para el coche/carro	**16**	driveway

El patio trasero		Backyard
silla de jardín	**17**	lawn chair
cortacésped/cortagrama	**18**	lawnmower
barraca/caseta para herramientas	**19**	tool shed
puerta con tela metálica	**20**	screen door
puerta trasera/de atrás	**21**	back door
agarrador/tirador/perilla	**22**	door knob
patio/cubierta/veranda	**23**	deck
asador/parrilla/barbacoa	**24**	barbecue/ (outdoor) grill
patio	**25**	patio
canal de desagüe/gotera	**26**	gutter
desagüe/caño	**27**	drainpipe
antena parabólica	**28**	satellite dish
antena de televisión	**29**	TV antenna
chimenea	**30**	chimney
puerta lateral	**31**	side door
cerca(o)/valla	**32**	fence

A. When are you going to repair the **lamppost**?
B. I'm going to repair it next Saturday.

[On the telephone]
A. Harry's Home Repairs.
B. Hello. Do you fix _____s?
A. No, we don't.
B. Oh, okay. Thank you.

[At work on Monday morning]
A. What did you do this weekend?
B. Nothing much. I repaired my _____ and my _____.

Do you like to repair things?
What things can you repair yourself?
What things can't you repair? Who repairs them?

EL EDIFICIO DE APARTAMENTOS/DEPARTAMENTOS

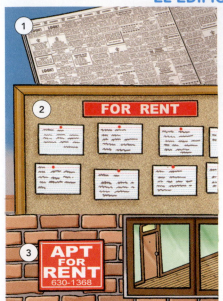

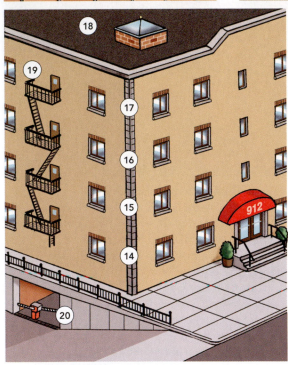

Búsqueda de apartamentos/ departamentos		**Looking for an Apartment**
anuncios/clasificados para apartamentos/ departamentos	**1**	apartment ads/ classified ads
tablero/mural/ tablón de anuncios	**2**	apartment listings
letrero de vacante	**3**	vacancy sign
Firma del contrato		**Signing a Lease**
arrendatario(a)/ inquilino(a)	**4**	tenant
arrendador(a)/ casero(a)	**5**	landlord
contrato de alquiler	**6**	lease
depósito	**7**	security deposit

La mudanza	**Moving In**	
camión de mudanzas	**8**	moving truck/ moving van
vecino(a)	**9**	neighbor
conserje	**10**	building manager
portero(a)	**11**	doorman
llave	**12**	key
cerradura/chapa	**13**	lock
primer piso	**14**	first floor
segundo piso	**15**	second floor
tercer piso	**16**	third floor
cuarto piso	**17**	fourth floor
techo	**18**	roof
escalera de emergencia	**19**	fire escape

garaje/estacionamiento/ aparcamiento con techo	**20**	parking garage
balcón	**21**	balcony
patio	**22**	courtyard
estacionamiento/ aparcamiento/ parqueadero	**23**	parking lot
espacio para estacionarse	**24**	parking space
piscina/alberca/ pileta	**25**	swimming pool
bañera/ tina de hidromasaje/ de terapia/tina-jacuzzi	**26**	whirlpool
basurero	**27**	trash bin
aire acondicionado	**28**	air conditioner

Vestíbulo/Lobby		Lobby		Pasillo/Corredor		Hallway
interfono/portero automático/eléctrico	**29**	intercom/ speaker		salida/escalera de emergencia	**38**	fire exit/ emergency stairway
timbre/chicharra	**30**	buzzer		alarma contra incendios	**39**	fire alarm
casilla/casillero postal/buzón	**31**	mailbox		extintor/sistema de aspersión contra incendios	**40**	sprinkler system
ascensor/elevador	**32**	elevator		superintendente/conserje/encargado(a)	**41**	superintendent
escalera	**33**	stairway		disparador/tobogán/conducto/ chuta para la basura	**42**	garbage chute/ trash chute
Puerta de entrada		**Doorway**				
mirilla	**34**	peephole		**Sótano**		**Basement**
cadena de seguridad/ antirrobo	**35**	(door) chain		depósito	**43**	storage room
cerrojo dormido/ cerrojo/seguro	**36**	dead-bolt lock		cuarto de almacenaje	**44**	storage locker
detector de humo	**37**	smoke detector		lavandería/cuarto de lavado/lavadero	**45**	laundry room
				verja de seguridad	**46**	security gate

[19–46]
A. Is there a **fire escape**?
B. Yes, there is. Do you want to see the apartment?
A. Yes, I do.

[19–46]

[Renting an apartment]
A. Let me show you around.
B. Okay.
A. This is the _____, and here's the _____.
B. I see.

[19–46]

[On the telephone]
A. Mom and Dad? I found an apartment.
B. Good. Tell us about it.
A. It has a/an _____ and a/an _____.
B. That's nice. Does it have a/an _____?
A. Yes, it does.

Do you or someone you know live in an apartment building? Tell about it.

PROBLEMAS DE MANTENIMIENTO Y REPARACIÓN DE LA CASA

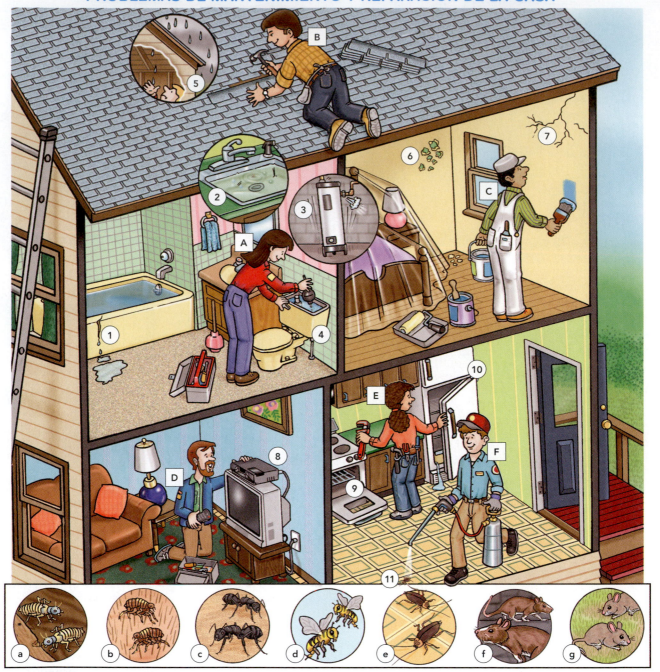

plomero(a)/fontanero(a) · **A plumber**

El agua de la tina/bañera se sale. · **1** The bathtub is leaking.

El lavabo/lavamanos está tapado. · **2** The sink is clogged.

El calentador de agua no funciona. · **3** The hot water heater isn't working.

El excusado/retrete/inodoro/ está descompuesto. · **4** The toilet is broken.

reparador(a) de techos · **B roofer**

El techo tiene goteras. · **5** The roof is leaking.

pintor(a) · **C (house) painter**

La pintura se está descascarillando. · **6** The paint is peeling.

La pared está cuarteada. · **7** The wall is cracked.

compañía de televisión por cable · **D cable TV company**

La señal no funciona. · **8** The cable TV isn't working.

reparador(a)/mecánico(a) · **E appliance repairperson**

La estufa no funciona. · **9** The stove isn't working.

El refrigerador está averiado/descompuesto. · **10** The refrigerator is broken.

fumigador(a) · **F exterminator/ pest control specialist**

Hay ____ en la cocina. · **11** There are ____ in the kitchen.

carcomas/comejenes/ termitas/termes · **a** termites

pulgas · **b** fleas

hormigas · **c** ants

abejas · **d** bees

cucarachas · **e** cockroaches

ratas · **f** rats

ratones · **g** mice

cerrajero(a) G locksmith
La cerradura está rota. **12** The lock is broken.

electricista H electrician
La luz de la entrada **13** The front light
no prende/se enciende. doesn't go on.
El timbre de la puerta **14** The doorbell
no suena. doesn't ring.
No hay luz en la sala. **15** The power is out in
the living room.

deshollinador(a) I chimneysweep
La chimenea está sucia. **16** The chimney is dirty.

ayudante J home repairperson/"handyman"
Los azulejos del baño **17** The tiles in the bathroom
están flojos. are loose.

carpintero(a) K carpenter
Los escalones están rotos. **18** The steps are broken.
La puerta no se abre. **19** The door doesn't open.

**servicio de calefacción y L heating and air
aire acondicionado conditioning service**
La calefacción está **20** The heating system is
descompuesta/rota. broken.
El aire acondicionado **21** The air conditioning isn't working.
no funciona.

A. What's the matter?
B. ___[1–21]___.
A. I think we should call a/an ___[A–L]___.

[1–21]
A. I'm having a problem in my apartment/house.
B. What's the problem?
A. _____.

[A–L]
A. Can you recommend a good _____?
B. Yes. You should call ....

What do you do when there are problems in your home? Do you fix things yourself, or do you call someone?

LA LIMPIEZA DE LA CASA

barrer el piso	**A**	sweep the floor
pasar la aspiradora	**B**	vacuum
trapear/fregar el piso	**C**	mop the floor
lavar las ventanas	**D**	wash the windows
sacudir/quitar el polvo	**E**	dust
encerar el piso	**F**	wax the floor
lustrar los muebles	**G**	polish the furniture
limpiar el (cuarto de) baño	**H**	clean the bathroom
sacar la basura	**I**	take out the garbage
escoba	**1**	broom
recogedor	**2**	dustpan
escobilla	**3**	whisk broom
barredor de alfombra	**4**	carpet sweeper
aspiradora	**5**	vacuum (cleaner)
accesorios para la aspiradora	**6**	vacuum cleaner attachments
bolsa para la aspiradora	**7**	vacuum cleaner bag
aspiradora de mano	**8**	hand vacuum

trapeador seco/mapo/mopa/mechudo	**9**	(dust) mop/(dry) mop
trapeador de esponja	**10**	(sponge) mop
trapeador/fregona	**11**	(wet) mop
papel toalla/papel absorbente	**12**	paper towels
líquido limpiaventanas	**13**	window cleaner
amoniaco/amoníaco	**14**	ammonia
limpión/trapo para limpiar/sacudir	**15**	dust cloth
plumero/sacudidor	**16**	feather duster
cera para el piso	**17**	floor wax
cera para muebles	**18**	furniture polish
limpiador en polvo/farola	**19**	cleanser
cepillo para limpiar el inodoro	**20**	scrub brush
esponja	**21**	sponge
cubo/cubeta	**22**	bucket/pail
basurero/bote para la basura/ tinaco/zafacón	**23**	trash can/ garbage can
contenedor de artículos renovables/reciclables	**24**	recycling bin

[A–I]
A. What are you doing?
B. I'm **sweep**ing **the floor**.

[1–24]
A. I can't find the **broom**.
B. Look over there!

[1–12, 15, 16, 20–24]
A. Excuse me. Do you sell _____(s)?
B. Yes. They're at the back of the store.
A. Thanks.

[13, 14, 17–19]
A. Excuse me. Do you sell _____?
B. Yes. It's at the back of the store.
A. Thanks.

What household cleaning chores do people do in your home? What things do they use?

MATERIALES DE MANTENIMIENTO

metro/vara de una yarda	**1**	yardstick	lubricante/aceite tres en uno	**15**	oil
matamoscas	**2**	fly swatter	goma de pegar/pegamento	**16**	glue
bomba/destapacaños	**3**	plunger	guantes de jardín	**17**	work gloves
linterna/lámpara/faro de mano	**4**	flashlight	insecticida/aerosol para	**18**	bug spray/
extensión	**5**	extension cord	matar insectos		insect spray
cinta de medir	**6**	tape measure	matacucarachas	**19**	roach killer
escalera	**7**	step ladder	lija	**20**	sandpaper
trampa para ratones/ratas/ratonera	**8**	mousetrap	pintura	**21**	paint
cinta para empacar/para pintores/	**9**	masking tape	disolvente/trementina/	**22**	paint thinner
masking tape			aguarrás/terpina		
cinta aisladora/aislante/de empalme	**10**	electrical tape	brocha	**23**	paintbrush/brush
cinta gris para sellar	**11**	duct tape	bandeja para la pintura	**24**	paint pan
baterías/pilas	**12**	batteries	rodillo	**25**	paint roller
foco/bombilla(o)	**13**	lightbulbs/bulbs	pistola para pintar	**26**	spray gun
fusibles	**14**	fuses			

A. I can't find the **yardstick**!
B. Look in the utility cabinet.
A. I did.
B. Oh! Wait a minute! I lent the **yardstick** to the neighbors.

[1–8, 23–26]

A. I'm going to the hardware store.
   Can you think of anything we need?
B. Yes. We need a/an _____.
A. Oh, that's right.

[9–22]

A. I'm going to the hardware store.
   Can you think of anything we need?
B. Yes. We need _____.
A. Oh, that's right.

What home supplies do you have?
How and when do you use each
one?

TOOLS AND HARDWARE
HERRAMIENTAS Y MATERIALES DE FERRETERÍA

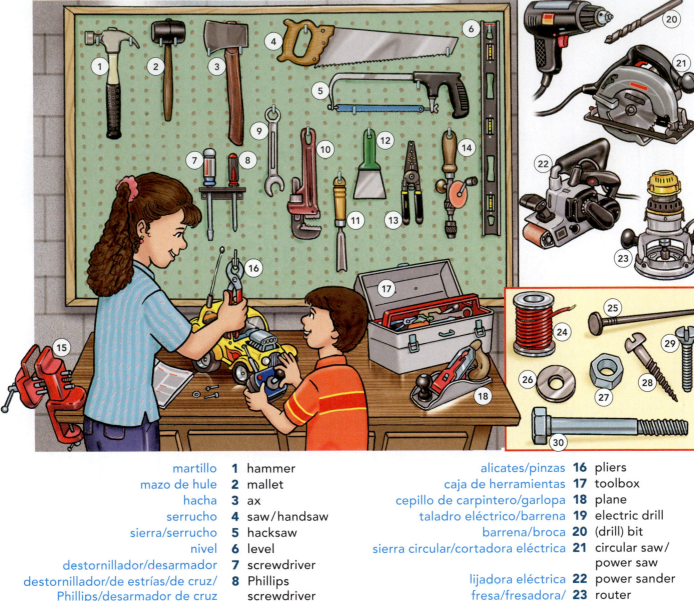

martillo	**1**	hammer	alicates/pinzas	**16**	pliers
mazo de hule	**2**	mallet	caja de herramientas	**17**	toolbox
hacha	**3**	ax	cepillo de carpintero/garlopa	**18**	plane
serrucho	**4**	saw/handsaw	taladro eléctrico/barrena	**19**	electric drill
sierra/serrucho	**5**	hacksaw	barrena/broca	**20**	(drill) bit
nivel	**6**	level	sierra circular/cortadora eléctrica	**21**	circular saw/
destornillador/desarmador	**7**	screwdriver			power saw
destornillador/de estrías/de cruz/	**8**	Phillips	lijadora eléctrica	**22**	power sander
Phillips/desarmador de cruz		screwdriver	fresa/fresadora/	**23**	router
llave/llave para tuercas	**9**	wrench	ranuradora eléctrica		
llave inglesa/	**10**	monkey wrench/	alambre	**24**	wire
de cremallera/perico		pipe wrench	clavo	**25**	nail
cincel	**11**	chisel	arandela/rondana	**26**	washer
raspador/espátula	**12**	scraper	tuerca	**27**	nut
pelador de cables	**13**	wire stripper	tornillo para madera	**28**	wood screw
taladro de mano/taladradora	**14**	hand drill	tornillo para metal	**29**	machine screw
torno/tornillo/prensa de banco	**15**	vise	perno	**30**	bolt

A. Can I borrow your **hammer**?
B. Sure.
A. Thanks.

* With 25–30, use: Could I borrow some _____s?

[1–15, 17–24]
A. Where's the _____?
B. It's on/next to/near/over/under the _____.

[16, 25–30]
A. Where are the _____s?
B. They're on/next to/near/over/under the _____.

Do you like to work with tools? What tools do you have in your home?

HERRAMIENTAS Y LABORES DE JARDINERÍA

cortar el césped/la grama/el zacate	**A**	mow the lawn
sembrar/plantar vegetales	**B**	plant vegetables
sembrar/plantar flores	**C**	plant flowers
regar las flores	**D**	water the flowers
barrer las hojas	**E**	rake leaves
recortar el seto	**F**	trim the hedge
podar los arbustos	**G**	prune the bushes
deshierbar	**H**	weed

cortacésped/cortagrama	**1**	lawnmower
lata/tanque de gasolina	**2**	gas can
cortadora de cordón/de línea	**3**	line trimmer
pala	**4**	shovel
semillas de vegetales	**5**	vegetable seeds
azadón/azada	**6**	hoe

palita de mano/jardín/palustre	**7**	trowel
carretilla	**8**	wheelbarrow
abono/fertilizante	**9**	fertilizer
manguera (de jardín)	**10**	(garden) hose
pitón/boca/boquilla	**11**	nozzle
rociador/regador/aspersor	**12**	sprinkler
regadera	**13**	watering can
rastrillo	**14**	rake
soplahojas	**15**	leaf blower
bolsa para la maleza/recortes de jardín	**16**	yard waste bag
tijeras de jardín	**17**	(hedge) clippers
podadora eléctrica	**18**	hedge trimmer
tijeras podadoras	**19**	pruning shears
escarda/escardilla(o)/almocafre	**20**	weeder

[A–H]
A. Hi! Are you busy?
B. Yes. I'm **mow**ing **the lawn**.

[1–20]
A. What are you looking for?
B. The **lawnmower**.

[A–H]
A. What are you going to do tomorrow?
B. I'm going to _____.

[1–20]
A. Can I borrow your _____?
B. Sure.

Do you ever work with any of these tools? Which ones? What do you do with them?

EN EL VECINDARIO I

panadería/pastelería/repostería	**1** bakery	guardería infantil	**9** child-care center / day-care center
banco	**2** bank	tintorería/lavandería en seco	**10** cleaners / dry cleaners
barbería/peluquería	**3** barber shop	clínica/consultorio	**11** clinic
librería	**4** book store	tienda de ropa	**12** clothing store
terminal de autobuses/camiones	**5** bus station	cafetería/café/cafetín	**13** coffee shop
confitería/tienda de confites/dulces	**6** candy store	tienda de computadoras/ordenadores	**14** computer store
agencia/distribuidora de carros	**7** car dealership	tienda/tiendita de abarrotes/colmado	**15** convenience store
puesto/tienda de tarjetas/ papelería	**8** card store	centro de fotocopias	**16** copy center

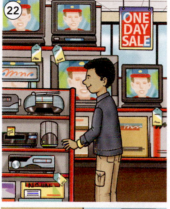

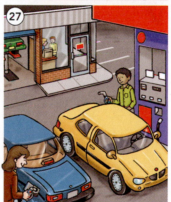
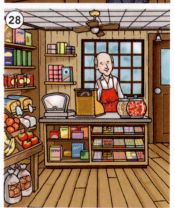

delicatessen/charcutería	**17**	delicatessen/deli
almacén	**18**	department store
tienda de descuentos	**19**	discount store
churrería/tienda de donas	**20**	donut shop
farmacia/droguería	**21**	drug store/pharmacy
tienda de electrónicos	**22**	electronics store
óptica/oculista	**23**	eye-care center/optician

cafetería/bar/merendero	**24**	fast-food restaurant
floristería/florería/florista	**25**	flower shop/florist
mueblería	**26**	furniture store
gasolinera/surtidor/estación/ bomba de gasolina	**27**	gas station/ service station
tienda/abarrotería/ bodega/colmado	**28**	grocery store

A. Where are you going?
B. I'm going to the **bakery**.

A. Hi! How are you today?
B. Fine. Where are you going?
A. To the _____. How about you?
B. I'm going to the _____.

A. Oh, no! I can't find my wallet/purse!
B. Did you leave it at the _____?
A. Maybe I did.

Which of these places are in your neighborhood?
(In my neighborhood there's a/an ....)

PLACES AROUND TOWN II

EN EL VECINDARIO II

salón de belleza/peluquería	**1**	hair salon
ferretería	**2**	hardware store
gimnasio/club	**3**	health club
hospital	**4**	hospital
hotel	**5**	hotel
heladería/refresquería/sorbetería	**6**	ice cream shop
joyería	**7**	jewelry store
lavandería pública/ automática/lavamático	**8**	laundromat

biblioteca	**9**	library
almacén/tienda de ropa de maternidad	**10**	maternity shop
motel	**11**	motel
cine	**12**	movie theater
almacén/tienda de música	**13**	music store
manicurista	**14**	nail salon
parque	**15**	park
tienda de mascotas	**16**	pet shop/ pet store

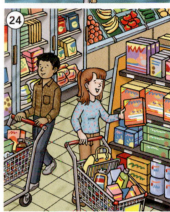

fotocentro/centro de revelado	**17**	photo shop	galería/centro comercial	**23**	(shopping) mall
pizzería	**18**	pizza shop	supermercado	**24**	supermarket
oficina de correos	**19**	post office	juguetería	**25**	toy store
restaurante	**20**	restaurant	estación de trenes	**26**	train station
escuela/instituto/colegio	**21**	school	agencia de viajes	**27**	travel agency
zapatería	**22**	shoe store	videocentro	**28**	video store

A. Where's the **hair salon**?
B. It's right over there.

A. Is there a/an _____ nearby?
B. Yes. There's a/an _____ around the corner.
A. Thanks.

A. Excuse me. Where's the _____?
B. It's down the street, next to the _____.
A. Thank you.

Which of these places are in your neighborhood?
(In my neighborhood there's a/an ....)

LA CIUDAD

juzgado/corte/tribunal	**1**	courthouse	estación de policía	**11**	police station
taxi	**2**	taxi/cab/taxicab	cárcel	**12**	jail
parada de taxis/piquera	**3**	taxi stand	acera/banqueta	**13**	sidewalk
taxista/conductor/ chofer de taxi	**4**	taxi driver/ cab driver	calle	**14**	street
			alumbrado/lámpara/farol/poste de luz	**15**	street light
hidrante/boca de riego	**5**	fire hydrant	estacionamiento/parqueadero/ aparcamiento	**16**	parking lot
basurero	**6**	trash container			
palacio de gobierno/ ayuntamiento/alcaldía	**7**	city hall	inspector(a) de estacionómetro/parquímetro	**17**	meter maid
			estacionómetro/parquímetro	**18**	parking meter
alarma contra incendios	**8**	fire alarm box	camión de la basura	**19**	garbage truck
buzón	**9**	mailbox	subterráneo/metro	**20**	subway
alcantarilla/desagüe/drenaje	**10**	sewer	estación del metro	**21**	subway station

puesto de periódicos	**22**	newsstand	parada/paradero de autobús/camión	**32** bus stop
semáforo	**23**	traffic light / traffic signal	autobús/bus/guagua/camión	**33** bus
cruce/intersección	**24**	intersection	conductor/chofer de autobús/busero	**34** bus driver
policía	**25**	police officer	edificio de oficinas	**35** office building
cruce de peatones/línea de seguridad	**26**	crosswalk	teléfono público	**36** public telephone
peatón(a)	**27**	pedestrian	letrero con el nombre de la calle	**37** street sign
repartidor/carretilla de helados/mantecados	**28**	ice cream truck	boca de la alcantarilla/del desagüe/del drenaje	**38** manhole
cuneta/empalme/bordillo/encintado	**29**	curb	motocicleta/moto	**39** motorcycle
estacionamiento/parqueadero de niveles	**30**	parking garage	buhonero/vendedor ambulante	**40** street vendor
estación de bomberos/bomba	**31**	fire station	cajero/ventanilla de servicio rápido	**41** drive-through window

A. Where's the _____?
B. On/In/Next to/Between/Across from/In front of/Behind/Under/Over the _____.

[An Election Speech]

If I am elected mayor, I'll take care of all the problems in our city. We need to do something about our _____s. We also need to do something about our _____s. And look at our _____s! We REALLY need to do something about THEM! We need a new mayor who can solve these problems. If I am elected mayor, we'll be proud of our _____s, _____s, and _____s again! Vote for me!

Go to an intersection in your city or town. What do you see? Make a list. Then tell about it.

DESCRIPCIÓN FÍSICA DE LAS PERSONAS/LA GENTE

niño(a)/niños(as)	1	child–children
bebé/nene(a)	2	baby/infant
niño(a) que empieza a hacer pinitos/a andar	3	toddler
niño	4	boy
niña	5	girl
adolescente	6	teenager
adulto	**7**	**adult**
hombre–hombres	8	man–men
mujer–mujeres	9	woman–women
persona mayor/ de edad avanzada/ de la tercera edad/ anciano(a)	10	senior citizen/ elderly person
edad		**age**
joven	11	young
maduro(a)/cuarentón(a)/ cincuentón(a)	12	middle-aged
mayor/de edad avanzada	13	old/elderly
estatura		**height**
alto(a)	14	tall
estatura promedio/ mediana	15	average height
bajo(a)	16	short
peso		**weight**
gordo(a)	17	heavy
de peso mediano	18	average weight
delgado(a)/fino(a)/ esbelto(a)	19	thin/slim
embarazada/ encinta	20	pregnant
discapacitado(a)	21	physically challenged
ciego(a)/tener problemas de la vista	22	vision impaired
sordo(a)/tener problemas de oído	23	hearing impaired

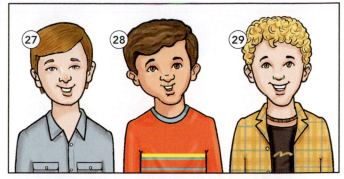

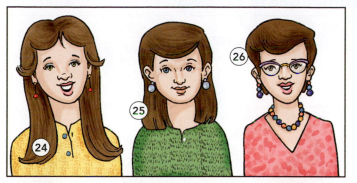

Descripción del pelo/cabello		Describing Hair
largo	24	long
hasta el hombro	25	shoulder length
corto	26	short
lacio/liso	27	straight
ondulado	28	wavy
rizado/ensortijado/crespo/ encrespado/chino/grifo	29	curly

negro	30	black
café/castaño/marrón	31	brown
rubio/mono/güero	32	blond
pelirrojo	33	red
cano/canoso/gris	34	gray
calvo(a)/pelón(a)	35	bald
barba	36	beard
bigote/mostacho	37	mustache

A. Tell me about *your brother.*
B. *He's a tall heavy boy* with *short curly brown* hair.

A. What does *your new boss* look like?
B. *She's average height,* and *she* has *long straight black* hair.

A. Can you describe *the person*?
B. *He's a tall thin middle-aged man.*
A. Anything else?
B. Yes. *He's bald*, and *he* has *a mustache.*

A. Can you describe *your grandmother*?
B. *She's a short thin elderly person* with *long wavy gray* hair.
A. Anything else?
B. Yes. *She's hearing impaired.*

Tell about yourself.

Tell about people in your family.

Tell about your favorite actor or actress or other famous person.

DESCRIPCIÓN DE PERSONAS/GENTE Y COSAS

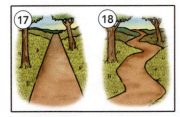
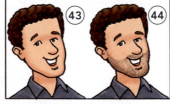

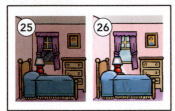

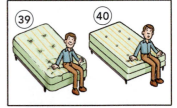

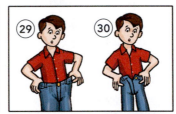
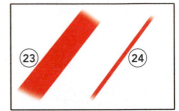

nuevo(a) – viejo(a)	1–2	new – old
joven – viejo(a)	3–4	young – old
alto(a) – bajo(a)	5–6	tall – short
largo(a) – corto(a)	7–8	long – short
grande – chiquito(a)/pequeño(a)	9–10	large/big – small/little
rápido(a) – lento(a)	11–12	fast – slow
gordo(a) - delgado(a)/flaco(a)	13–14	heavy/fat – thin/skinny
pesado(a) – liviano(a)	15–16	heavy – light
recto(a) – sinuoso(a)/curvo(a)	17–18	straight – crooked
liso(a) – rizado(a)/encrespado(a)	19–20	straight – curly
ancho(a) – angosto(a)/estrecho(a)	21–22	wide – narrow
grueso(a) – delgado(a)	23–24	thick – thin
oscuro(a) – claro(a)/con luz	25–26	dark – light
alto(a) – bajo(a)	27–28	high – low
flojo(a)/holgado(a) – estrecho(a)/apretado(a)	29–30	loose – tight
bueno(a) – malo(a)	31–32	good – bad
caliente – frío(a)	33–34	hot – cold
ordenado(a) – desordenado(a)	35–36	neat – messy
limpio(a) – sucio(a)	37–38	clean – dirty
suave – duro(a)	39–40	soft – hard
fácil – difícil/duro(a)	41–42	easy – difficult/hard
terso(a)/liso(a) – áspero(a)	43–44	smooth – rough
escandaloso(a) – quieto(a)/tranquilo(a)/callado(a)	45–46	noisy/loud – quiet
casado(a) – soltero(a)	47–48	married – single

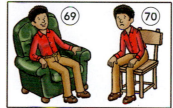

rico(a) – pobre	**49–50**	rich/wealthy – poor	
bonito(a) – feo(a)	**51–52**	pretty/beautiful – ugly	
guapo(a) – feo(a)	**53–54**	handsome – ugly	
mojado(a) – seco(a)	**55–56**	wet – dry	
abierto(a) – cerrado(a)	**57–58**	open – closed	
lleno(a) – vacío(a)	**59–60**	full – empty	
caro(a) – barato(a)	**61–62**	expensive – cheap/inexpensive	

elegante – sencillo(a)	**63–64**	fancy – plain
brillante – opaco(a)	**65–66**	shiny – dull
afilado(a) – romo(a)/desafilado(a)	**67–68**	sharp – dull
cómodo(a) – incómodo(a)	**69–70**	comfortable – uncomfortable
honesto(a)/honrado(a) – deshonesto(a)	**71–72**	honest – dishonest

[1–2]
A. Is your car **new**?
B. No. It's **old**.

1–2	Is your car _____?	25–26	Is the room _____?	49–50	Is your uncle _____?
3–4	Is he _____?	27–28	Is the bridge _____?	51–52	Is the witch _____?
5–6	Is your sister _____?	29–30	Are the pants _____?	53–54	Is the pirate _____?
7–8	Is his hair _____?	31–32	Are your neighbor's children _____?	55–56	Are the clothes _____?
9–10	Is their dog _____?	33–34	Is the water _____?	57–58	Is the door _____?
11–12	Is the train _____?	35–36	Is your desk _____?	59–60	Is the pitcher _____?
13–14	Is your friend _____?	37–38	Are the windows _____?	61–62	Is that restaurant _____?
15–16	Is the box _____?	39–40	Is the mattress _____?	63–64	Is the dress _____?
17–18	Is the road _____?	41–42	Is the homework _____?	65–66	Is your kitchen floor _____?
19–20	Is her hair _____?	43–44	Is your skin _____?	67–68	Is the knife _____?
21–22	Is the tie _____?	45–46	Is your neighbor _____?	69–70	Is the chair _____?
23–24	Is the line _____?	47–48	Is your sister _____?	71–72	Is he _____?

A. Tell me about your ....
B. He's/She's/It's/They're _____.

A. Do you have a/an _____ ....?
B. No. I have a/an _____ ....

Describe yourself.
Describe a person you know.
Describe some things in your home.
Describe some things in your community.

DESCRIPCIÓN DE ESTADOS FÍSICOS Y EMOTIVOS/DE ÁNIMO

estar cansado(a)	**1**	tired	estar lleno(a)/satisfecho(a)	**9**	full
tener sueño/estar soñoliento(a)	**2**	sleepy	estar contento(a)	**10**	happy
estar agotado(a)	**3**	exhausted	estar triste	**11**	sad/unhappy
estar enfermo(a)	**4**	sick/ill	sentirse desgraciado(a)/infeliz	**12**	miserable
tener calor	**5**	hot	estar entusiasmado(a)/emocionado (a)	**13**	excited
tener frío	**6**	cold	estar decepcionado(a)	**14**	disappointed
tener hambre	**7**	hungry	estar contrariado(a)	**15**	upset
tener sed	**8**	thirsty	estar molesto(a)/contrariado(a)	**16**	annoyed

estar enfadado(a)/disgustado(a)/enojado(a)	**17** angry/mad	estar preocupado(a)	**26** worried
estar furioso(a)	**18** furious	estar asustado(a)/tener miedo	**27** scared/afraid
estar harto(a)/colmado(a)/asqueado(a)	**19** disgusted	estar aburrido(a)	**28** bored
estar frustrado(a)	**20** frustrated	estar orgulloso(a)	**29** proud
estar sorprendido(a)	**21** surprised	estar avergonzado(a)	**30** embarrassed
estar atónito(a)/turbado(a)/consternado(a)/ estupefacto(a)/pasmado(a)	**22** shocked	estar celoso(a)	**31** jealous
sentirse solo(a)	**23** lonely	estar confundido(a)/desconcertado(a)/ enredado(a)/hecho(a) un lío	**32** confused
echar de menos/tener morriña/nostalgia	**24** homesick		
estar nervioso(a)	**25** nervous		

A. You look _____.
B. I am. I'm VERY _____.

A. Are you _____?
B. No. Why do you ask? Do I LOOK _____?
A. Yes. You do.

What makes you happy? sad? mad?

What do you do when you feel nervous? annoyed?

Do you ever feel embarrassed? When?

LAS FRUTAS

Spanish		English		Spanish		English
manzana	**1** apple	higo	**12** fig	mandarina	**23** tangerine
durazno/melocotón	**2** peach	coco	**13** coconut	uvas	**24** grapes
pera	**3** pear	aguacate	**14** avocado	cerezas	**25** cherries
banana/guineo/plátano	**4** banana	melón	**15** cantaloupe	ciruelas pasas	**26** prunes
plátano verde/grande	**5** plantain	melón verde/dulce/chino/	**16** honeydew	dátiles	**27** dates
ciruela	**6** plum	de Indias	(melon)	uvas pasas/pasitas	**28** raisins
albaricoque/	**7** apricot	sandía/melón de agua	**17** watermelon	nueces	**29** nuts
chabacano/damasco		piña	**18** pineapple	frambuesas	**30** raspberries
nectarina	**8** nectarine	toronja/pomelo	**19** grapefruit	arándanos	**31** blueberries
kiwi	**9** kiwi	lima/limón (amarillo)	**20** lemon	fresas	**32** strawberries
papaya/fruta bomba	**10** papaya	lima/limón (verde)	**21** lime		
mango	**11** mango	naranja/china	**22** orange		

[1–23]
A. This **apple** is delicious!
   Where did you get it?
B. At *Sam's Supermarket.*

[24–32]
A. These **grapes** are delicious!
   Where did you get them?
B. At *Franny's Fruit Stand.*

A. I'm hungry. Do we have any fruit?
B. Yes. We have _____s* and
   _____s.*

* With 15–19, use:
   We have _____ and _____.

A. Do we have any more _____s?†
B. No. I'll get some more when I go
   to the supermarket.

† With 15–19 use:
   Do we have any more _____?

What are your favorite fruits?
Which fruits don't you like?

Which of these fruits grow where you live?

Name and describe other fruits you know.

LOS VEGETALES/LAS VERDURAS

Spanish	#	English
apio	1	celery
maíz/elote	2	corn
brécol/brócoli	3	broccoli
coliflor	4	cauliflower
espinaca	5	spinach
perejil	6	parsley
espárrago	7	asparagus
berenjena	8	eggplant
lechuga	9	lettuce
repollo/col	10	cabbage
bok choy	11	bok choy
calabacita/calabacín	12	zucchini
calabaza pequeña	13	acorn squash
zapallo/güira(o)	14	butternut squash
ajo	15	garlic

Spanish	#	English
guisante/chícharo/petit pois	16	pea
habichuelas tiernas/ejotes/judías verdes	17	string bean/green bean
haba	18	lima bean
frijol negro	19	black bean
frijol rojo/colorado habichuelas coloradas poroto	20	kidney bean
repollito/col de bruselas	21	brussels sprout
pepino/pepinillo	22	cucumber
tomate/jitomate	23	tomato
zanahoria	24	carrot
rábano	25	radish
hongo/seta/champiñón	26	mushroom

Spanish	#	English
alcachofa	27	artichoke
papa/patata	28	potato
batata dulce/camote	29	sweet potato
batata (anaranjada)	30	yam
pimiento verde	31	green pepper/sweet pepper
pimiento rojo/pimiento morrón	32	red pepper
chile/pimiento jalapeño	33	jalapeño (pepper)
chile colorado	34	chili pepper
remolacha/betabel	35	beet
cebolla	36	onion
cebollino(a)/cebollín/escalonia	37	scallion/green onion
nabo	38	turnip

A. What do we need from the supermarket?
B. We need **celery*** and **peas.†**

* 1–15   † 16–38

A. How do you like the
   ___[1–15]___ / ___[16–38]___s?
B. It's/They're delicious.

A. *Bobby*? Finish your vegetables!
B. But you KNOW I hate
   ___[1–15]___ / ___[16–38]___s!
A. I know. But it's/they're good for you!

Which vegetables do you like?
Which vegetables don't you like?

Which of these vegetables grow where you live?

Name and describe other vegetables you know.

CARNES, AVES, PESCADOS Y MARISCOS

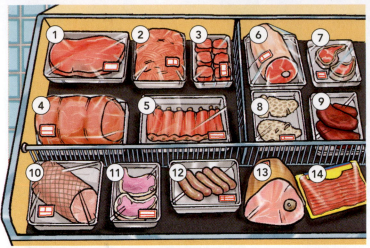

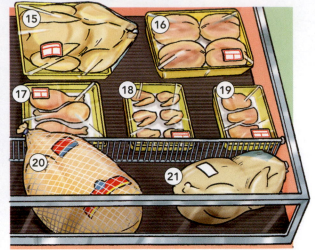

Carnes	Meat	
filete/bistec/bisté/bife	**1**	steak
carne molida	**2**	ground beef
carne para guisar/cocer/estofado	**3**	stewing beef
carne para asar	**4**	roast beef
costillas	**5**	ribs
pierna de cordero	**6**	leg of lamb
chuletas de cordero	**7**	lamb chops
tripa/mondongo/callos/menudo	**8**	tripe
hígado	**9**	liver
puerco/cerdo	**10**	pork
chuletas de puerco/de cerdo	**11**	pork chops
salchichones/chorizos/longaniza/salchichas	**12**	sausages
jamón	**13**	ham
tocino/tocineta/panceta/bacón/beicon	**14**	bacon

Aves	Poultry	
pollo/gallina	**15**	chicken
pechugas de pollo/gallina	**16**	chicken breasts
muslos de pollo/gallina	**17**	chicken legs/drumsticks
alitas/alas de pollo/gallina	**18**	chicken wings
encuentros/caderas de pollo/gallina	**19**	chicken thighs

pavo/guajolote	**20**	turkey
pato	**21**	duck

Pescados y mariscos	Seafood	
PESCADOS	FISH	
salmón	**22**	salmon
mero	**23**	halibut
abadejo/bacalao	**24**	haddock
lenguado	**25**	flounder
trucha	**26**	trout
bagro/bagre/barbo	**27**	catfish
filete de lenguado/de suela	**28**	filet of sole
MARISCOS	SHELLFISH	
gambas/langostinos/camarones	**29**	shrimp
conchuelas/vieiras/veneras/ callos de hacha	**30**	scallops
cangrejos	**31**	crabs
almejas	**32**	clams
mejillones	**33**	mussels
ostras	**34**	oysters
langosta	**35**	lobster

A. I'm going to the supermarket. What do we need?
B. Please get some **steak**.
A. **Steak**? All right.

A. Excuse me. Where can I find _____?
B. Look in the _____ Section.
A. Thank you.

A. This/These _____ looks/ look very fresh!
B. Let's get some for dinner.

Do you eat meat, poultry, or seafood? Which of these foods do you like?

Which of these foods are popular in your countr

PRODUCTOS LÁCTEOS, JUGOS Y BEBIDAS

Productos lácteos	Dairy Products		Jugos/Zumos	Juices		Bebidas	Beverages
leche	**1** milk		jugo de manzana	**15** apple juice		soda/gaseosa/	**23** soda
leche baja en grasa	**2** low-fat milk		jugo de piña	**16** pineapple juice		refresco	
leche descremada/	**3** skim milk		jugo de toronja/	**17** grapefruit juice		soda de dieta	**24** diet soda
desgrasada			pomelo			agua embotellada	**25** bottled water
leche con chocolate	**4** chocolate milk		jugo de tomate	**18** tomato juice			
jugo de naranja/	**5** orange juice*		jugo de uvas	**19** grape juice		**Café y té**	**Coffee and Tea**
de china*			ponche de frutas	**20** fruit punch		café	**26** coffee
queso	**6** cheese		cartón/paquete de	**21** juice paks		café	**27** decaffeinated
mantequilla	**7** butter		jugos			descafeinado	coffee/decaf
margarina	**8** margarine		jugo/zumo/bebida en	**22** powdered		café instantáneo	**28** instant coffee
crema agria/crema	**9** sour cream		polvo/instantánea	drink mix		té	**29** tea
queso crema	**10** cream cheese					tisana/infusión de	**30** herbal tea
requesón/cuajada	**11** cottage cheese					hierbas/yerbas	
yogur/leche búlgara	**12** yogurt					chocolate en polvo	**31** cocoa/hot
soja/soya/tofu*	**13** tofu*						chocolate mix
huevos	**14** eggs						

*El jugo de naranja y el tofu no son productos lácteos,
pero usualmente se les encuentra en esta sección.

A. I'm going to the supermarket to get some **milk**.
Do we need anything else?
B. Yes. Please get some **apple juice**.

A. Excuse me. Where can I find _____?
B. Look in the _____ Section.
A. Thanks.

A. Look! _____ is/are on sale this week!
B. Let's get some!

Which of these foods do you like?

Which of these foods are good for you?

Which brands of these foods do you buy?

DELICATESSEN/CHARCUTERÍA: CARNES FRÍAS, PRODUCTOS CONGELADOS Y APERITIVOS

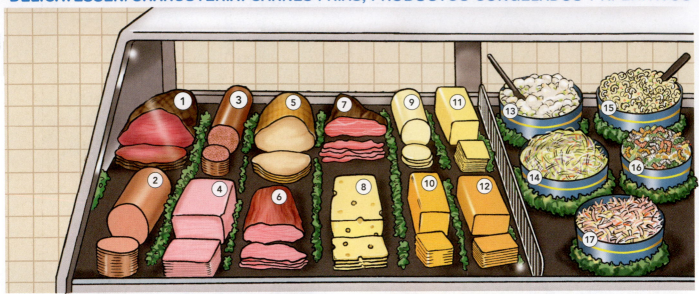

Delicatessen/Charcutería	Deli		Productos congelados	Frozen Foods
carne (de vaca) asada/rosbif	1	roast beef	helado	18 ice cream
mortadela	2	bologna	vegetales congelados	19 frozen vegetables
salami	3	salami	comida congelada /platos congelados	20 frozen dinners
jamón	4	ham	concentrado de limonada congelada	21 frozen lemonade
pavo/guajolote	5	turkey	concentrado de jugo de naranja/	22 frozen orange juice
carne adobada/en salmuera/	6	corned beef	de china congelado	
salpresa/cornbif				
pastrami	7	pastrami	**Aperitivos/Botanas/Antojitos/**	**Snack Foods**
queso suizo	8	Swiss cheese	**Pasabocas**	
provolone	9	provolone	papas/papitas/patatas fritas	23 potato chips
queso americano	10	American cheese	fritos de tortilla/totoposte/totopo	24 tortilla chips
mozzarella	11	mozzarella	pretzels	25 pretzels
queso cheddar	12	cheddar cheese	nueces	26 nuts
ensalada de papas/patatas	13	potato salad	palomitas/rosetas/hojuelas/	27 popcorn
ensalada de repollo/col	14	cole slaw	rositas de maíz	
ensalada de coditos	15	macaroni salad		
ensalada de pasta	16	pasta salad		
ensalada de mariscos	17	seafood salad		

A. Should we get some **roast beef**?
B. Good idea. And let's get some **potato salad**.

ABARROTES/PROVISIONES

Productos envasados/ empaquetados	Packaged Goods		mantequilla de maní/ cacahuete/cacahuate/ crema de cacahuate	14	peanut butter	sazón/aliño aderezo para ensaladas	29	salad dressing
cereal	1	cereal						
galletas	2	cookies	Condimentos/especias y salsas	Condiments		Panadería y pastelería	Baked Goods	
galletas saladas/de soda	3	crackers	salsa de tomate/catsup	15	ketchup	pan	30	bread
coditos/macarrones cortos	4	macaroni	mostaza	16	mustard	bollos/ panecillos	31	rolls
fideos/tallarines	5	noodles	encurtido picado	17	relish	bollos/	32	English
espaguetis	6	spaghetti	encurtidos	18	pickles	panecillos		muffins
arroz	7	rice	aceitunas	19	olives	pan de pita	33	pita bread
			sal	20	salt	bizcocho/torta/	34	cake
Productos enlatados	Canned Goods		pimienta	21	pepper	pastel/ponqué		
sopa	8	soup	especias/condimentos	22	spices			
atún enlatado	9	tuna (fish)	salsa china/de soja/soya	23	soy sauce	Productos para	Baking	
vegetales/verduras enlatados(as)	10	(canned) vegetables	mayonesa	24	mayonnaise	hornear	Products	
fruta enlatada	11	(canned) fruit	aceite para cocinar	25	(cooking) oil	harina	35	flour
			aceite de oliva	26	olive oil	azúcar	36	sugar
Mermeladas y confituras	Jams and Jellies		salsa	27	salsa	harina preparada para bizcocho	37	cake mix
mermelada	12	jam	vinagre	28	vinegar			
jalea	13	jelly						

A. I got **cereal** and **soup**. What else is on the shopping list?
B. **Ketchup** and **bread**.

A. Excuse me. I'm looking for _____.
B. It's/They're next to the _____.

A. Pardon me. I'm looking for _____.
B. It's/They're between the _____ and the _____.

Which of these foods do you like?

Which brands of these foods do you buy?

ARTÍCULOS PARA EL HOGAR, EL BEBÉ Y LAS MASCOTAS

Productos de papel/desechables	Paper Products		Artículos para el bebé	Baby Products
servilletas	**1** napkins		cereal	**15** baby cereal
vasos de cartón/desechables	**2** paper cups		papillas/colados	**16** baby food
pañuelos desechables/kleenex	**3** tissues		fórmula	**17** formula
pajillas/popotes/carrizos/sorbetos	**4** straws		toallitas húmedas desechables	**18** wipes
platos de cartón/desechables	**5** paper plates		pañales desechables	**19** (disposable) diapers
papel toalla	**6** paper towels			
papel higiénico/sanitario	**7** toilet paper		**Comida para mascotas**	**Pet Food**
			comida para gatos	**20** cat food
Artículos para el hogar	**Household Items**		comida para perros	**21** dog food
bolsitas plásticas para sándwiches	**8** sandwich bags			
bolsas para la basura	**9** trash bags			
jabón	**10** soap			
jabón líquido	**11** liquid soap			
papel de aluminio	**12** aluminum foil			
plástico para envolver	**13** plastic wrap			
papel encerado/de cera	**14** waxed paper			

A. Excuse me. Where can I find **napkins**?
B. **Napkins**? Look in Aisle 4.

[7, 10–17, 20, 21]
A. We forgot to get _____!
B. I'll get it. Where is it?
A. It's in Aisle _____.

[1–6, 8, 9, 18, 19]
A. We forgot to get _____!
B. I'll get them. Where are they?
A. They're in Aisle _____.

What do you need from the supermarket?
Make a complete shopping list!

EL SUPERMERCADO

pasillo/corredor	**1** aisle	empacador(a)	**14** bagger/packer
cliente	**2** shopper/customer	caja rápida	**15** express checkout (line)
carretilla/carrito	**3** shopping basket		
fila para pagar	**4** checkout line	periódico	**16** tabloid (newspaper)
mostrador de chequeo/caja	**5** checkout counter	revista	**17** magazine
cinta/banda transportadora	**6** conveyor belt	lector óptico	**18** scanner
caja registradora	**7** cash register	bolsa plástica/de plástico	**19** plastic bag
carrito/carretilla	**8** shopping cart	frutas y verduras	**20** produce
chicle/goma de masticar	**9** (chewing) gum	gerente	**21** manager
pastilla/caramelo/dulce	**10** candy	empleado(a)	**22** clerk
cupones	**11** coupons	pesa/balanza	**23** scale
cajero(a)	**12** cashier	recicladora/reembolsadora para latas	**24** can-return machine
bolsa/cartucho/talego de papel	**13** paper bag	recicladora/reembolsadora para botellas	**25** bottle-return machine

[1–8, 11–19, 21–25]
A. This is a gigantic supermarket!
B. It is! Look at all the **aisle**s!

[9, 10, 20]
A. This is a gigantic supermarket!
B. It is. Look at all the **produce**!

Where do you usually shop for food? Do you go to a supermarket, or do you go to a small grocery store? Describe the place where you shop.

Describe the differences between U.S. supermarkets and food stores in your country.

ENVASES, RECIPIENTES Y MEDIDAS DE CANTIDAD

bolsa	**1** bag	cabeza	**9** head	barra	**16** stick
botella	**2** bottle	frasco/tarro/pote	**10** jar	tubo	**17** tube
caja/cajeta/cajetita	**3** box	hogaza(s)/barra(s) de pan	**11** loaf–loaves	pinta	**18** pint
racimo/manojo/mazo	**4** bunch	paquete/cajetilla/cajeta	**12** pack	cuarto de galón	**19** quart
lata	**5** can	paquete/bulto	**13** package	medio galón	**20** half-gallon
cartón	**6** carton	rollo	**14** roll	galón	**21** gallon
envase	**7** container	cartón/paquete/	**15** six-pack	litro	**22** liter
docena	**8** dozen*	bulto de seis artículos		libra	**23** pound

* "a dozen eggs," NO "a dozen of eggs"

A. Please get a **bag** of *flour* when you go to the supermarket.
B. A **bag** of *flour*? Okay.

A. Please get two **bottles** of *ketchup* when you go to the supermarket.
B. Two **bottles** of *ketchup*? Okay.

[At home]

A. What did you get at the supermarket?
B. I got _____, _____, and _____.

[In a supermarket]

A. Is this the express checkout line?
B. Yes, it is. Do you have more than eight items?
A. No. I only have _____, _____, and _____.

Open your kitchen cabinets and refrigerator. Make a list of all the things you find.

What do you do with empty bottles, jars, and cans? Do you recycle them, reuse them, or throw them away?

PESOS Y MEDIDAS

| cucharadita | teaspoon | cucharada | tablespoon | una onza | 1 (fluid) ounce |
| cdta. | tsp. | cda. | Tbsp. | 1 oz. líquida | 1 fl. oz. |

una taza	cup	una pinta	pint	un cuarto de galón	quart	un galón	gallon
	c.		pt.		qt.		gal.
8 ozs. líquidas	8 fl. ozs.	16 ozs. líquidas	16 fl. ozs.	32 ozs. líquidas	32 fl. ozs.	128 ozs. líquidas	128 fl. ozs.

A. How much water should I put in?
B. The recipe says to add one _____ of water.

A. This fruit punch is delicious! What's in it?
B. Two _____s of apple juice, three _____ of orange juice, and a _____ of grape juice.

una onza	an ounce	un cuarto de libra	a quarter of a pound	media libra	half a pound	tres cuartos de libra	three-quarters of a pound	una libra	a pound
		¼ lb.	1/4 lb.	½ lb.	1/2 lb.	¾ lb.	3/4 lb.	1 lb.	lb.
1 oz.	oz.	4 ozs.	4 ozs.	8 ozs.	8 ozs.	12 ozs.	12 ozs.	16 ozs.	16 ozs.

A. How much roast beef would you like?
B. I'd like _____, please.
A. Anything else?
B. Yes. Please give me _____ of Swiss cheese.

A. This chili tastes very good! What did you put in it?
B. _____ of ground beef, _____ of beans, _____ of tomatoes, and _____ of chili powder.

RECETAS Y PREPARACIÓN DE ALIMENTOS

corte (a)	**1**	cut (up)
pique (pica)	**2**	chop (up)
corte(a)/rebane(a)	**3**	slice
ralle(a)	**4**	grate
pele(a)/monde(a)	**5**	peel
parta(e)	**6**	break
bata(e)	**7**	beat
revuelva(e)	**8**	stir
eche(a)/vierta(e)	**9**	pour
añada(e)	**10**	add
combine(a) ____ y ____	**11**	combine ____ and ____
mezcle(a) ____ y ____	**12**	mix ____ and ____
ponga (pon) ____ en ____	**13**	put ____ in ____

cocine(a)	**14**	cook
hornee(a)	**15**	bake
hierva(e)	**16**	boil
ase(a) a la parrilla	**17**	broil
cuezca/cueza (cuece) al vapor	**18**	steam
fría(e)	**19**	fry
guise(a)/saltee(a)	**20**	saute
cuezca/cueza(cuece) a fuego lento	**21**	simmer
ase(a)/hornee(a)	**22**	roast
ase(a) a la parrilla	**23**	barbecue / grill
saltee(a)/sofría(e)	**24**	stir-fry
cuezca/cueza(cuece)/cocine(a) en el microondas	**25**	microwave

A. Can I help you?
B. Yes. Please **cut up** the vegetables.

[1–25]
A. What are you doing?
B. I'm _____ing the ....

[14–25]
A. How long should I _____ the ....?
B. _____ the .... for .... minutes/seconds.

What's your favorite recipe? Give instructions and use the units of measure on page 57. For example:

Mix a cup of flour and two tablespoons of sugar.
Add half a pound of butter.
Bake at 350° (degrees) for twenty minutes.

UTENSILIOS DE COCINA

Spanish	#	English
cuchara bola para servir helados	1	ice cream scoop
abrelatas	2	can opener
abrebotellas	3	bottle opener
mondador/pelapapas	4	(vegetable) peeler
batidor de mano	5	(egg) beater
tapadera/tapa	6	lid/cover/top
olla/cacerola/cazo	7	pot
sartén	8	frying pan/skillet
olla de baño María	9	double boiler
wok/disco chino	10	wok
cucharón	11	ladle
colador	12	strainer
espátula	13	spatula

Spanish	#	English
rejilla para cocer al vapor	14	steamer
cuchillo	15	knife
triturador/machacador de ajos	16	garlic press
rallo/rallador	17	grater
bandeja/fuente/refractario	18	casserole dish
bandeja de asar/hornear	19	roasting pan
parrilla de asar/hornear/pavera	20	roasting rack
trinchante	21	carving knife
cacerola	22	saucepan
colador	23	colander

Spanish	#	English
minutero	24	kitchen timer
rodillo/rolo	25	rolling pin
molde para tartas	26	pie plate
mondador	27	paring knife
plancha/bandeja para hornear galletas	28	cookie sheet
molde de hacer galletas	29	cookie cutter
tazón/cuenco	30	(mixing) bowl
batidor de mano	31	whisk
taza de medir	32	measuring cup
cuchara de medir	33	measuring spoon
molde para bizcochos/hornear/pasteles	34	cake pan
cuchara de madera	35	wooden spoon

A. Could I possibly borrow your **ice cream scoop**?
B. Sure. I'll be happy to lend you my **ice cream scoop**.
A. Thanks.

A. What are you looking for?
B. I can't find the _____.
A. Look in that drawer/in that cabinet/
on the counter/next to the _____/
....

[A Commercial]
Come to *Kitchen World*! We have
everything you need for your kitchen, from
_____s and _____s, to _____s
and _____s. Are you looking for a new
_____? Is it time to throw out your old
_____? Come to *Kitchen World* today!
We have everything you need!

What kitchen utensils and
cookware do you have in
your kitchen?

Which things do you use
very often?

Which things do you
rarely use?

COMIDA RÁPIDA/AL PASO/AL INSTANTE

hamburguesa	**1** hamburger		helado de yogur	**15** frozen yogurt
hamburguesa con queso/quesoburguesa	**2** cheeseburger		batido de leche/malteada	**16** milkshake
perro caliente/hot dog	**3** hot dog		soda/gaseosa	**17** soda
bocadillo/emparedado/sándwich de pescado	**4** fish sandwich		tapas	**18** lids
bocadillo/emparedado/sándwich de pollo	**5** chicken sandwich		vasos de cartón	**19** paper cups
pollo frito	**6** fried chicken		pajillas/popotes/carrizos/	**20** straws
papas fritas	**7** french fries		sorbetos	
nachos	**8** nachos		servilletas	**21** napkins
taco	**9** taco		cubiertos plásticos/de plástico	**22** plastic utensils
burrito	**10** burrito		salsa de tomate/catsup	**23** ketchup
pedazo de pizza	**11** slice of pizza		mostaza	**24** mustard
tazón de chile con carne	**12** bowl of chili		mayonesa	**25** mayonnaise
ensalada	**13** salad		encurtido de pepinillos	**26** relish
helado	**14** ice cream		sazón/aliño/aderezo para ensaladas	**27** salad dressing

A. May I help you?
B. Yes. I'd like a/an ___[1–5, 9–17]___/
an order of ___[6–8]___.

A. Excuse me. We're almost out of ___[18–27]___.
B. I'll get some more from the supply room. Thanks for telling me.

Do you go to fast-food restaurants? Which ones?
How often? What do you order?

Are there fast-food restaurants in your country?
Are they popular? What foods do they have?

EN LA CAFETERÍA Y LOS SÁNDWICHES

churro/dona/buñuelo/llanta	**1** donut	chocolate caliente	**20** hot chocolate
pan dulce/bollo/bollito	**2** muffin	leche	**21** milk
bagel	**3** bagel	bocadillo/emparedado/sándwich de atún	**22** tuna fish sandwich
bollo/dulce/panecillo	**4** bun	bocadillo/emparedado/sándwich de huevo	**23** egg salad sandwich
pan dulce danés	**5** danish/pastry	bocadillo/emparedado/sándwich de pollo	**24** chicken salad sandwich
bisquet/panecillo	**6** biscuit	bocadillo/emparedado/ sándwich de jamón con queso	**25** ham and cheese sandwich
croissant/cuernito	**7** croissant		
huevos	**8** eggs	bocadillo/emparedado/ sándwich de carne en salmuera/cornbif	**26** corned beef sandwich
panqueques/hot cakes	**9** pancakes		
waffles/gofres	**10** waffles	bocadillo/emparedado/ sándwich de tomate con lechuga y tocino	**27** BLT/bacon, lettuce, and tomato sandwich
pan tostado/tostada	**11** toast		
tocino/tocineta	**12** bacon	bocadillo/emparedado/ sándwich de carne (asada)/rosbif	**28** roast beef sandwich
chorizos/salchichas	**13** sausages		
papas estilo casero	**14** home fries	pan blanco/blando/suave/de molde/de agua	**29** white bread
café	**15** coffee	pan integral/de trigo	**30** whole wheat bread
café descafeinado	**16** decaf coffee	pan sirio/de pita	**31** pita bread
té	**17** tea	pan integral de centeno/negro	**32** pumpernickel
té frío/helado	**18** iced tea	pan de centeno	**33** rye bread
limonada	**19** lemonade	un panecito/panecillo/bollo	**34** a roll
		un mollete/pan de barra	**35** a submarine roll

A. May I help you?
B. Yes. I'd like a ____[1–7]____/an order of ____[8–14]____, please.
A. Anything to drink?
B. Yes. I'll have a small/medium-size/large/extra-large ____[15–21]____.

A. I'd like a ____[22–28]____ on ____[29–35]____, please.
B. What do you want on it?
A. Lettuce/tomato/mayonnaise/mustard/...

Do you like these foods? Which ones? Where do you get them? How often do you have them?

lleve los clientes a la mesa	**A**	seat the customers
vierta/sirva el agua	**B**	pour the water
tome/anote la orden	**C**	take the order
sirva la comida	**D**	serve the meal
anfitriona	**1**	hostess
anfitrión	**2**	host
cliente/comensal	**3**	diner/patron/customer
butaca/reservado/privado	**4**	booth
mesa	**5**	table
silla alta/trona	**6**	high chair

asiento elevador	**7**	booster seat
menú/carta	**8**	menu
canasta/canastilla/cesta para pan	**9**	bread basket
ayudante de camarero(a)	**10**	busperson
mesera/camarera	**11**	waitress/server
mesero/camarero	**12**	waiter/server
barra de ensaladas	**13**	salad bar
comedor	**14**	dining room
cocina	**15**	kitchen
chef	**16**	chef

[4–9]
A. Would you like a **booth**?
B. Yes, please.

[10–12]
A. Hello. My name is *Julie*, and I'll be your **waitress** this evening.
B. Hello.

[1, 2, 13–16]
A. This restaurant has a wonderful **salad bar**.
B. I agree.

limpie la mesa	**E** clear the table
pague la cuenta	**F** pay the check
deje una propina	**G** leave a tip
ponga/arregle la mesa	**H** set the table

cuarto para lavar platos	**17** dishroom
lavaplatos/lavavajillas	**18** dishwasher
bandeja/charola	**19** tray
carrito de postres	**20** dessert cart
cuenta	**21** check
propina	**22** tip
plato para la ensalada	**23** salad plate
plato para el pan y la mantequilla	**24** bread-and-butter plate
plato llano	**25** dinner plate

plato hondo/sopero	**26** soup bowl
vaso/copa para el agua	**27** water glass
copa	**28** wine glass
taza	**29** cup
platito/platillo	**30** saucer
servilleta	**31** napkin

juego de cubiertos/cuchillería silverware
tenedor/trinche para la ensalada	**32** salad fork
tenedor	**33** dinner fork
cuchillo	**34** knife
cucharita/cucharilla/cuchara de té	**35** teaspoon
cuchara para la sopa	**36** soup spoon
cuchillo para la mantequilla	**37** butter knife

[A–H]
A. Please _____.
B. All right. I'll _____ right away.

[23–37]
A. Excuse me. Where does the _____ go?
B. It goes { to the left of the _____.
to the right of the _____.
on the _____.
between the _____ and the _____.

[1, 2, 10–12, 16, 18]
A. Do you have any job openings?
B. Yes. We're looking for a _____.

[23–37]
A. Excuse me. I dropped my _____.
B. That's okay. I'll get you another _____ from the kitchen.

Tell about a restaurant you know. Describe the place and the people. (Is the restaurant large or small? How many tables are there? How many people work there? Is there a salad bar? . . .)

UN MENÚ

coctel/copa de frutas	**1** fruit cup/ fruit cocktail	antipasto/entremés **10** antipasto (plate)	fideos **22** noodles
jugo de tomate	**2** tomato juice	ensalada estilo César **11** Caesar salad	vegetales/ **23** mixed
coctel de camarones/ de gambas	**3** shrimp cocktail	pastel/budín de **12** meatloaf carne molida	verduras mixtos(as) vegetables
alitas de pollo	**4** chicken wings	filete/bistec de costilla/ **13** roast beef/	bizcocho/torta/ **24** chocolate
nachos	**5** nachos	asado/bife/rosbif prime rib	pastel de cake
cáscaras de papa rellenas	**6** potato skins	pollo al horno/asado **14** baked chicken	chocolate
		pescado a la parrilla **15** broiled fish	pastel/tarta de **25** apple pie
ensalada mixta	**7** tossed salad/ garden salad	espaguetis con **16** spaghetti and albóndigas meatballs	manzanas
			helado **26** ice cream
ensalada griega	**8** Greek salad	chuleta de ternera **17** veal cutlet	gelatina **27** jello
ensalada de espinacas	**9** spinach salad	una papa al horno/asada **18** a baked potato	pudín/budín **28** pudding
		puré de papas **19** mashed potatoes	copa de **29** ice cream
		papas fritas **20** french fries	helado/ sundae
		arroz **21** rice	mantecado especial/ sundae

[Ordering dinner]

A. May I take your order?
B. Yes, please. For the appetizer, I'd like the _____[1–6]_____.
A. And what kind of salad would you like?
B. I'll have the _____[7–11]_____.
A. And for the main course?
B. I'd like the _____[12–17]_____, please.
A. What side dish would you like with that?
B. Hmm. I think I'll have _____[18–23]_____.

[Ordering dessert]

A. Would you care for some dessert?
B. Yes. I'll have _____[24–28]_____/an _____[29]_____.

Tell about the food at a restaurant you know.
What's on the menu?

What are some typical foods on the menus of
restaurants in your country?

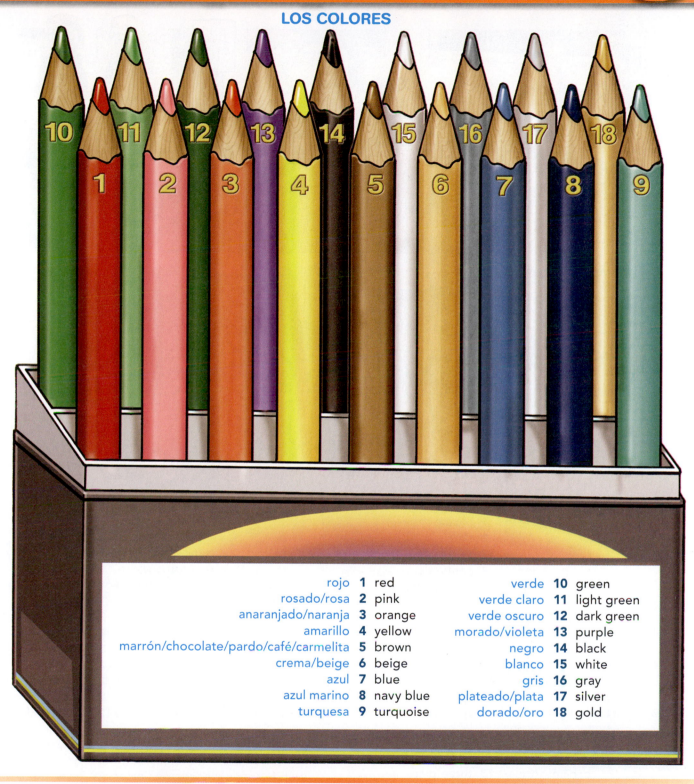

rojo	1	red		verde	10	green
rosado/rosa	2	pink		verde claro	11	light green
anaranjado/naranja	3	orange		verde oscuro	12	dark green
amarillo	4	yellow		morado/violeta	13	purple
marrón/chocolate/pardo/café/carmelita	5	brown		negro	14	black
crema/beige	6	beige		blanco	15	white
azul	7	blue		gris	16	gray
azul marino	8	navy blue		plateado/plata	17	silver
turquesa	9	turquoise		dorado/oro	18	gold

A. What's your favorite color?
B. **Red.**

A. I like your _____ shirt.
You look very good in _____.
B. Thank you. _____ is my
favorite color.

A. My TV is broken.
B. What's the matter with it?
A. People's faces are _____,
the sky is _____, and the
grass is _____!

Do you know the flags of different countries?
What are the colors of flags you know?

What color makes you happy? What color
makes you sad? Why?

LA ROPA

blusa	**1** blouse		corbata	**14** tie/necktie
falda	**2** skirt		uniforme	**15** uniform
camisa	**3** shirt		camiseta/playera	**16** T-shirt
pantalones	**4** pants/slacks		pantalones cortos/shorts	**17** shorts
camisa de mangas cortas	**5** sport shirt		vestido/traje de maternidad	**18** maternity dress
pantalones vaqueros/jeans/ de mezclilla/mahones	**6** jeans		mono/mameluco/overol/guardapolvo	**19** jumpsuit
polo/camisa/jersey de punto	**7** knit shirt/jersey		chaleco	**20** vest
vestido/traje	**8** dress		mameluco/trajecito júmper/júmper/mono	**21** jumper
suéter/con cuello de pico	**9** sweater		blazer/chaqueta cruzada	**22** blazer
chaqueta/saco	**10** jacket		túnica	**23** tunic
chaqueta/saco informal/ deportiva(o)/chaquetón/ campera/americana	**11** sport coat/ sport jacket/ jacket		leotardos/mallas	**24** leggings
			overol/mono/mameluco	**25** overalls
traje sastre/vestido de chaqueta/de dos piezas	**12** suit		camisa de cuello de tortuga/cisne	**26** turtleneck
			esmoquin/smóking	**27** tuxedo
conjunto/traje/ vestido de tres piezas/terno	**13** three-piece suit		corbata de gato/de lazo/de pajarita/ mariquita/corbatín	**28** bow tie
			vestido/traje de noche/de fiesta/ formal/de etiqueta	**29** (evening) gown

A. I think I'll wear my new **blouse** today.
B. Good idea!

A. I really like your _____.
B. Thank you.
A. Where did you get it/them?
B. At ....

A. Oh, no! I just ripped
my _____!
B. What a shame!

What clothing items in this lesson do you wear?

What color clothing do you like to wear?

What do you wear at work or at school? at parties?
at weddings?

ROPA PARA RESGUARDARSE DEL TIEMPO

Spanish	#	English	Spanish	#	English
abrigo/gabán/sobretodo	1	coat	paraguas/parasol/sombrilla	15	umbrella
abrigo/gabán/sobretodo	2	overcoat	poncho (de agua)/jorongo/sarape	16	poncho
sombrero	3	hat	capote corto/chamarra para lluvia/chubasquero	17	rain jacket
chaqueta/cazadora/chompa/chamarra	4	jacket	botas de goma/de caucho/hule/para la lluvia	18	rain boots
bufanda	5	scarf/muffler	gorro/gorra de esquiar	19	ski hat
abrigo tejido/de punto/suéter abierto	6	sweater jacket	abrigo/chaqueta para esquiar	20	ski jacket
leotardos/mallas	7	tights	guantes	21	gloves
gorra/cachucha	8	cap	máscara de esquiar/pasamontañas	22	ski mask
chaqueta de cuero	9	leather jacket	abrigo de plumas de ganso/acolchonado	23	down jacket
gorra de béisbol	10	baseball cap	mitones/guantes enteros	24	mittens
chaqueta/impermeable contra el viento	11	windbreaker	abrigo de invierno/pelliza/parka	25	parka
capote/impermeable	12	raincoat	anteojos/lentes/gafas para sol	26	sunglasses
sombrero impermeable	13	rain hat	orejeras	27	ear muffs
gabardina/trinchera/impermeable	14	trench coat	chaleco de plumas de ganso/acolchonado/acojinado	28	down vest

A. What's the weather like today?
B. It's cool/cold/raining/snowing.
A. I think I'll wear my _____.

[1–6, 8–17, 19, 20, 22, 23, 25, 28]
A. May I help you?
B. Yes, please. I'm looking for a/an _____.

[7, 18, 21, 24, 26, 27]
A. May I help you?
B. Yes, please. I'm looking for _____.

What do you wear outside when the weather is cool?/when it's raining?/when it's very cold?

ROPA DE DORMIR Y ROPA INTERIOR

pijama/piyama	**1** pajamas	calzones largos/térmicos	**11** long underwear/ long johns
camisón	**2** nightgown	medias/tobilleras/calcetines/calcetas	**12** socks
camisa de dormir	**3** nightshirt	panty bikini/pantaleta bikini	**13** (bikini) panties
bata de baño/albornoz	**4** bathrobe/robe	panty/pantaleta/calzonario/ braga/bombacha	**14** briefs/ underpants
zapatillas/babuchas/ pantuflas/chinelas	**5** slippers	sostenedor/sostén/brassiere/bra	**15** bra
mameluco/pelele/ pijamita de una pieza	**6** blanket sleeper	camisola/justillo	**16** camisole
camiseta	**7** undershirt/T-shirt	peticote de falda/medio fondo/enagua	**17** half slip
calzoncillos/trusas	**8** (jockey) shorts/ underpants/briefs	peticote/fondo entero/enagua/combinación	**18** (full) slip
calzoncillos bóxer/largos	**9** boxer shorts/boxers	medias	**19** stockings
suspensorios	**10** athletic supporter/ jockstrap	pantimedias	**20** pantyhose
		leotardos/mallas	**21** tights
		calcetines	**22** knee-highs
		calcetines/medias/tobilleras/tobimedias largas	**23** knee socks

A. I can't find my new _____.
B. Did you look in the bureau/dresser/closet?
A. Yes, I did.
B. Then it's/they're probably in the wash.

What sleepwear items do you wear? What sleepwear items do people in your family wear?

ROPA DEPORTIVA Y CALZADO

camiseta sin mangas	**1**	tank top	leotardo	**12** leotard
pantalones/calzones cortos/ pantaloncillos/shorts	**2**	running shorts	zapatos	**13** shoes
vincha/bandana	**3**	sweatband	zapatos de tacón alto	**14** (high) heels
traje para correr/ traje deportivo/ chándal	**4**	jogging suit/ running suit/ warm-up suit	zapatos de tacón bajo	**15** pumps
			mocasines	**16** loafers
camiseta/playera	**5**	T-shirt	zapatillas deportivas/tenis	**17** sneakers/athletic shoes
pantalones cortos/calzones/ pantaloncillos de Lycra/malla	**6**	lycra shorts/ bike shorts	zapatillas para jugar tenis	**18** tennis shoes
sudadera	**7**	sweatshirt	zapatillas para correr	**19** running shoes
pantalones de sudadera	**8**	sweatpants	zapatillas de botín alto/ medio botín/tenis altos	**20** high-tops/ high-top sneakers
batín	**9**	cover-up	sandalias	**21** sandals
vestido/traje de baño/ bañador	**10**	swimsuit/bathing suit	chancletas/chinelas/pantuflas	**22** thongs/flip-flops
			botas	**23** boots
traje de baño/bañador	**11**	swimming trunks/ swimsuit/bathing suit	botas de trabajo	**24** work boots
			botas para escalar	**25** hiking boots
			botas de vaquero	**26** cowboy boots
			mocasines	**27** moccasins

[1–12]
A. Excuse me. I found this/these _____ in the dryer. Is it/Are they yours?
B. Yes. It's/They're mine. Thank you.

[13–27]
A. Are those new _____?
B. Yes, they are.
A. They're very nice.
B. Thanks.

Do you exercise? What do you do?
What kind of clothing do you wear when you exercise?

What kind of shoes do you wear when you go to work or to school?
when you exercise? when you relax at home?
when you go out with friends or family members?

JOYERÍA Y ACCESORIOS DE VESTIR

anillo/sortija	**1** ring	tirantes	**14** suspenders
anillo de compromiso	**2** engagement ring	reloj/reloj de pulsera	**15** watch/wrist watch
anillo de matrimonio	**3** wedding ring/wedding band	pañuelo	**16** handkerchief
aretes/pendientes/pantallas	**4** earrings	llavero	**17** key ring/key chain
collar	**5** necklace	monedero	**18** change purse
collar de perlas	**6** pearl necklace/pearls/ string of pearls	billetera/cartera	**19** wallet
		cinturón/correa	**20** belt
cadena	**7** chain	bolso/bolsa/cartera	**21** purse/handbag/pocketbook
collar de cuentas	**8** beads	carriel/bolsa de correa	**22** shoulder bag
prendedor/broche	**9** pin/brooch	bolsa/bolsón	**23** tote bag
dije/colgante/relicario	**10** locket	maleta para libros/mochila	**24** book bag
pulsera/brazalete	**11** bracelet	mochila/mochila de excursión	**25** backpack
pasador/hebilla de cabello	**12** barrette	bolsa para maquillaje/necessaire	**26** makeup bag
gemelos/mancuernas/yuntas	**13** cuff links	portafolios/maletín	**27** briefcase

A. Oh, no! I think I lost my **ring**!
B. I'll help you look for it.

A. Oh, no! I think I lost my **earrings**!
B. I'll help you look for them.

[In a store]
A. Excuse me. Is this/Are these
_____ on sale this week?
B. Yes. It's/They're half price.

[On the street]
A. Help! Police! Stop that man/woman!
B. What happened?!
A. He/She just stole my _____
and my _____!

Do you like to wear jewelry? What jewelry do you have?

In your country, what do men, women, and children use to carry their things?

DESCRIPCIÓN DE LA ROPA

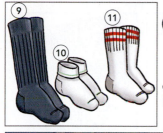

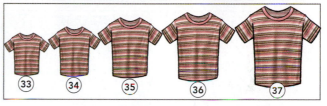

Tipos de ropa	Types of Clothing		camisa de franela/lanilla	**19** flannel *shirt*
camisa de mangas largas	**1** long-sleeved shirt		*blusa* de poliéster	**20** polyester *blouse*
camisa de mangas cortas	**2** short-sleeved shirt		*vestido/traje* de hilo/lino	**21** linen *dress*
camisa sin mangas	**3** sleeveless shirt		*bufanda* de seda	**22** silk *scarf*
camisa de cuello de tortuga/cisne	**4** turtleneck (shirt)		*suéter* de lana	**23** wool *sweater*
			sombrero de paja	**24** straw *hat*
suéter con cuello en V/de pico	**5** V-neck sweater			
cárdigan/suéter abierto con botones	**6** cardigan sweater		**Patrones**	**Patterns**
jersey/suéter con cuello cerrado	**7** crewneck sweater		de rayas/de rayitas	**25** striped
suéter con cuello de tortuga/cisne	**8** turtleneck sweater		de cuadros/de cuadritos	**26** checked
			de diseño a cuadros escocés	**27** plaid
calcetines/medias/tobilleras/ tobimedias largas	**9** knee-high socks		punteado(a) de bolas/bolitas (motitas)	**28** polka-dotted
medias cortas/calcetas	**10** ankle socks		estampado(a)	**29** patterned/print
medias/calcetines deportivas(os)	**11** crew socks		floreado(a)	**30** flowered/floral
			paisley/pesle	**31** paisley
aretes	**12** pierced earrings		azul sólido	**32** solid *blue*
aretes de pinza/de presión	**13** clip-on earrings			
			Tallas/Tamaños	**Sizes**
Tipos de material/tela	**Types of Material**		petite/extra pequeño(a)	**33** extra-small
pantalones de pana/cordoncillo	**14** corduroy *pants*		pequeño(a)	**34** small
botas de cuero	**15** leather *boots*		mediano(a)	**35** medium
medias de nailon/nylon	**16** nylon *stockings*		grande	**36** large
camiseta/playera de algodón	**17** cotton *T-shirt*		extra grande	**37** extra-large
chaqueta/chamarra de mezclilla	**18** denim *jacket*			

[1–24]
A. May I help you?
B. Yes, please. I'm looking for a *shirt*.*
A. What kind?
B. I'm looking for a *long-sleeved shirt*.

* With 9–16: I'm looking for _____.

[25–32]
A. How do you like this _____ tie/shirt/skirt?
B. Actually, I prefer that _____ one.

[33–37]
A. What size are you looking for?
B. _____.

Describe your favorite clothing items. For each item, tell about the color, the type of material, the size, and the pattern.

PROBLEMAS Y ARREGLOS DE LA ROPA

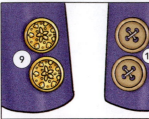

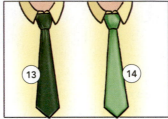
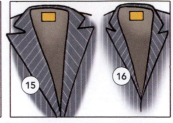

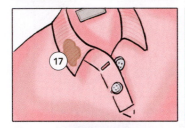

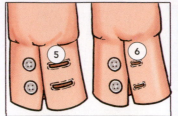

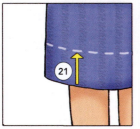
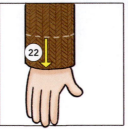

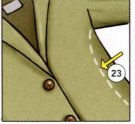

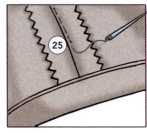

largo(a) – corto(a)	**1–2** long – short	*cuello* manchado	**17** stained *collar*
estrecho(a) – ancho(a)/flojo(a)	**3–4** tight – loose/baggy	*bolsillo* desgarrado/roto	**18** ripped/torn *pocket*
grande – chico(a)	**5–6** large/big – small	*cierre/cremallera* roto(a)	**19** broken *zipper*
alto(a) – bajo(a)	**7–8** high – low	le falta *un botón*	**20** missing *button*
elaborado(a) – sencillo(a)	**9–10** fancy – plain	subirle la basta/el dobladillo a *la falda*	**21** shorten the *skirt*
grueso(a)/pesado(a) – delgado(a)/liviano(a)	**11–12** heavy – light	alargar *las mangas*	**22** lengthen the *sleeves*
		meterle a la costura de *la chaqueta*	**23** take in the *jacket*
oscuro(a) – claro(a)	**13–14** dark – light	sacarle a la costura de *los pantalones*	**24** let out the *pants*
ancho(a) – angosto(a)	**15–16** wide – narrow	remendar *la costura*	**25** fix/repair the *seam*

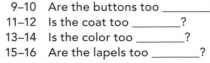

[1–2]
A. Are the sleeves too **long**?
B. No. They're too **short**.

1–2 Are the sleeves too _____?	9–10 Are the buttons too _____?
3–4 Are the pants too _____?	11–12 Is the coat too _____?
5–6 Are the buttonholes too _____?	13–14 Is the color too _____?
7–8 Are the heels too _____?	15–16 Are the lapels too _____?

[17–20]
A. What's the matter with it?
B. It has a **stained** *collar*.

[21–25]
A. Please **shorten** the *skirt*.
B. **Shorten** the *skirt*? Okay.

Tell about the differences between clothing people wear now and clothing people wore a long time ago.

LAVANDERÍA

separar la ropa	**A**	sort the laundry
meter la ropa en la lavadora	**B**	load the washer
sacar la ropa de la lavadora	**C**	unload the washer
meter la ropa en la secadora	**D**	load the dryer
colgar/tender la ropa en el tendedero	**E**	hang clothes on the clothesline
planchar	**F**	iron
doblar la ropa	**G**	fold the laundry
colgar la ropa	**H**	hang up clothing
guardar la ropa	**I**	put things away
ropa sucia	**1**	laundry
ropa clara	**2**	light clothing
ropa oscura	**3**	dark clothing
canasta para la ropa sucia	**4**	laundry basket
bolsa para la ropa sucia	**5**	laundry bag
lavadora/lavadora automática	**6**	washer/washing machine
detergente en polvo	**7**	laundry detergent
suavizador/suavizante	**8**	fabric softener
blanqueador/lejía/cloro	**9**	bleach

ropa mojada	**10**	wet clothing
secadora	**11**	dryer
filtro para la pelusa	**12**	lint trap
quitaestática	**13**	static cling remover
tendedero	**14**	clothesline
horquillas/ganchos/pinzas pinches para tender ropa	**15**	clothespin
plancha/planchar	**16**	iron
tabla de planchar	**17**	ironing board
ropa arrugada	**18**	wrinkled clothing
ropa planchada	**19**	ironed clothing
almidón en aerosol	**20**	spray starch
ropa limpia	**21**	clean clothing
clóset/armario/ropero	**22**	closet
gancho para colgar ropa	**23**	hanger
gaveta/cajón	**24**	drawer
repisa-repisas	**25**	shelf-shelves

[A–I]
A. What are you doing?
B. I'm _____ing.

[4–6, 11, 14–17, 23]
A. Excuse me. Do you sell _____s?
B. Yes. They're at the back of the store.
A. Thank you.

[7–9, 13, 20]
A. Excuse me. Do you sell _____?
B. Yes. It's at the back of the store.
A. Thank you.

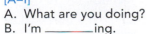

Who does the laundry in your home? What things does this person use?

EL ALMACÉN/LA TIENDA DE DEPARTAMENTOS

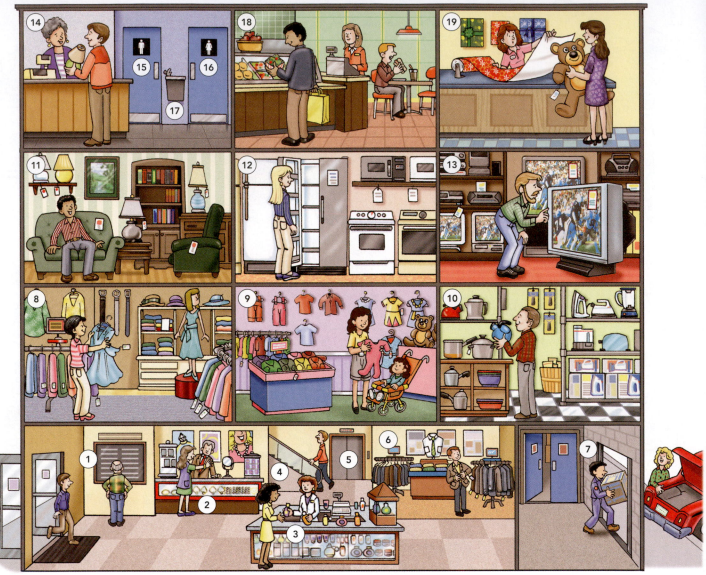

guía/directorio	**1**	(store) directory
Joyería	**2**	Jewelry Counter
Perfumería	**3**	Perfume Counter
escalera eléctrica/ automática/mecánica	**4**	escalator
ascensor/elevador	**5**	elevator
Sección de ropa de caballero	**6**	Men's Clothing Department
área de entrega de mercancía	**7**	customer pickup area
Sección de ropa de damas	**8**	Women's Clothing Department
Sección de ropa de niños	**9**	Children's Clothing Department

Sección de artículos para el hogar/ de cocina	**10**	Housewares Department
Sección de muebles	**11**	Furniture Department/ Home Furnishings Department
Sección de electrodomésticos	**12**	Household Appliances Department
Sección de electrónica/ aparatos electrónicos	**13**	Electronics Department
Mostrador de servicio al cliente	**14**	Customer Assistance Counter/ Customer Service Counter
servicios/baños para caballeros	**15**	men's room
servicios/baños para damas	**16**	ladies' room
fuente/bebedero	**17**	water fountain
cafetería/refresquería	**18**	snack bar
Mostrador para envolver regalos	**19**	Gift Wrap Counter

A. Excuse me. Where's the **store directory**?
B. It's over there, next to the **Jewelry Counter**.
A. Thanks.
B. You're welcome.

A. Excuse me. Do you sell *ties**?
B. Yes. You can find *ties** in the ___[6, 8–13]___ /at the ___[2, 3]___ on the first/second/third/fourth floor.
A. Thank you.

**ties/bracelets/dresses/toasters/. . .*

Describe a department store you know. Tell what is on each floor.

DE COMPRAS

20% OFF

Medium
100% Cotton

Dry Clean Only

$30.00 $24.00

$24.00
1.20 Tax
$25.20

comprar	**A**	buy
devolver	**B**	return
cambiar	**C**	exchange
probarse/ponerse	**D**	try on
pagar	**E**	pay for
obtener información	**F**	get some information about

letrero para anuncio de ofertas/descuentos/rebajas	**1**	sale sign
etiqueta	**2**	label
etiqueta con el precio	**3**	price tag
recibo	**4**	receipt
descuento/rebaja	**5**	discount
talla/tamaño	**6**	size
material	**7**	material

cuidado de la ropa	**8**	care instructions
precio normal/regular	**9**	regular price
precio de descuento	**10**	sale price
precio	**11**	price
impuesto de ventas	**12**	sales tax
precio total	**13**	total price

A. May I help you?
B. Yes, please. I want to _____[A–F]_____ this item.
A. Certainly. I'll be glad to help you.

A. { What's the _____[5–7, 9–13]_____?
{ What are the _____[8]_____?
B. _____.
A. Are you sure?
B. Yes. Look at the _____[1–4]_____!

Which stores in your area have sales? How often?

Tell about something you bought on sale.

EQUIPO DE VIDEO Y SONIDO

televisor/televisión	**1** TV/television	disco	**20** record
televisor/televisión de plasma	**2** plasma TV	tornamesa/giradiscos/	**21** turntable
televisor/televisión de cristal líquido	**3** LCD TV	tocadiscos	
televisor/televisión de proyección	**4** projection TV	CD/disco compacto	**22** CD/compact disc
televisor/televisión portátil	**5** portable TV	reproductor de CD/discos	**23** CD player
control remoto	**6** remote (control)	compactos	
DVD/disco de video digital	**7** DVD	sintonizador	**24** tuner
reproductor de video digital/DVD	**8** DVD player	audiocinta/audiocasete	**25** (audio)tape/(audio)cassette
video/videocasete/	**9** video/videocassette/	casetera	**26** tape deck/cassette deck
videocinta	videotape	bocinas/altavoces/	**27** speakers
videocasetera/videograbadora/	**10** VCR/videocassette	altoparlantes	
videoreproductora	recorder	equipo estereofónico	**28** portable stereo system/
videocámara/	**11** camcorder/	portátil	boombox
cámara de video	video camera	reproductor de CD	**29** portable/personal
paquete de pilas/baterías	**12** battery pack	portátil	CD player
cargador de pilas/baterías	**13** battery charger	tocacintas/	**30** portable/personal
radio	**14** radio	tocacasetes portátil	cassette player
radio reloj despertador	**15** clock radio	audífonos/auriculares	**31** headphones
radio de onda corta	**16** shortwave radio	lector de MP3/reproductor	**32** portable/personal
grabadora de cintas	**17** tape recorder/	de audio digital portátil	digital audio player
magnetofónicas	cassette recorder	sistema de videojuego	**33** video game system
micrófono	**18** microphone	videojuego/cartucho/	**34** video game
equipo estereofónico/de estéreo/	**19** stereo system/	paquete de videojuego	
de estereofonía	sound system	videojuego manual	**35** hand-held video game

A. May I help you?
B. Yes, please. I'm looking for a **TV**.

* With 27 & 31, use: I'm looking for _____.

A. I like your new _____.
Where did you get it/them?
B. At .....(name of store)....

A. Which company makes the best
_____?
B. In my opinion, the best _____
is/are made by ....

What video and audio equipment do you have or want?

In your opinion, which brands of video and audio equipment are the best?

TELÉFONOS Y CÁMARAS

Spanish	#	English
teléfono	1	telephone/phone
teléfono portátil/inalámbrico	2	cordless phone
teléfono celular/móvil	3	cell phone/cellular phone
batería/pila	4	battery
cargador de baterías/pilas	5	battery charger
contestadora automática	6	answering machine
mensáfono/buscapersonas	7	pager
asistente digital personal/PDA	8	PDA/electronic personal organizer
máquina de fax/transmisor-receptor electrónico	9	fax machine
calculadora de bolsillo	10	(pocket) calculator
sumadora/calculadora	11	adding machine
regulador de voltaje	12	voltage regulator
adaptador	13	adapter
cámara de 35 milímetros	14	(35 millimeter) camera
lente	15	lens
rollo de película/film	16	film
visor/lente zoom	17	zoom lens
cámara digital	18	digital camera
tarjeta de memoria	19	memory disk
trípode	20	tripod
flash removible	21	flash (attachment)
estuche de la cámara	22	camera case
proyector de transparencias/diapositivas	23	slide projector
pantalla	24	(movie) screen

A. Can I help you?
B. Yes. I want to buy a **telephone.***

* With 16, use: I want to buy _____.

A. Excuse me. Do you sell _____s?*
B. Yes. We have a large selection of _____s.

* With 16, use the singular.

A. Which _____ is the best?
B. This one here. It's made by ....(company)..........

What kind of telephone do you use?

Do you have a camera? What kind is it?
What do you take pictures of?

Does anyone you know have an answering machine?
When you call, what message do you hear?

COMPUTADORAS/ORDENADORES

Hardware/Equipo/Soporte físico	**Computer Hardware**		
computadora/ordenador personal	**1** (desktop) computer	ratón fijo con pelota de barrido/ trackball	**13** track ball
CPU/procesadora central/ disco duro/base	**2** CPU/central processing unit	módem	**14** modem
monitor/pantalla electrónica	**3** monitor/screen	protector de sobrevoltaje	**15** surge protector
lector de CD-ROM	**4** CD-ROM drive	impresora	**16** printer
disco CD-ROM	**5** CD-ROM	escáner	**17** scanner
unidad de disquete	**6** disk drive	cable	**18** cable
disquete	**7** (floppy) disk		
teclado	**8** keyboard	**Programa (informático)/ de computadora**	**Computer Software**
ratón	**9** mouse	procesador de textos	**19** word-processing program
pantalla plana/ de cristal líquido	**10** flat panel screen/ LCD screen	procesador de hoja de cálculo	**20** spreadsheet program
microcomputadora/laptop/portátil	**11** notebook computer	programa informático educativo	**21** educational software program
palanca	**12** joystick	juego de computadora	**22** computer game

A. Can you recommend a good **computer**?
B. Yes. This **computer** here is excellent.

A. Is that a new _____?
B. Yes.
A. Where did you get it?
B. At ...... *(name of store)* ......

A. May I help you?
B. Yes, please. Do you sell _____s?
A. Yes. We carry a complete line of _____s.

Do you use a computer? When?

In your opinion, how have computers changed the world?

LA JUGUETERÍA

juego de mesa/tablero	**1**	board game
rompecabezas	**2**	(jigsaw) puzzle
juguete para armar/mecano	**3**	construction set
bloques/cubitos	**4**	(building) blocks
pelota/balón	**5**	rubber ball
pelota/balón de playa	**6**	beach ball
cubito/cubeta y palita	**7**	pail and shovel
muñeca	**8**	doll
ropa de muñeca	**9**	doll clothing
casa de muñecas	**10**	doll house
muebles para la casa de muñecas	**11**	doll house furniture
muñeco mecánico	**12**	action figure
peluche	**13**	stuffed animal
carrito de juguete	**14**	matchbox car
camión de juguete	**15**	toy truck
juego de carros de carrera	**16**	racing car set
juego de trenes	**17**	train set
modelo para armar	**18**	model kit
juego de laboratorio/química	**19**	science kit
juego de intercomunicador/walki talki	**20**	walkie-talkie (set)
aro/hula hoop	**21**	hula hoop
cuerda/soga/reata/comba	**22**	jump rope
burbujas/pompas de jabón	**23**	bubble soap
figuritas/estampas/tarjetas	**24**	trading cards
crayolas/lápices de cera/crayones	**25**	crayons
marcadores/lápices de felpa/plumones	**26**	(color) markers
cuaderno de dibujos/para pintar/colorear	**27**	coloring book
cartulina para actividades manuales	**28**	construction paper
juego de pintura	**29**	paint set
plastilina/masilla	**30**	(modeling) clay
calcomanía/pegatina	**31**	stickers
bicicleta	**32**	bicycle
triciclo	**33**	tricycle
vagón/vagoneta	**34**	wagon
monopatín/patineta	**35**	skateboard
columpios	**36**	swing set
casa de juguete	**37**	play house
piscina/alberca/pileta infantil inflable/chapoteadero	**38**	kiddie pool/inflatable pool

A. Excuse me. I'm looking for (a/an) _____(s) for my *grandson*.*
B. Look in the next aisle.
A. Thank you.

* grandson/granddaughter/. . .

A. I don't know what to get my ....-year-old son/daughter for his/her birthday.
B. What about (a) _____?
A. Good idea! Thanks.

A. Mom/Dad? Can we buy this/these _____?
B. No, *Johnny*. Not today.

What toys are most popular in your country?

What were your favorite toys when you were a child?

EL BANCO

hacer un depósito	A	make a deposit
sacar dinero/hacer un retiro	B	make a withdrawal
cambiar/cobrar un cheque	C	cash a check
comprar cheques de viajero	D	get traveler's checks
abrir una cuenta	E	open an account
pedir un préstamo	F	apply for a loan
cambiar divisas/dinero/efectivo	G	exchange currency
ficha de depósito	1	deposit slip
ficha de retiro	2	withdrawal slip
cheque	3	check

cheques de viajero	4	traveler's check
libreta de banco	5	bankbook/passbook
tarjeta para cajero automático	6	ATM card
tarjeta de crédito	7	credit card
caja/caja fuerte/de caudales	8	(bank) vault
caja de seguridad	9	safe deposit box
cajero(a)	10	teller
guardia de seguridad	11	security guard
cajero automático	12	ATM (machine)/ cash machine
funcionario(a) de banco	13	bank officer

[A–G]
A. Where are you going?
B. I'm going to the bank.
I have to _____.

[5–7]
A. What are you looking for?
B. My _____. I can't find it anywhere!

[8–13]
A. How many _____s does the State Street Bank have?
B. ....

Do you have a bank account? What kind? Where? What do you do at the bank?

Do you ever use traveler's checks? When?

Do you have a credit card? What kind? When do you use it?

FINANZAS

Formas de pago — Forms of Payment

dinero en efectivo	1	cash
cheque	2	check
número del cheque	a	check number
número de la cuenta	b	account number
tarjeta de crédito	3	credit card
número de la tarjeta de crédito	a	credit card number
orden de pago/giro postal/telegráfico	4	money order
cheques de viajero	5	traveler's check

Cuentas del hogar — Household Bills

renta/arriendo/alquiler	6	rent
hipoteca	7	mortgage payment
cuenta de la electricidad	8	electric bill
cuenta del teléfono	9	telephone bill
cuenta del gas	10	gas bill
cuenta de la calefacción	11	oil bill/heating bill
cuenta del agua	12	water bill
cuenta de la televisión por cable	13	cable TV bill
pago del automóvil	14	car payment
cuenta de la tarjeta de crédito	15	credit card bill

Finanzas familiares — Family Finances

reconciliar la cuenta de cheques	16	balance the checkbook
hacer/escribir un cheque	17	write a check
hacer banca en línea/banco virtual	18	bank online
chequera/talonario de cheques	19	checkbook
registro de cheques	20	check register
estado de cuenta mensual	21	monthly statement

Uso del cajero automático — Using an ATM Machine

inserte la tarjeta de cajero automático	22	insert the ATM card
ingrese/teclee su número de identificación personal	23	enter your PIN number/personal identification number
elija la transacción que desee realizar	24	select a transaction
haga su depósito	25	make a deposit
retire el dinero	26	withdraw/get cash
transfiera fondos	27	transfer funds
retire su tarjeta	28	remove your card
retire el comprobante/recibo/resguardo de la transacción	29	take your transaction slip/receipt

A. Can I pay by ___[1, 2]___ / with a ___[3–5]___ ?
B. Yes. We accept ___[1]___ / ___[2–5]___ s.

A. What are you doing?
B. I'm paying the ___[6–15]___ .
   I'm ___[16–18]___ ing.
   I'm looking for the ___[19–21]___ .

A. What should I do?
B. ___[22–29]___ .

What household bills do you receive?
How much do you pay for the different bills?

Who takes care of the finances in your household? What does that person do?

Do you use ATM machines?
If you do, how do you use them?

LA OFICINA DE CORREOS

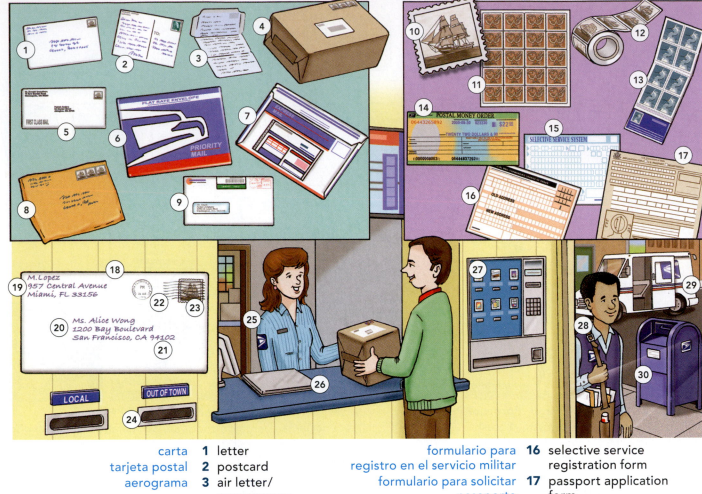

carta	**1**	letter	formulario para registro en el servicio militar	**16** selective service registration form
tarjeta postal	**2**	postcard	formulario para solicitar pasaporte	**17** passport application form
aerograma	**3**	air letter/ aerogramme	sobre	**18** envelope
paquete	**4**	package/parcel	remitente	**19** return address
primera clase	**5**	first class	destinatario	**20** mailing address
urgente	**6**	priority mail	código/área postal	**21** zip code
entrega inmediata/ expreso	**7**	express mail/ overnight mail	sello postal/matasellos	**22** postmark
paquete postal/encomienda	**8**	parcel post	sello postal/estampilla/timbre	**23** stamp/postage
correo certificado	**9**	certified mail	buzón	**24** mail slot
sello postal/estampilla/timbre	**10**	stamp	empleado(a) de correos	**25** postal worker/postal clerk
pliego de sellos/estampillas	**11**	sheet of stamps	báscula	**26** scale
rollo de sellos/estampillas	**12**	roll of stamps	máquina de estampillas	**27** stamp machine
libreta de sellos/estampillas	**13**	book of stamps	cartero(a)	**28** letter carrier/mail carrier
giro/giro postal/telegráfico	**14**	money order	camión de correos	**29** mail truck
formulario de cambio de domicilio	**15**	change-of-address form	buzón	**30** mailbox

[1–4]
A. Where are you going?
B. To the post office. I have to mail a/an _____.

[5–9]
A. How do you want to send it?
B. _____, please.

[10–17]
A. Next!
B. I'd like a _____, please.
A. Here you are.

[19–21, 23]
A. Do you want me to mail this letter?
B. Yes, thanks.
A. Oops! You forgot the _____!

How often do you go to the post office? What do you do there?   Tell about the postal system in your country.

LA BIBLIOTECA

Spanish	#	English		Spanish	#	English
catálogo en línea	1	online catalog		CD/discos compactos	17	CDs
catálogo/tarjetero/fichero	2	card catalog		videocintas	18	videotapes
autor	3	author		programa de computadora/informático	19	(computer) software
título	4	title		disco de video digital/DVD	20	DVDs
carnet/tarjeta de identificación	5	library card		sección de lenguas/idomas extranjeros(as)	21	foreign language section
fotocopiadora	6	copier/photocopier/copy machine		libros en lenguas/idiomas extranjeros(as)	22	foreign language books
estantes/librero/librería	7	shelves		sección de referencias/consultas	23	reference section
sección infantil	8	children's section		microfilm	24	microfilm
libros infantiles	9	children's books		lector de microfilm	25	microfilm reader
sección de publicaciones periódicas/revistas académicas	10	periodical section		diccionario	26	dictionary
boletines/revistas académicas	11	journals		enciclopedia	27	encyclopedia
revistas	12	magazines		atlas	28	atlas
periódicos	13	newspapers		mostrador de la sección de consultas	29	reference desk
sección audiovisual	14	media section		bibliotecario(a) de la sección de consulta	30	(reference) librarian
libros grabados/hablantes	15	books on tape		mostrador de préstamos	31	checkout desk
audiocintas/audiocasetes	16	audiotapes		empleado(a) de biblioteca	32	library clerk

[1, 2, 6–32]
A. Excuse me. Where's/Where are the _____?
B. Over there, at/near/next to the _____.

[8–23, 26–28]
A. Excuse me. Where can I find a/an ___[26–28]___/___[9, 11–13, 15–20, 22]___?
B. Look in the ___[8, 10, 14, 21, 23]___ over there.

A. I'm having trouble finding a book.
B. Do you know the ___[3–4]___?
A. Yes. ....

A. Excuse me. I'd like to check out this ___[26–28]___/these ___[11–13]___.
B. I'm sorry. It/They must remain in the library.

Do you go to a library? Where? What does this library have?

Tell about how you use the library.

INSTITUCIONES COMUNITARIAS

comisaría/estación/cuartel de policía	**A** police station
cuartel/estación de bomberos	**B** fire station
hospital/sanatorio	**C** hospital
palacio de gobierno/ayuntamiento	**D** town hall/city hall
centro recreativo	**E** recreation center
basurero público	**F** dump
guardería infantil	**G** child-care center
centro para personas mayores	**H** senior center
iglesia	**I** church
sinagoga	**J** synagogue
mezquita	**K** mosque
templo	**L** temple
telefonista para llamadas de emergencia	**1** emergency operator
policía	**2** police officer
radiopatrulla/patrulla/coche de policía	**3** police car
vehículo autobomba	**4** fire engine

bombero(a)	**5** firefighter
sala de emergencias	**6** emergency room
paramédico	**7** EMT/paramedic
ambulancia	**8** ambulance
alcalde/intendente municipal	**9** mayor/city manager
sala de reuniones	**10** meeting room
gimnasio	**11** gym
director de actividades	**12** activities director
salón de juegos	**13** game room
piscina/pileta/alberca	**14** swimming pool
recogedor de basura	**15** sanitation worker
centro de reciclaje/reutilización	**16** recycling center
auxiliar de guardería infantil	**17** child-care worker
guardería infantil	**18** nursery
cuarto de juegos	**19** playroom
enfermero(a) geriátrico(a)/ especialista en adultos mayores	**20** eldercare worker/ senior care worker

[A–L]
A. Where are you going?
B. I'm going to the _____.

[1, 2, 5, 7, 12, 15, 17, 20]
A. What do you do?
B. I'm a/an _____.

[3, 4, 8]
A. Do you hear a siren?
B. Yes. There's a/an _____ coming up behind us.

What community institutions are in your city or town? Where are they located?

Which community institutions do you use? When?

CRÍMENES Y EMERGENCIAS

choque/accidente	**1** car accident		asesinato	**12** murder
incendio	**2** fire		apagón	**13** blackout/power outage
explosión	**3** explosion		escape/fuga de gas	**14** gas leak
robo	**4** robbery		tubería de agua principal rota	**15** water main break
robo a una casa	**5** burglary		cable eléctrico roto	**16** downed power line
atraco	**6** mugging		derrame de sustancias químicas	**17** chemical spill
secuestro	**7** kidnapping		descarrilamiento de trenes	**18** train derailment
niño(a) perdido(a)	**8** lost child		vandalismo	**19** vandalism
robo de automóvil/carro/coche	**9** car jacking		violencia de pandillas	**20** gang violence
robo a un banco	**10** bank robbery		conductores ebrios	**21** drunk driving
asalto/ataque	**11** assault		tráfico de drogas	**22** drug dealing

[1–13]
A. I want to report a/an _____.
B. What's your location?
A. ....

[14–18]
A. Why is this street closed?
B. It's closed because of a _____.

[19–22]
A. I'm very concerned about the amount of _____ in our community.
B. I agree. _____ is a very serious problem.

Is there much crime in your community? Tell about it.

Have you ever experienced a crime or emergency? What happened?

EL CUERPO HUMANO

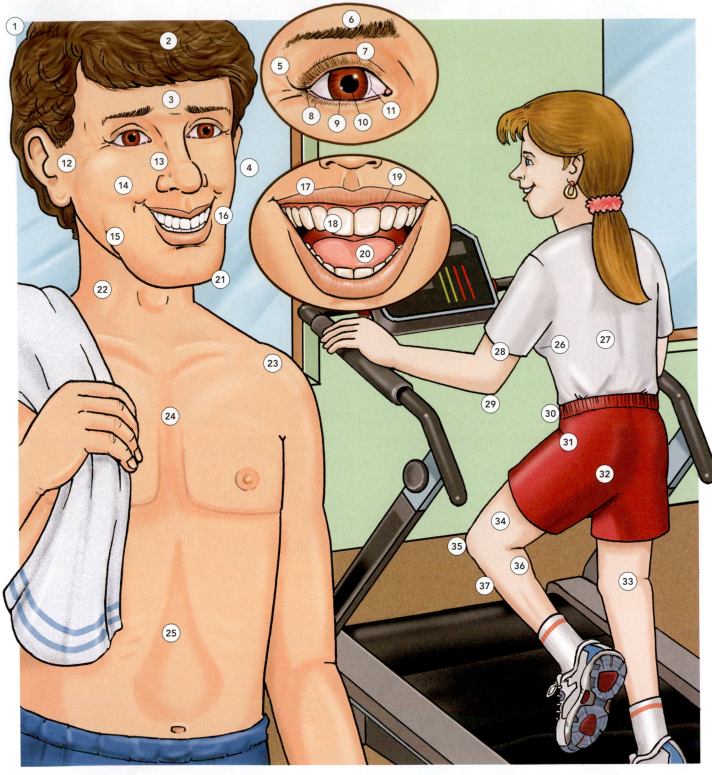

cabeza	1	head	pupila	10	pupil	diente(s)	18	tooth–teeth	brazo	28	arm
cabello/	2	hair	córnea	11	cornea	encías	19	gums	codo	29	elbow
pelo			oreja	12	ear	lengua	20	tongue	cintura	30	waist
frente	3	forehead	nariz	13	nose	mentón/barbilla	21	chin	cadera	31	hip
cara	4	face	mejilla/	14	cheek	cuello	22	neck	nalgas	32	buttocks
ojo	5	eye	pómulo			hombro	23	shoulder	pierna	33	leg
ceja	6	eyebrow	mandíbula/	15	jaw	pecho	24	chest	muslo	34	thigh
párpado	7	eyelid	quijada			abdomen/vientre	25	abdomen	rodilla	35	knee
pestañas	8	eyelashes	boca	16	mouth	seno/busto/pecho	26	breast	pantorrilla	36	calf
iris	9	iris	labio	17	lip	espalda	27	back	espinilla	37	shin

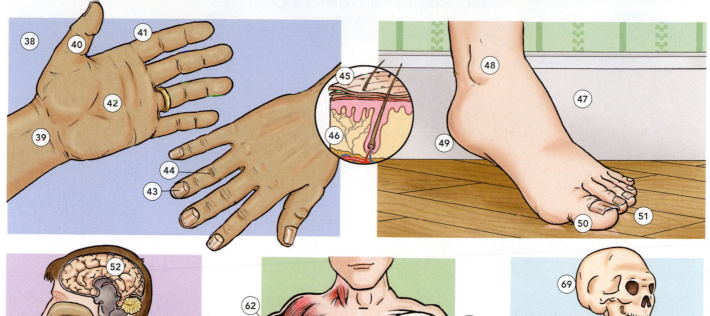

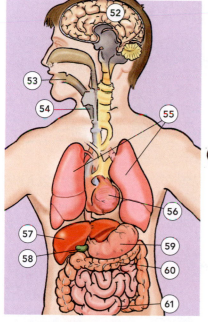

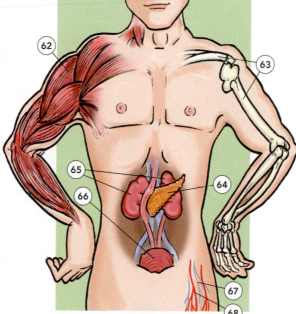

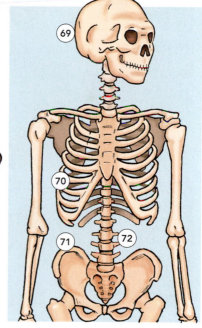

mano	**38**	hand	dedo del pie	**50**	toe	músculos	**62**	muscles
muñeca	**39**	wrist	uña del dedo del pie	**51**	toenail	huesos	**63**	bones
pulgar	**40**	thumb	cerebro	**52**	brain	páncreas	**64**	pancreas
dedo	**41**	finger	garganta	**53**	throat	riñones	**65**	kidneys
palma	**42**	palm	esófago	**54**	esophagus	vejiga	**66**	bladder
uña	**43**	fingernail	pulmones	**55**	lungs	venas	**67**	veins
nudillo	**44**	knuckle	corazón	**56**	heart	arterias	**68**	arteries
piel	**45**	skin	hígado	**57**	liver	cráneo	**69**	skull
nervio	**46**	nerve	vesícula biliar	**58**	gallbladder	caja torácica	**70**	ribcage
pie	**47**	foot	estómago	**59**	stomach	pelvis	**71**	pelvis
tobillo	**48**	ankle	intestino grueso	**60**	large intestine	columna vertebral/	**72**	spinal column/
talón	**49**	heel	intestino delgado	**61**	small intestine	espina dorsal		spinal cord

A. My doctor checked my **head** and said everything is okay.
B. I'm glad to hear that.

[1, 3–7, 12–29, 31–51]

A. Ooh!
B. What's the matter?
{ My _____ hurts!
{ My _____s hurt!

[52–72]

A. My doctor wants me to have some tests.
B. Why?
A. She's concerned about my _____.

Describe yourself as completely as you can.

Which parts of the body are most important at school? at work? when you play your favorite sport?

MALESTARES, SÍNTOMAS Y LESIONES

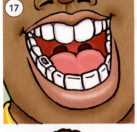

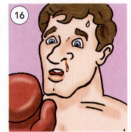

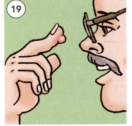

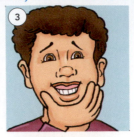

dolor de cabeza	1	headache
dolor de oído	2	earache
dolor de muelas/dientes	3	toothache
dolor de estómago	4	stomachache
dolor de espalda	5	backache
dolor de garganta	6	sore throat
fiebre/calentura	7	fever/temperature
catarro/resfriado	8	cold
tos	9	cough
infección	10	infection
sarpullido/salpullido	11	rash
picadura/picada	12	insect bite
quemadura de sol	13	sunburn
tortícolis	14	stiff neck
moquear	15	runny nose
hemorragia nasal	16	bloody nose
caries	17	cavity
ampolla	18	blister
verruga	19	wart
hipo	20	(the) hiccups
escalofrío	21	(the) chills
calambre/retortijón	22	cramps
diarrea	23	diarrhea
dolor en el pecho	24	chest pain
jadeo	25	shortness of breath
laringitis	26	laryngitis

A. What's the matter?
B. I have a/an _____[1–19]_____ .

A. What's the matter?
B. I have _____[20–26]_____ .

Spanish	#	English
desmayo	27	faint
(tener) mareo	28	dizzy
tener náuseas	29	nauseous
hinchazón del abdomen/gases	30	bloated
congestionado(a)	31	congested
agotado(a)	32	exhausted
tos	33	cough
estornudo	34	sneeze
respiración sibilante	35	wheeze
eructo	36	burp
vómito	37	vomit/throw up
sangrado	38	bleed
torcedura de pie	39	twist
arañazo	40	scratch
raspadura/rasguño	41	scrape
moretón/magulladura/cardenal	42	bruise
quemadura	43	burn
lesionarse	44	hurt–hurt
cortarse	45	cut–cut
torcedura	46	sprain
dislocación	47	dislocate
fracturarse	48	break–broke
hinchazón	49	swollen
comezón/picazón	50	itchy

A. What's the problem?
B. { I feel [27–30] .
{ I'm [31–32] .
{ I've been [33–38] ing a lot.

A. What happened?
B. { I [39–45] ed my ....
{ I think I [46–48] ed my ....
{ My .... is/are [49–50] .

A. How do you feel?
B. Not so good. / Not very well. / Terrible!
A. What's the matter?
B. .... , ... , and ....
A. I'm sorry to hear that.

Tell about the last time you didn't feel well. What was the matter?

Tell about a time you hurt yourself. What happened? How? What did you do about it?

What do you do when you have a cold? a stomachache? an insect bite? the hiccups?

PRIMEROS AUXILIOS

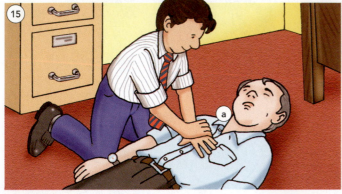 

manual de primeros auxilios	**1** first-aid manual		venda elástica	**12**	elastic bandage/ Ace™ bandage
maletín/botiquín de primeros auxilios	**2** first-aid kit		aspirina	**13**	aspirin
tirita/curita	**3** (adhesive) bandage/ Band-Aid™		analgésico sin aspirina	**14**	non-aspirin pain reliever
toallita antiséptica	**4** antiseptic cleansing wipe		respiración artificial/ resucitación cardiopulmonar	**15**	CPR (cardiopulmonary resuscitation)
almohadilla estéril	**5** sterile (dressing) pad		no tiene pulso	**a**	has no pulse
agua oxigenada	**6** hydrogen peroxide		respiración artificial/asistida	**16**	rescue breathing
ungüento antibiótico	**7** antibiotic ointment		no está respirando	**b**	isn't breathing
gasa	**8** gauze		la maniobra de Heimlich	**17**	the Heimlich maneuver
esparadrapo/ cinta adhesiva	**9** adhesive tape		está atorado/se está asfixiando	**c**	is choking
pinzas	**10** tweezers		entablillar	**18**	splint
crema antihistamínica	**11** antihistamine cream		se rompió un dedo	**d**	broke a finger
			torniquete	**19**	tourniquet
			está sangrando	**e**	is bleeding

A. Do we have any ____[3–5, 12]____ s/ ____[6–11, 13, 14]____ ?
B. Yes. Look in the first-aid kit.

A. Help! My friend ____[a–e]____ !
B. I can help!
{ I know how to do ____[15–17]____ .
{ I can make a ____[18, 19]____ .

Do you have a first-aid kit? If you do, what's in it? If you don't, where can you buy one?

Tell about a time when you gave or received first aid.

Where can a person learn first aid in your community?

EMERGENCIAS MÉDICAS Y ENFERMEDADES/DOLENCIAS

   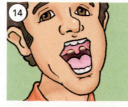 
 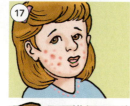   
  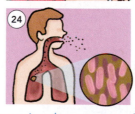 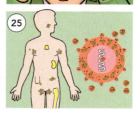

Spanish	#	English
herido(a)/lastimado(a)	1	hurt/injured
en estado de choque	2	in shock
inconsciente	3	unconscious
insolación	4	heatstroke
congelado(a)/daño en el cuerpo por el frío	5	frostbite
ataque al corazón	6	heart attack
reacción alérgica	7	allergic reaction
tragar veneno	8	swallow poison
sobredosis de medicinas/drogas	9	overdose on drugs
caerse	10	fall–fell
sufrir un choque eléctrico	11	get–got an electric shock
influenza/gripe	12	the flu/influenza
infección de oído	13	an ear infection
infección (de estreptococos) en la garganta	14	strep throat
sarampión	15	measles
paperas	16	mumps
varicela/viruela loca	17	chicken pox
asma	18	asthma
cáncer	19	cancer
depresión	20	depression
diabetes	21	diabetes
afección del corazón	22	heart disease
presión alta/hipertensión	23	high blood pressure/hypertension
tuberculosis	24	TB/tuberculosis
SIDA*	25	AIDS*

* Síndrome de Inmunodeficiencia Adquirida * Acquired Immune Deficiency Syndrome

A. What happened?
B. My .... is ___[1–3]___. has ___[4–5]___. is having a/an ___[6–7]___. ___[8–11]___ ed.
A. What's your location?
B. ...(address)...

A. My .... is sick.
B. What's the matter?
A. He/She has ___[12–25]___.
B. I'm sorry to hear that.

Tell about a medical emergency that happened to you or someone you know.

Which illnesses in this lesson are you familiar with?

EL EXAMEN MÉDICO

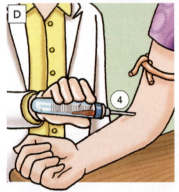

medir*le* y pesar*le*	**A** measure *your* height and weight	báscula/balanza	**1** scale
tomar*le* la temperatura	**B** take *your* temperature	termómetro	**2** thermometer
tomar*le* la presión arterial	**C** check *your* blood pressure	manómetro	**3** blood pressure gauge
sacar*le* sangre	**D** draw some blood	aguja/jeringa/jeringuilla	**4** needle/syringe
hacer*le* algunas preguntas sobre *su* salud	**E** ask *you* some questions about *your* health	consultorio	**5** examination room
examinar*le* los ojos, oídos, nariz y garganta	**F** examine *your* eyes, ears, nose, and throat	camilla de examen/ mesa de reconocimiento	**6** examination table
escuchar*le* el corazón	**G** listen to *your* heart	cartilla para medir la vista	**7** eye chart
tomar*le* una radiografía del pecho	**H** take a chest X-ray	estetoscopio	**8** stethoscope
		máquina de rayos X/ radiografías	**9** X-ray machine

[A–H]

A. Now I'm going to **measure your height and weight**.

B. All right.

[A–H]

A. What did the doctor/nurse do during the examination?

B. She/He **measured my height and weight**.

[1–3, 5–9]

A. So, how do you like our new **scale?**

B. It's very nice, doctor.

How often do you have a medical exam? What does the doctor/nurse do?

PROCEDIMIENTOS MÉDICOS Y DENTALES

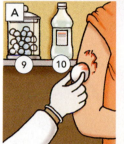

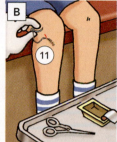

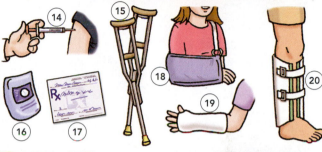

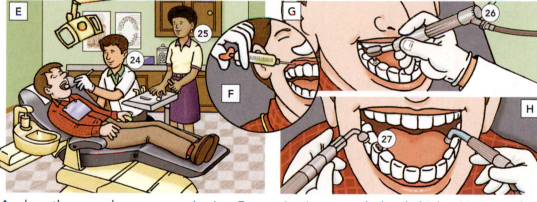

limpiar la herida	**A**	clean the wound
coser/suturar la herida	**B**	close the wound
vendar la herida	**C**	dress the wound
limpiar*le* los dientes	**D**	clean *your* teeth
examinar*le* los dientes	**E**	examine *your* teeth
poner*le* una inyección con anestesia/ Novocaína™	**F**	give *you* a shot of anesthetic/ Novocaine™
taladrar el diente/la caries	**G**	drill the cavity
rellenar la cavidad/el diente	**H**	fill the tooth

Spanish	Number	English
sala de espera	**1**	waiting room
recepcionista	**2**	receptionist
tarjeta de seguro médico	**3**	insurance card
formulario para la historia/ el historial clínico(a)	**4**	medical history form

Spanish	Number	English
consultorio	**5**	examination room
médico/ doctor	**6**	doctor/ physician
paciente	**7**	patient
enfermero(a)	**8**	nurse
motas/bolas de algodón	**9**	cotton balls
alcohol	**10**	alcohol
sutura/puntos	**11**	stitches
gasa	**12**	gauze
esparadrapo	**13**	tape
inyección	**14**	injection/ shot
muletas	**15**	crutches

Spanish	Number	English
bolsa de hielo	**16**	ice pack
receta médica	**17**	prescription
cabestrillo	**18**	sling
yeso/enyesado/ escayola	**19**	cast
férula/entablillado	**20**	brace
higienista dental	**21**	dental hygienist
mascarilla/máscara	**22**	mask
guantes	**23**	gloves
dentista	**24**	dentist
asistente (del dentista)	**25**	dental assistant
fresa/taladro	**26**	drill
empaste/relleno	**27**	filling

A. Now I'm going to { give you (a/an) ____ [A–H] .
____ [14–17] .
put your .... in a ____ [18–20] . }

B. Okay.

A. I need { ____ [9, 10, 12, 13, 23] .
a ____ [22, 26] . }

B. Here you are.

Tell about a personal experience you had with a medical or dental procedure.

MEDICAL ADVICE

RECOMENDACIONES MÉDICAS

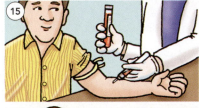
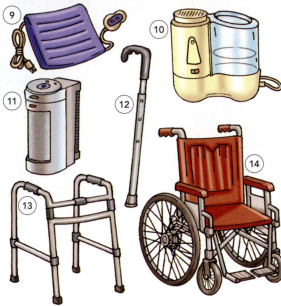

guardar cama	1	rest in bed	purificador de aire	11	air purifier
tomar líquidos	2	drink fluids	bastón	12	cane
hacer gárgaras	3	gargle	andadera	13	walker
ponerse a dieta	4	go on a diet	silla de ruedas	14	wheelchair
hacer ejercicio	5	exercise	análisis/pruebas de sangre	15	blood work/blood tests
tomar vitaminas	6	take vitamins	exámenes médicos/análisis	16	tests
ver a un especialista	7	see a specialist	fisioterapia	17	physical therapy
recibir tratamiento de acupuntura	8	get acupuncture	operación/cirugía	18	surgery
bolsa caliente/almohadilla eléctrica	9	heating pad	consejo personal/psicoterapia	19	counseling
humidificador	10	humidifier	frenos	20	braces

A. I think { you should _____ [1–8] .
you should use a/an _____ [9–14] .
you need _____ [15–20] .

B. I see.

A. What did the doctor say?

B. The doctor thinks { I should _____ [1–8] .
I should use a/an _____ [9–14] .
I need _____ [15–20] .

Tell about medical advice a doctor gave you. What did the doctor say? Did you follow the advice?

REMEDIOS/MEDICINAS

aspirina **1** aspirin	gotas para los ojos **10** eye drops
píldoras para el resfriado/catarro **2** cold tablets	ungüento/pomada **11** ointment
vitaminas **3** vitamins	pomada/crema **12** cream/creme
jarabe para la tos **4** cough syrup	loción **13** lotion
analgésico sin aspirina **5** non-aspirin pain reliever	píldora **14** pill
pastillas para la tos **6** cough drops	tableta/pastilla **15** tablet
pastillas para la garganta **7** throat lozenges	cápsula **16** capsule
antiácido en tabletas **8** antacid tablets	cápsula comprimida **17** caplet
descongestionante nasal (en **9** decongestant spray/	cucharadita/cuchara de té **18** teaspoon
atomizador/spray) nasal spray	cucharada/cuchara sopera **19** tablespoon

[1–13]

A. What did the doctor say?

B. { She/He told me to take _____[1–4]_____ /a _____[5]_____.
   { She/He told me to use _____[6–13]_____.

[14–19]

A. What's the dosage?

B. One _____ every four hours.

What medicines in this lesson do you have at home? What other medicines do you have?

What do you take or use for a fever? a headache? a stomachache? a sore throat? a cold? a cough?

Tell about any medicines in your country that are different from the ones in this lesson.

MÉDICOS ESPECIALISTAS

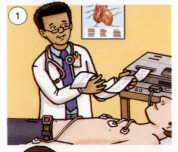

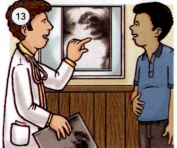

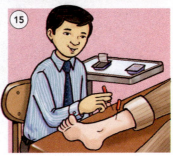

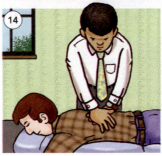

cardiólogo(a)	**1**	cardiologist	audiólogo(a)	**9**	audiologist
ginecólogo(a)	**2**	gynecologist	fisioterapeuta	**10**	physical therapist
pediatra	**3**	pediatrician	psicoterapeuta/terapeuta	**11**	counselor/therapist
geriatra	**4**	gerontologist	psiquiatra	**12**	psychiatrist
alergista/alergólogo(a)	**5**	allergist	gastroenterólogo(a)	**13**	gastroenterologist
ortopeda/ortopedista	**6**	orthopedist	quiropráctico(a)	**14**	chiropractor
oftalmólogo(a)	**7**	ophthalmologist	acupuntor(a)/acupunturista	**15**	acupuncturist
otorrinolaringólogo(a)	**8**	ear, nose, and throat (ENT) specialist	ortodoncista	**16**	orthodontist

A. I think you need to see a specialist.
I'm going to refer you to a/an _____.
B. A/An _____?
A. Yes.

A. When is your next appointment with the _____?
B. It's at ......(time)...... on .....(date)........

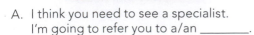

Do you or members of your family see any of these medical specialists? Which ones?

EL HOSPITAL

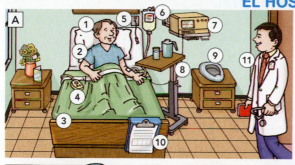

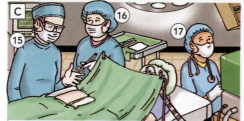

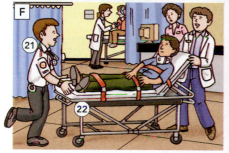

Spanish	#	English
cuarto del/ de la paciente	**A**	**patient's room**
paciente	1	patient
bata de hospital	2	hospital gown
cama de hospital	3	hospital bed
control de la cama	4	bed control
timbre	5	call button
venoclisis/intravenosa	6	I.V.
monitor/pantalla con control de signos vitales	7	vital signs monitor
mesa de cama	8	bed table
cuña/paleta/bacín/ cómodo/silleta	9	bed pan
cuadrícula/hoja clínica	10	medical chart
médico(a)/doctor(a)	11	doctor/physician
estación de enfermeros(as)	**B**	**nurse's station**
enfermero(a)	12	nurse
especialista en dietética	13	dietitian
asistente de enfermero(a)	14	orderly

Spanish	#	English
sala de operaciones/quirófano	**C**	**operating room**
cirujano(a)	15	surgeon
enfermero(a)/quirúrgico(a)	16	surgical nurse
anestesiólogo(a)/anestesista	17	anesthesiologist
sala de espera	**D**	**waiting room**
voluntario(a)	18	volunteer
sala de partos	**E**	**birthing room/delivery room**
ginecólogo(a)/obstetra	19	obstetrician
enfermera comadrona/partera	20	midwife/nurse-midwife
sala de emergencias	**F**	**emergency room / ER**
paramédico(a)	21	emergency medical technician/EMT
camilla	22	gurney
departamento de radiología	**G**	**radiology department**
técnico(a) radiólogo(a)	23	X-ray technician
radiólogo	24	radiologist
laboratorio	**H**	**laboratory/lab**
técnico de laboratorio	25	lab technician

A. This is your ____[2–10]____.
B. I see.

A. Do you work here?
B. Yes. I'm a/an ____[11–21, 23–25]____.

A. Where's the ____[11–21, 23–25]____?
B. She's/He's { in the ____[A, C–H]____.
at the ____[B]____.

Tell about an experience you or a family member had in the hospital.

HIGIENE PERSONAL

me estoy cepillando los dientes	**A**	**brush *my* teeth**	*me estoy* secando el pelo/cabello	**H**	**dry *my* hair**
cepillo de dientes	**1**	toothbrush	secador(a) de pelo/cabello	**11**	hair dryer/ blow dryer
pasta de dientes/crema dental	**2**	toothpaste			
estoy usando el hilo dental	**B**	**floss *my* teeth**	*me estoy* peinando	**I**	**comb *my* hair**
seda/hilo dental/hilo de dientes	**3**	dental floss	peine/peinilla	**12**	comb
estoy haciendo gárgaras	**C**	**gargle**	*me estoy* cepillando el pelo/cabello	**J**	**brush *my* hair**
antiséptico/enjuague bucal	**4**	mouthwash	cepillo para el pelo/cabello	**13**	(hair) brush
me estoy blanqueando los dientes	**D**	**whiten *my* teeth**	*me estoy* arreglando el pelo/ cabello	**K**	**style *my* hair**
blanqueador de dientes	**5**	teeth whitener	peinilla caliente/alisadora/ tenazas eléctricas/moldeador/ rizador de pelo/cabello	**14**	hot comb/ curling iron
me estoy bañando en la tina	**E**	**bathe/take a bath**			
jabón	**6**	soap	fijador/spray para el pelo/cabello	**15**	hairspray
baño de burbujas/espuma	**7**	bubble bath	fijador/gel para el pelo/cabello	**16**	hair gel
			gancho/horquilla/pasador	**17**	bobby pin
me estoy bañando/duchando	**F**	**take a shower**	pasador/hebilla/barra para el pelo/ cabello	**18**	barrette
gorra(o) de baño	**8**	shower cap			
me estoy lavando el pelo/cabello	**G**	**wash *my* hair**	pinza/sujetador de pelo/cabello	**19**	hairclip
champú	**9**	shampoo			
acondicionador/enjuague	**10**	conditioner/rinse			

me estoy afeitando/rasurando	**L shave**	crema/loción para el cuerpo	**35** body lotion
crema para afeitarse/rasurarse	**20** shaving cream	talco/polvo	**36** powder
maquinilla de afeitar/rastrillo	**21** razor	colonia/perfume	**37** cologne/perfume
hoja de navaja	**22** razor blade	bloqueador solar/loción protectora	**38** sunscreen
máquina de afeitar eléctrica	**23** electric shaver		
astringente	**24** styptic pencil	**me estoy maquillando**	**O put on makeup**
loción para después de afeitar	**25** aftershave (lotion)	colorete	**39** blush/rouge
		base para el maquillaje	**40** foundation/base
me estoy arreglando las uñas	**M do my nails**	crema/loción humectante	**41** moisturizer
lima de metal para las uñas	**26** nail file	polvo para la cara	**42** face powder
lima de cartón para las uñas	**27** emery board	delineador de ojos	**43** eyeliner
cortaúñas	**28** nail clipper	sombra para los ojos	**44** eye shadow
cepillo de uñas	**29** nail brush	rímel/pintador de pestañas	**45** mascara
tijeras	**30** scissors	lápiz de cejas	**46** eyebrow pencil
esmalte de uñas/barniz	**31** nail polish	pintalabios/lápiz de labios/	**47** lipstick
acetona/quitaesmalte de uñas	**32** nail polish remover	carmín/bilé	
me estoy poniendo . . .	**N put on . . .**	**me estoy lustrando los zapatos**	**P polish my shoes**
desodorante	**33** deodorant	betún/cera para zapatos	**48** shoe polish
crema/loción para las manos	**34** hand lotion	cordones de zapatos/agujetas	**49** shoelaces

[A–M, N (33–38), O, P]
A. What are you doing?
B. I'm _____ing.

[1, 8, 11–14, 17–19, 21–24, 26–30, 46, 49]
A. Excuse me. Where can I find
   _____(s)?
B. They're in the next aisle.

[2–7, 9, 10, 15, 16, 20, 25, 31–45, 47, 48]
A. Excuse me. Where can I find
   _____?
B. It's in the next aisle.

Which of these personal care products do you use?

You're going on a trip. Make a list of the personal care products you need to take with you.

EL CUIDADO DEL BEBÉ

darle la comida	**A feed**	palillo de algodón/hisopo	**15** cotton swab
papillas/comidas de bebé en frasquitos o tarritos/colados	**1** baby food	loción para niños	**16** baby lotion
babero	**2** bib	cargar	**D hold**
biberón/mamadera/tetero/mamila	**3** bottle	chupete/consuelo/chupón	**17** pacifier
chupón/chupete/tetina/tetilla/mamadera	**4** nipple	chupador/chupón/mordedera	**18** teething ring
fórmula/leche en polvo	**5** formula	amamantar	**E nurse**
vitaminas en líquido/en gotas	**6** (liquid) vitamins	vestir	**F dress**
cambiarle el pañal	**B change the baby's diaper**	mecer/arrullar	**G rock**
pañal desechable	**7** disposable diaper	guardería infantil	**19** child-care center
pañal de tela/algodón	**8** cloth diaper	trabajador(a) de guardería infantil	**20** child-care worker
imperdible/alfiler de gancho/seguridad	**9** diaper pin	mecedora	**21** rocking chair
toallitas húmedas desechables	**10** (baby) wipes	leerle a	**H read to**
polvo/talco para niños	**11** baby powder	armario	**22** cubby
pañal entrenador/pull up	**12** training pants	jugar con	**I play with**
pomada/ungüento	**13** ointment	juguetes	**23** toys
bañar	**C bathe**		
champú para niños	**14** baby shampoo		

A. What are you doing?

B. { I'm _____[A, C–I]_____ ing the baby.
    I'm _____[B]_____ ing.

A. Do we need anything from the store?

B. Yes. We need some more { [2–4, 7–9, 15, 17, 18] s
                     [1, 5, 6, 10–14, 16] .

In your opinion, which are better: cloth diapers or disposable diapers? Why?   Tell about baby products in your country.

TIPOS DE ESCUELA

jardín de la infancia/preescolar/kínder	**1**	preschool/nursery school	institución que imparte los dos primeros años de una carrera y educación para adultos	**7** community college
escuela primaria	**2**	elementary school	universidad	**8** college
primer ciclo de escuela secundaria/liceo (grados séptimo a noveno)	**3**	middle school/junior high school	universidad	**9** university
segundo ciclo de escuela secundaria/instituto/bachillerato	**4**	high school	escuela de postgrado/posgrado	**10** graduate school
escuela para adultos	**5**	adult school	facultad de leyes	**11** law school
escuela de artes y oficios/vocacional	**6**	vocational school/trade school	facultad de medicina	**12** medical school

A. Are you a student?
B. Yes. I'm in ___[1–4, 8, 10–12]___.

A. Are you a student?
B. Yes. I go to a/an ___[5–7, 9]___.

A. Is this apartment building near a/an _____?
B. Yes. ___(name of school)___ is nearby.

A. Tell me about your previous education.
B. I went to ___(name of school)___.
A. Did you like it there?
B. Yes. It was an excellent _____.

What types of schools are there in your community? What are their names, and where are they located?

What types of schools have you gone to?

Where? When? What did you study?

LA ESCUELA

oficina/administración	**A**	(main) office
dirección/rectoría	**B**	principal's office
enfermería	**C**	nurse's office
consejería	**D**	guidance office
salón/sala de clases/aula	**E**	classroom
pasillo/corredor	**F**	hallway
casillero	**a**	locker
laboratorio de ciencias	**G**	science lab
gimnasio	**H**	gym/gymnasium
vestidor	**a**	locker room
pista	**I**	track
gradería/gradas	**a**	bleachers
campo de juego	**J**	field
auditorio	**K**	auditorium
cafetería	**L**	cafeteria

biblioteca	**M**	library
secretario(a) de la escuela	**1**	clerk/(school) secretary
director(a)	**2**	principal
enfermero(a)	**3**	(school) nurse
consejero(a)	**4**	(guidance) counselor
maestro(a)/profesor(a)	**5**	teacher
subdirector(a)	**6**	assistant principal/vice-principal
guardia de seguridad	**7**	security officer
maestro(a) de ciencias	**8**	science teacher
maestro(a) de educación física	**9**	P.E. teacher
entrenador(a)	**10**	coach
portero(a)/afanador(a)	**11**	custodian
empleado(a) de la cafetería	**12**	cafeteria worker
supervisor(a) de la cafetería	**13**	lunchroom monitor
bibliotecario(a)	**14**	(school) librarian

A. Where are you going?
B. I'm going to the _____[A–D, G–M]_____.
A. Do you have a hall pass?
B. Yes. Here it is.

A. Where's the _____[1–14]_____?
B. He's/She's in the _____[A–M]_____.

Describe the school where you study English. Tell about the rooms, offices, and people.

Tell about differences between the school in this lesson and schools in your country.

CURSOS/MATERIAS

 1

 2

3

4

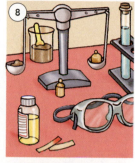 5

 6

7

8

9

 10

 11

 12

 13

14

 15

 16

17

 18

 19

 20

matemáticas	**1**	math/mathematics	informática/computación **11**	computer science
inglés	**2**	English	español **12**	Spanish
historia	**3**	history	francés **13**	French
geografía	**4**	geography	economía doméstica **14**	home economics
gobierno/civismo	**5**	government	artes industriales/taller **15**	industrial arts/shop
ciencias	**6**	science	comercio/negocios **16**	business education
biología	**7**	biology	educación física **17**	physical education/P.E.
química	**8**	chemistry	curso para aprender a manejar/conducir **18**	driver's education/driver's ed
física	**9**	physics	arte **19**	art
salud/higiene	**10**	health	música **20**	music

A. What do you have next period?
B. **Math**. How about you?
A. **English**.
B. There's the bell. I've got to go.

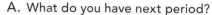

What is/was your favorite subject? Why?

In your opinion, what's the most interesting subject?
the most difficult subject? Why do you think so?

ACTIVIDADES EXTRACURRICULARES

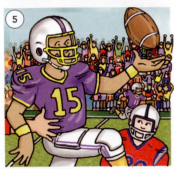

banda	**1** band		periódico estudiantil	**9** school newspaper
orquesta	**2** orchestra		anuario	**10** yearbook
coro	**3** choir/chorus		revista literaria	**11** literary magazine
drama/teatro	**4** drama		equipo/cuadrilla de luces y sonido	**12** A.V. crew
fútbol americano	**5** football		club de oratoria	**13** debate club
animadores(as)	**6** cheerleading/pep squad		club de informática/computación	**14** computer club
asociación de estudiantes	**7** student government		club de relaciones internacionales	**15** international club
servicio comunitario	**8** community service		club de ajedrez	**16** chess club

A. Are you going home right after school?
B. { No. I have ___[1–6]___ practice.
{ No. I have a ___[7–16]___ meeting.

What extracurricular activities do/did you participate in?

Which extracurricular activities in this lesson are there in schools in your country? What other activities are there?

MATEMÁTICAS

Arithmetic   Aritmética

$$2+1=3 \qquad 8-3=5 \qquad 4\times2=8 \qquad 10\div2=5$$

suma addition	resta subtraction	multiplicación multiplication	división division
2 **plus** 1 **equals*** 3.	8 **minus** 3 **equals*** 5.	4 **times** 2 **equals*** 8.	10 **divided by** 2 **equals*** 5.

*You can also say: **is**

A. How much is *two plus one*?
B. *Two plus one* equals / is *three*.

Make conversations for the arithmetic problems above and others.

Fractions   Fracciones

1/4 — one quarter / one fourth

1/3 — one third

1/2 — one half / half

2/3 — two thirds

3/4 — three quarters / three fourths

A. Is this on sale?
B. Yes. It's _____ off the regular price.

A. Is the gas tank almost empty?
B. It's about _____ full.

Percents   Porcentajes

10% — ten percent

50% — fifty percent

75% — seventy-five percent

100% — one-hundred percent

A. How did you do on the test?
B. I got _____ percent of the answers right.

A. What's the weather forecast?
B. There's a _____ percent chance of rain.

Types of Math   Tipos de matemáticas

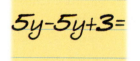  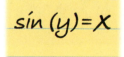 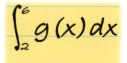 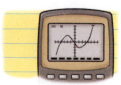

$5y-5y+3=$ — algebra / álgebra

geometry / geometría

$\sin(y)=x$ — trigonometry / trigonometría

$\int_{2}^{6} g(x)\,dx$ — calculus / cálculo

statistics / estadística

A. What math course are you taking this year?
B. I'm taking _____.

Are you good at math?

What math courses do / did you take in school?

Tell about something you bought on sale. How much off the regular price was it?

Research and discuss: What percentage of people in your country live in cities? live on farms? work in factories? vote in general elections?

MEDIDAS Y FORMAS GEOMÉTRICAS

Medidas		Measurements
altura	**1**	height
ancho/anchura	**2**	width
profundidad	**3**	depth
largo/longitud	**4**	length
pulgada	**5**	inch
pie-pies	**6**	foot–feet
yarda	**7**	yard
centímetro	**8**	centimeter
metro	**9**	meter
distancia	**10**	distance
milla	**11**	mile
kilómetro	**12**	kilometer

Líneas		**Lines**
línea recta	**13**	straight line
línea curva	**14**	curved line

líneas paralelas	**15**	parallel lines
líneas perpendiculares	**16**	perpendicular lines

Formas geométricas		**Geometric Shapes**
cuadrado	**17**	square
lado		**a** side
rectángulo	**18**	rectangle
base		**a** length
altura		**b** width
diagonal		**c** diagonal
triángulo rectángulo	**19**	right triangle
vértice		**a** apex
ángulo recto		**b** right angle
base		**c** base
hipotenusa		**d** hypotenuse

triángulo isósceles	**20**	isosceles triangle
ángulo agudo		**a** acute angle
ángulo obtuso		**b** obtuse angle
círculo	**21**	circle
centro		**a** center
radio		**b** radius
diámetro		**c** diameter
circunferencia		**d** circumference
elipse	**22**	ellipse/oval

Sólidos/Figuras tridimensionales		**Solid Figures**
cubo	**23**	cube
cilindro	**24**	cylinder
esfera	**25**	sphere
cono	**26**	cone
pirámide	**27**	pyramid

[1–9]
A. What's the ____ [1–4] ?
B. .... ____ [5–9] (s).

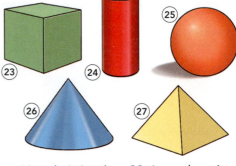

[11–12]
A. What's the distance?
B. .... _____ (s).

1 inch (1") = 2.54 centimeters (cm)
1 foot (1') = 0.305 meters (m)
1 yard (1 yd.) = 0.914 meters (m)
1 mile (mi.) = 1.6 kilometers (km)

[17–22]
A. Who can tell me what shape this is?
B. I can. It's a/an _____.

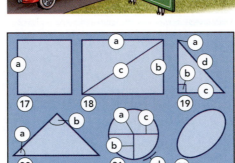

[23–27]
A. Who knows what figure this is?
B. I do. It's a/an _____.

[13–27]
A. This painting is magnificent!
B. Hmm. I don't think so. It just looks like a lot of _____s and _____s to me!

EL IDIOMA INGLÉS: LENGUAJE Y REDACCIÓN

Types of Sentences & Parts of Speech   **Tipos de oraciones y elementos del habla**

A Students study in the new library.
     ① ② ③ ④ ⑤

C Read page nine.

B Do they study hard?
     ⑥ ⑦

D This cake is fantastic!

declarativo **A** declarative	sustantivo **1** noun	adjetivo **5** adjective
interrogativo **B** interrogative	verbo **2** verb	pronombre **6** pronoun
imperativo **C** imperative	preposición **3** preposition	adverbio **7** adverb
exclamativo **D** exclamatory	artículo **4** article	

We study English every day.

A. What type of sentence is this?
B. It's a/an _____[A–D]_____ sentence.

The student is tired.

A. What part of speech is this?
B. It's a/an _____[1–7]_____.

Punctuation Marks & the Writing Process   Signos de puntuación y el proceso de la escritura

punto **8** period	recolectar y asociar ideas **16** brainstorm ideas	
signo de interrogación **9** question mark	organizar *mis* ideas **17** organize *my* ideas	
signo de exclamación **10** exclamation point	escribir un borrador **18** write a first draft	
coma **11** comma	título **a** title	
apóstrofe **12** apostrophe	párrafo **b** paragraph	
comillas **13** quotation marks	corregir/revisar/editar **19** make corrections/revise/edit	
dos puntos **14** colon	recibir reacciones/comentarios **20** get feedback	
punto y coma **15** semi-colon	pasar en limpio/escribir la copia final **21** write a final copy/rewrite	

A. Did you find any mistakes?
B. Yes. You forgot to put a/an _____[8–15]_____ in this sentence.

A. Are you working on your composition?
B. Yes. I'm _____[16–21]_____ing.

LA LITERATURA Y LA ESCRITURA

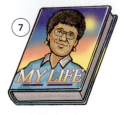

ficción	**1** fiction	artículo periodístico	**11** newspaper article
novela	**2** novel	editorial	**12** editorial
cuento	**3** short story	carta	**13** letter
poesía/poemas	**4** poetry/poems	tarjeta postal	**14** postcard
no ficción	**5** non-fiction	nota	**15** note
biografía	**6** biography	invitación	**16** invitation
autobiografía	**7** autobiography	nota de agradecimiento	**17** thank-you note
ensayo	**8** essay	memorándum/memoranda	**18** memo
trabajo/reporte/ informe escolar	**9** report	mensaje por correo electrónico/e-mail	**19** e-mail
artículo de revista	**10** magazine article	mensaje instantáneo	**20** instant message

A. What are you doing?

B. I'm writing $\begin{cases} \underline{\hspace{1cm}[1, 4, 5]\hspace{1cm}}. \\ \text{a/an } \underline{\hspace{1cm}[2, 3, 6-20]\hspace{1cm}}. \end{cases}$

What kind of literature do you like to read? What are some of your favorite books? Who is your favorite author?

Do you like to read newspapers and magazines? Which ones do you read?

Do you sometimes send or receive letters, postcards, notes, e-mail, or instant messages? Tell about the people you communicate with, and how.

GEOGRAFÍA

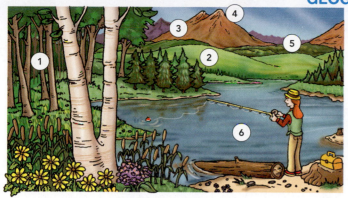

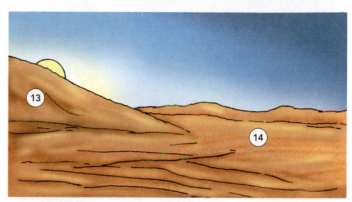

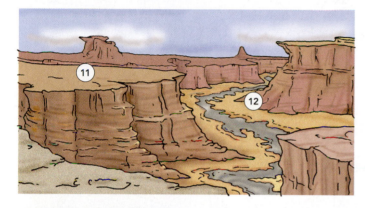

bosque	**1**	forest/woods		duna	**13**	dune/sand dune
colina	**2**	hill		desierto	**14**	desert
cordillera/sierra	**3**	mountain range		selva tropical/jungla	**15**	jungle
cumbre	**4**	mountain peak		playa/costa	**16**	seashore/shore
valle	**5**	valley		bahía	**17**	bay
lago	**6**	lake		océano	**18**	ocean
llanuras	**7**	plains		isla	**19**	island
pradera	**8**	meadow		península	**20**	peninsula
arroyo/quebrada/riachuelo	**9**	stream/brook		selva húmeda/tropical	**21**	rainforest
laguna/charca/estanque	**10**	pond		río	**22**	river
meseta	**11**	plateau		cascada (pequeña)/	**23**	waterfall
cañón	**12**	canyon		catarata (grande)		

A. { Isn't this a beautiful _____?!
     { Aren't these beautiful _____s?!
B. Yes. It's/They're magnificent!

Tell about the geography of your country.
Describe the different geographic features.

Have you seen some of the geographic
features in this lesson? Which ones? Where?

CIENCIAS

Equipo para el laboratorio de ciencias	Science Equipment
microscopio	**1** microscope
computadora/ordenador	**2** computer
platina	**3** slide
caja de Petri/de cultivos	**4** Petri dish
matraz	**5** flask
embudo	**6** funnel
vaso de precipitados	**7** beaker
tubo de ensayo/probeta	**8** test tube
fórceps/tenazas	**9** forceps
pinzas para crisol	**10** crucible tongs
mechero de Bunsen	**11** Bunsen burner
probeta graduada	**12** graduated cylinder
imán	**13** magnet
prisma	**14** prism
gotero	**15** dropper
productos químicos	**16** chemicals
balanza/báscula	**17** balance
balanza/báscula	**18** scale

El método científico	The Scientific Method
presentar el problema	**A** state the problem
formular una hipótesis	**B** form a hypothesis
planear un procedimiento	**C** plan a procedure
realizar el procedimiento	**D** do a procedure
anotar las observaciones	**E** make/record observations
sacar conclusiones	**F** draw conclusions

A. What do we need to do this procedure?
B. We need a/an/the ___[1–18]___.

A. How is your experiment coming along?
B. I'm getting ready to ___[A–F]___.

Do you have experience with the scientific equipment in this lesson? Tell about it.

What science courses do/did you take in school?

Think of an idea for a science experiment.
What question about science do you want to answer? State the problem.
What do you think will happen in the experiment? Form a hypothesis.
How can you test your hypothesis? Plan a procedure.

EL UNIVERSO

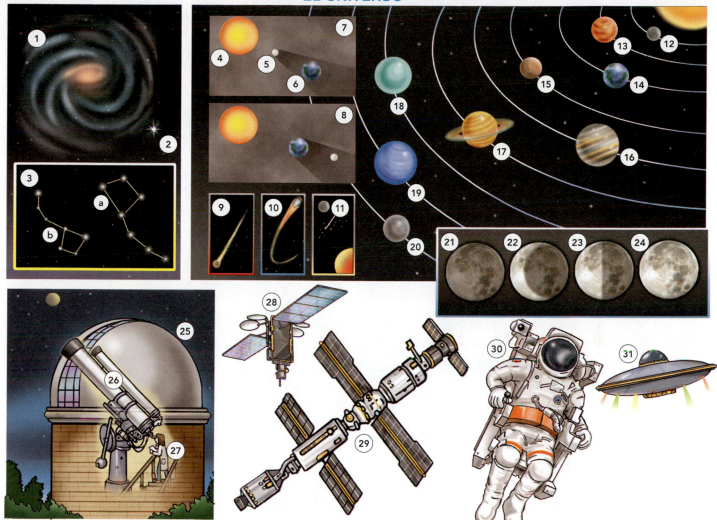

El universo		**The Universe**
galaxia	1	galaxy
estrella	2	star
constelación	3	constellation
La Osa Mayor	a	The Big Dipper
La Osa Menor	b	The Little Dipper
El sistema solar		**The Solar System**
sol	4	sun
luna	5	moon
planeta	6	planet
eclipse solar	7	solar eclipse
eclipse lunar	8	lunar eclipse
meteoro/bólido/ estrella fugaz	9	meteor
cometa/bólido/ estrella fugaz	10	comet
asteroide	11	asteroid
Mercurio	12	Mercury
Venus	13	Venus
La Tierra	14	Earth
Marte	15	Mars
Júpiter	16	Jupiter
Saturno	17	Saturn
Urano	18	Uranus
Neptuno	19	Neptune
Plutón	20	Pluto
luna nueva	21	new moon
cuarto creciente	22	crescent moon
media luna	23	quarter moon
luna llena	24	full moon
Astronomía		**Astronomy**
observatorio	25	observatory
telescopio	26	telescope
astrónomo(a)	27	astronomer
La exploración espacial		**Space Exploration**
satélite	28	satellite
estación espacial	29	space station
astronauta/cosmonauta	30	astronaut
platillo volador/ volante/ OVNI/UFO	31	U.F.O./ Unidentified Flying Object/ flying saucer

[1–24]
A. Is that (a/an/the) _____?
B. I'm not sure. I think it might be (a/an/the) _____.

[28–30]
A. Is the _____ ready for tomorrow's launch?
B. Yes. "All systems are go!"

Pretend you are an astronaut traveling in space. What do you see?

Draw and name a constellation you are familiar with.

Do you think space exploration is important? Why?

Have you ever seen a U.F.O.? Do you believe there is life in outer space? Why?

PROFESIONES Y OFICIOS I

What's the problem?

contador/contable	1	accountant
actor	2	actor
actriz	3	actress
arquitecto(a)	4	architect
pintor(a)	5	artist
montador(a)/ensamblador(a)/ armador(a)	6	assembler
niñero(a)/canguro	7	babysitter
panadero(a)	8	baker
peluquero(a)/barbero(a)	9	barber
albañil	10	bricklayer/mason
hombre de negocios	11	businessman
mujer de negocios	12	businesswoman
carnicero(a)	13	butcher
carpintero(a)	14	carpenter
cajero(a)	15	cashier
chef/cocinero(a)	16	chef/cook
auxiliar de guardería infantil	17	child day-care worker
ingeniero(a) de informática	18	computer software engineer
obrero(a)	19	construction worker
portero(a)/afanador(a)	20	custodian/janitor
representante para servicios a clientes	21	customer service representative
anotador(a) de datos	22	data entry clerk

repartidor(a)	**23** delivery person	jardinero(a)/paisajista	**32** gardener/landscaper
estibador(a)	**24** dockworker	costurero(a)	**33** garment worker
ingeniero(a)	**25** engineer	peluquero(a)	**34** hairdresser
obrero(a)	**26** factory worker	ayudante/asistente de salud	**35** health-care aide/attendant
granjero(a)/agricultor(a)	**27** farmer	ayudante/asistente	**36** home health aide/
bombero(a)	**28** firefighter	de salud en casa	home attendant
pescador(a)	**29** fisher	encargado(a) de la casa/amo(a) de casa	**37** homemaker
empleado(a) de cafetería	**30** food-service worker	sirviente(a)/criado(a)/	**38** housekeeper
maestro(a) de obras/capataz	**31** foreman	empleado(a) de servicio doméstico	

A. What do you do?
B. I'm an **accountant**. How about you?
A. I'm a **carpenter**.

[At a job interview]

A. Are you an experienced _____?
B. Yes. I'm a very experienced _____.

A. How long have you been a/an _____?
B. I've been a/an _____ for .... months/years.

Which of these occupations do you think are the most interesting? the most difficult? Why?

PROFESIONES Y OFICIOS II

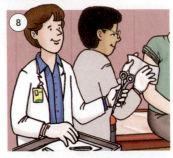

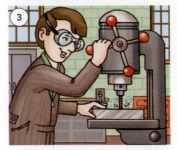

periodista/reportero(a)	**1**	journalist/reporter
abogado(a)	**2**	lawyer
maquinista	**3**	machine operator
cartero(a)	**4**	mail carrier/letter carrier
director(a)/gerente/ administrador(a)	**5**	manager
manicurista	**6**	manicurist
mecánico(a)	**7**	mechanic
técnico(a) sanitario(a)/ asistente médico(a)	**8**	medical assistant/ physician assistant
mensajero(a)	**9**	messenger/courier
mozo(a) de mudanzas	**10**	mover
músico	**11**	musician
pintor(a)	**12**	painter
boticario(a)/farmacéutico(a)/farmacista	**13**	pharmacist
fotógrafo(a)	**14**	photographer
piloto	**15**	pilot
policía	**16**	police officer
empleado(a) de correos	**17**	postal worker
recepcionista/recepcionista-telefonista	**18**	receptionist
reparador(a)/mecánico(a)	**19**	repairperson
vendedor(a)	**20**	salesperson

basurero(a)/recolector(a) de basura	21	sanitation worker/ trash collector
secretario(a)	22	secretary
guardia de seguridad	23	security guard
soldado	24	serviceman
soldada	25	servicewoman
empleado(a) de almacén	26	stock clerk
tendero(a)/comerciante	27	store owner/shopkeeper
supervisor(a)	28	supervisor
sastre(a)	29	tailor

maestro(a)/profesor(a)	30	teacher/instructor
agente de ventas por teléfono	31	telemarketer
traductor(a)/intérprete	32	translator/interpreter
agente de viajes	33	travel agent
camionero(a)	34	truck driver
veterinario(a)	35	veterinarian/vet
mesero/camarero	36	waiter/server
mesera/camarera	37	waitress/server
soldador(a)	38	welder

A. What's your occupation?
B. I'm a **journalist**.
A. A **journalist**?
B. Yes. That's right.

A. Are you still a _____?
B. No. I'm a _____.
A. Oh. That's interesting.

A. What kind of job would you like in the future?
B. I'd like to be a _____.

Do you work? What's your occupation?

What are the occupations of people in your family?

ACTIVIDADES RELACIONADAS CON EL TRABAJO

actuar	**1** act		manejar/conducir *un camión*	**11**	drive *a truck*
armar/montar *componentes*	**2** assemble *components*		archivar	**12**	file
ayudar a *pacientes*	**3** assist *patients*		pilotear *un avión*	**13**	fly *an airplane*
hornear	**4** bake		cultivar *vegetales*	**14**	grow *vegetables*
hacer/construir *cosas*	**5** build *things*/construct *things*		vigilar/cuidar *edificios*	**15**	guard *buildings*
limpiar	**6** clean		administrar *un restaurante*	**16**	manage *a restaurant*
cocinar	**7** cook		cortar *el césped*	**17**	mow *lawns*
repartir *pizzas*	**8** deliver *pizzas*		manejar *herramientas/máquinas*	**18**	operate *equipment*
diseñar *edificios*	**9** design *buildings*		pintar	**19**	paint
dibujar/trazar	**10** draw		tocar *el piano*	**20**	play the *piano*

27 Por favor complete esto.

32 Да. Yes.

preparar *la comida*	**21**	prepare *food*
reparar/componer/ arreglar *cosas*	**22**	repair *things*/ fix *things*
vender *autos/ carros/coches*	**23**	sell *cars*
servir *comida*	**24**	serve *food*
coser	**25**	sew
cantar	**26**	sing
hablar *español*	**27**	speak *Spanish*

supervisar *empleados*	**28**	supervise *people*
cuidar a *gente mayor*	**29**	take care of *elderly people*
hacer inventario	**30**	take inventory
enseñar	**31**	teach
traducir	**32**	translate
mecanografiar/teclear	**33**	type
usar *una caja registradora*	**34**	use *a cash register*
lavar *platos*	**35**	wash *dishes*
escribir	**36**	write

A. Can you **act**?
B. Yes, I can.

A. Do you know how to _____?
B. Yes. I've been _____ing for years.

A. Tell me about your skills.
B. I can _____, and I can _____.

Tell about your job skills.
What can you do?

JOB SEARCH
EN BUSCA DE EMPLEO

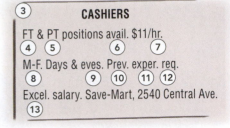

Tipos de anuncios	Types of Job Ads	En busca de empleo	Job Search
letrero de se busca ayuda	**1** help wanted sign	responder a un anuncio	**A** respond to an ad
tablero de anuncios	**2** job notice/announcement	solicitar información	**B** request information
anuncio/clasificado/ de empleo	**3** classified ad/want ad	solicitar una entrevista	**C** request an interview
		preparar el currículum vítae	**D** prepare a resume
Abreviaturas en los anuncios	**Job Ad Abbreviations**	vestirse de manera apropiada	**E** dress appropriately
		llenar una solicitud	**F** fill out an application (form)
tiempo completo	**4** full-time	ir a una entrevista	**G** go to an interview
tiempo parcial/medio tiempo	**5** part-time	hablar sobre sus aptitudes y habilidades	**H** talk about your skills and qualifications
disponible	**6** available	hablar sobre suexperiencia laboral	**I** talk about your experience
por hora	**7** hour	pedir información acerca del sueldo	**J** ask about the salary
de lunes a viernes	**8** Monday through Friday		
por las tardes	**9** evenings	pedir información acerca de los subsidios y prestaciones laborales	**K** ask about the benefits
previo(a)	**10** previous		
experiencia	**11** experience	escribir una nota de agradecimiento	**L** write a thank-you note
se requiere	**12** required		
excelente	**13** excellent	ser contratado(a)/nombrado(a)	**M** get hired

A. How did you find your job?
B. I found it through a ____[1–3]____.

A. How was your job interview?
B. It went very well.
A. Did you ___[D–F, H–M]___?
B. Yes, I did.

Tell about a job you are familiar with. What are the skills and qualifications required for the job? What are the hours? What is the salary?

Tell about how people you know found their jobs.

Tell about your own experience with a job search or a job interview.

recepción	**A** reception area	báscula de cartas	**6** postal scale	gerente	**23** office manager
sala de	**B** conference	máquina para sellos	**7** postage meter	estante/armario de	**24** supply
conferencias	room	ayudante de oficina	**8** office assistant	artículos de oficina	cabinet
cuarto del correo	**C** mailroom	buzón	**9** mailbox	estante/armario de	**25** storage
área de trabajo	**D** work area	cubículo	**10** cubicle	almacenaje	cabinet
oficina	**E** office	silla giratoria	**11** swivel chair	vendedora	**26** vending
cuarto de artículos	**F** supply	máquina de escribir	**12** typewriter	automática	machine
de oficina	room	calculadora/sumadora	**13** adding machine	fuente	**27** water cooler
cuarto de	**G** storage	fotocopiadora	**14** copier/photocopier	cafetera eléctrica	**28** coffee machine
almacenaje	room	trituradora de papel	**15** paper shredder	tablero	**29** message
salón de	**H** employee	guillotina	**16** paper cutter	(de anuncios)	board
empleados	lounge	archivista	**17** file clerk	tomar un mensaje	**a** take a message
perchero	**1** coat rack	archivador/archivero	**18** file cabinet	hacer una	**b** give a
ropero	**2** coat closet	secretario(a)	**19** secretary	presentación	presentation
recepcionista	**3** receptionist	estación/módulo	**20** computer	clasificar el correo	**c** sort the mail
mesa de reuniones/	**4** conference	de computadora	workstation	fotocopiar/copiar	**d** make copies
conferencias	table	jefe(a)/empleador(a)	**21** employer/boss	archivar	**e** file
tablero para	**5** presentation	asistente	**22** administrative assistant	escribir	**f** type a letter
presentaciones	board	administrativo(a)		una carta	

[A–H]
A. Where's ......(name)......?
B. He's / She's in the _____.

[1–29]
A. What do you think of the new _____?
B. He's / She's / It's very nice.

[a–f]
A. What's ......(name)...... doing?
B. He's / She's _____ing.

Describe a workplace you are familiar with. Tell about the rooms, the areas, and the employees.

EQUIPO Y ARTÍCULOS DE OFICINA

escritorio	**1** desk	libretita de notas autoadhesivas	**11** Post-It note pad	etiqueta postal	**24** mailing label
engrapadora/ presilladora/ grapadora	**2** stapler	agenda personal	**12** organizer/ personal planner	cartucho de tinta para máquina de escribir cartucho de tinta para impresora	**25** typewriter cartridge **26** ink cartridge
bandeja tamaño carta/apilable	**3** letter tray/ stacking tray	liga/goma clip/sujetador	**13** rubber band **14** paper clip	sello de goma	**27** rubber stamp
agenda rotatoria	**4** rotary card file	grapa	**15** staple	almohadilla de tinta/ tampón	**28** ink pad
carpeta de felpa	**5** desk pad	tachuela	**16** thumbtack		
agenda	**6** appointment book	chinche/chincheta	**17** pushpin	lápiz adhesivo	**29** glue stick
		libreta tamaño legal	**18** legal pad	goma/pegamento	**30** glue
tablilla con sujetapapeles	**7** clipboard	carpeta/fólder	**19** file folder	pegalotodo/ goma sintética	**31** rubber cement
libreta de notas/ memorandas	**8** note pad/ memo pad	ficha	**20** index card	líquido corrector	**32** correction fluid
		sobre	**21** envelope	cinta pegante de celofán	**33** cellophane tape/ clear tape
sacapuntas eléctrico	**9** electric pencil sharpener	papel para escribir cartas/ con membrete	**22** stationery/ letterhead (paper)	cinta pegante canela para empacar	**34** packing tape/ sealing tape
calendario de escritorio	**10** desk calendar	sobre paquete/ acolchado	**23** mailer		

A. My desk is a mess!
   I can't find my __[2–12]__ !
B. Here it is next to your __[2–12]__ .

A. Could you get some more
   __[13–21, 23–29]__ s / __[22, 30–34]__
from the supply room?
B. Some more __[13–21, 23–29]__ s /
   __[22, 30–34]__ ? Sure. I'd be happy to.

Which supplies and equipment do you use? What do you use them for?

Which supplies in this lesson do you have at home? at school?

LA FÁBRICA

reloj marcador/checador	**1**	time clock	embalador(a)/empacador(a)	**12** packer
tarjetas de asistencia	**2**	time cards	portacarga/montacarga	**13** forklift
vestidor	**3**	locker room	ascensor de carga	**14** freight elevator
cadena/línea de montaje	**4**	(assembly) line	circular del sindicato	**15** union notice
obrero(a)/operario(a)	**5**	(factory) worker	buzón de sugerencias	**16** suggestion box
estación de trabajo	**6**	work station	sección/departamento de envíos	**17** shipping department
supervisor(a) de cadena de montaje	**7**	line supervisor	encargado(a) de envíos	**18** shipping clerk
supervisor(a) de control de calidad	**8**	quality control supervisor	carrito manual/diablito	**19** hand truck/dolly
máquina	**9**	machine	muelle de carga	**20** loading dock
cinta transportadora	**10**	conveyor belt	oficina de pagos/de nómina	**21** payroll office
almacén/depósito	**11**	warehouse	oficina de personal	**22** personnel office

A. Excuse me. I'm a new employee.
 Where's/Where are the _____?
B. Next to/Near/In/On the _____.

A. Have you seen *Tony*?
B. Yes. *He's* in/on/at/next to/near
 the _____.

Are there any factories where you live? What kind?
What are the working conditions there?

What products do factories in your country produce?

almádena/mazo	**1** sledgehammer	andamio	**12** scaffolding	casa remolque/ tráiler	**21** trailer
pico	**2** pickax	volquete	**13** dump truck	muro en seco/	**22** drywall
pala	**3** shovel	pala cargadora mecánica	**14** front-end loader	muro ensamblable	
carretilla	**4** wheelbarrow	grúa	**15** crane	madera	**23** wood/lumber
taladro/ neumático perforador	**5** jackhammer/ pneumatic drill	grúa (con plataforma movible)	**16** cherry picker	madera contrachapada	**24** plywood
planos	**6** blueprints	bulldozer/tractor	**17** bulldozer	fibra aislante	**25** insulation
escalera	**7** ladder	tractor excavador(a)	**18** backhoe	alambre	**26** wire
cinta métrica	**8** tape measure	revolvedora de concreto/hormigonera	**19** concrete mixer truck	ladrillo	**27** brick
cinturón para herramientas	**9** toolbelt	concreto/hormigón	**a** concrete	teja	**28** shingle
palustre/paleta/llana	**10** trowel	camioneta de carga/ pickup	**20** pickup truck	tubo	**29** pipe
mezcladora de cemento/ mortero	**11** cement mixer			viga/trabe	**30** girder/beam
cemento	**a** cement				

A. Could you get me that/those ___[1–10]___?
B. Sure.

A. Watch out for that ___[11–21]___!
B. Oh! Thanks for the warning!

A. Do we have enough ___[22–26]___ / ___[27–30]___s?
B. I think so.

What building materials is your home made of?
When was it built?

Describe a construction site near your home or school.
Tell about the construction equipment and the materials.

SEGURIDAD LABORAL

casco de construcción	1	hard hat/helmet
tapones para oídos	2	earplugs
anteojos protectores/ gafas protectoras	3	goggles
chaleco de seguridad	4	safety vest
botas protectoras	5	safety boots
protector para los dedos de los pies	6	toe guard
faja/arnés de soporte	7	back support
orejeras protectoras	8	safety earmuffs
redecilla	9	hairnet
mascarilla/máscara	10	mask
guantes de látex	11	latex gloves
mascarilla filtrante	12	respirator
visor para soldar/ gafas de seguridad	13	safety glasses
inflamable	14	flammable
venenoso(a)	15	poisonous
corrosivo(a)	16	corrosive
radioactivo(a)	17	radioactive
peligroso(a)	18	dangerous
peligroso(a)	19	hazardous
peligro de agente biológico infeccioso/ patógeno tóxico	20	biohazard
peligro de electrocución	21	electrical hazard
botiquín/maletín de primeros auxilios	22	first-aid kit
extinguidor/ extintor de incendios	23	fire extinguisher
desfibrilador	24	defibrillator
salida de emergencia	25	emergency exit

A. Don't forget to wear your ___[1–13]___!
B. Thanks for reminding me.

A. Be careful!
- That material is ___[14–17]___!
- That machine is ___[18]___!
- That work area is ___[19]___!
- That's a ___[20]___! / That's an ___[21]___!

B. Thanks for the warning.

A. Where's the ___[22–25]___?
B. It's over there.

Have you ever used any of the safety equipment in this lesson? What have you used? When? Where?

Where do you see people using safety equipment in your community?

EL TRANSPORTE PÚBLICO

autobús/bus/ guagua/camión	**A**	**bus**	taquilla/ ventanilla	**12**	ticket window	torniquete/contador de entrada	**21**	turnstile

autobús/bus/ guagua/camión — **A bus**
parada/paradero — **1** bus stop
ruta — **2** bus route
pasajero(a) — **3** passenger/rider
tarifa — **4** (bus) fare
billete de trasbordo — **5** transfer
conductor(a)/chofer de autobús/busero(a) — **6** bus driver
estación de autobuses — **7** bus station
boletería/taquilla — **8** ticket counter
billete/pasaje/boleto — **9** ticket
maletero — **10** baggage compartment/ luggage compartment

tren B train
estación del tren — **11** train station

taquilla/ ventanilla — **12** ticket window
tablero de llegadas y salidas — **13** arrival and departure board
mostrador de información — **14** information booth
horarios — **15** schedule/ timetable
andén — **16** platform
riel/vía — **17** track
cobrador(a) — **18** conductor

metro/ subterráneo C subway
estación del metro — **19** subway station
ficha — **20** (subway) token

torniquete/contador de entrada — **21** turnstile
tarjeta de pasaje/ boleto prepagado — **22** fare card
máquina expendedora de pasajes/boletos — **23** fare card machine

taxi D taxi
parada de taxis/ piquera — **24** taxi stand
taxi — **25** taxi/cab/ taxicab
taxímetro — **26** meter
taxista/ chofer de taxi — **27** cab driver/ taxi driver

transbordador/ ferry E ferry

[A–E]
A. How are you going to get there?
B. { I'm going to take the __[A–C, E]__ .
    { I'm going to take a __[D]__ .

[1, 7, 8, 10–19, 21, 23–25]
A. Excuse me. Where's the _____?
B. Over there.

How do you get to different places in your community? Describe public transportation where you live.

In your country, can you travel far by train or by bus? Where can you go? How much do tickets cost? Describe the buses and trains.

TIPOS DE VEHÍCULOS

sedán	**1** sedan	limusina	**12** limousine
cupé/carro de tres puertas/hatchback	**2** hatchback	camión remolque/grúa	**13** tow truck
convertible/descapotable	**3** convertible	camper(o)/caravana/remolque	**14** R.V. (recreational vehicle)/camper
carro/coche deportivo	**4** sports car		
carro/coche híbrido	**5** hybrid	camión de mudanzas	**15** moving van
camioneta/vagoneta	**6** station wagon	camión	**16** truck
camioneta todoterreno/cuatro por cuatro/utilitaria	**7** S.U.V. (sport utility vehicle)	tráiler/camión con remolque/acoplado	**17** tractor trailer/semi
todoterreno/jeep	**8** jeep	bicicleta	**18** bicycle/bike
furgoneta/van/camioneta repartidora	**9** van	ciclomotor/bicimoto	**19** motor scooter
minivan/minibús/microbús	**10** minivan	scooter/motoneta/vespa	**20** moped
camioneta de carga/pickup	**11** pickup truck	motocicleta	**21** motorcycle

A. What kind of vehicle are you looking for?
B. I'm looking for a **sedan**.

A. Do you drive a/an _____?
B. No. I drive a/an _____.

A. I just saw an accident between a/an _____ and a/an _____!
B. Was anybody hurt?
A. No. Fortunately, nobody was hurt.

What are the most common types of vehicles in your country?

What's your favorite type of vehicle? Why? In your opinion, which company makes the best one?

PARTES Y MANTENIMIENTO DEL AUTOMÓVIL/COCHE/CARRO

parachoques/paragolpes	**1**	bumper	tanque de gasolina	**25** gas tank
luces delanteras/faros	**2**	headlight	gato	**26** jack
luz direccional/intermitente	**3**	turn signal	llanta de repuesto/refacción	**27** spare tire
señal de estacionamiento/ luz de aparcamiento/posición	**4**	parking light	llave de cruz/cruceta	**28** lug wrench
			señales de peligro/bengala	**29** flare
guardafango/guardabarros/salpicadera	**5**	fender	cables de conexión/reactivadores/ pasacorriente	**30** jumper cables
llanta/neumático/goma	**6**	tire		
tapacubos/embellecedor/pollera/copa	**7**	hubcap	bujías	**31** spark plugs
capó del motor/cofre	**8**	hood	filtro	**32** air filter
parabrisas/cristal delantero	**9**	windshield	motor	**33** engine
limpiaparabrisas/cepillo/limpiadores	**10**	windshield wipers	sistema de inyección de combustible	**34** fuel injection system
espejo lateral/retrovisor exterior	**11**	side mirror		
portaequipaje/parrilla	**12**	roof rack	radiador	**35** radiator
media luna/tragaluz/ quemacocos/claraboya	**13**	sunroof	manguera/manga del radiador	**36** radiator hose
			banda/correa del ventilador	**37** fan belt
antena	**14**	antenna	alternador	**38** alternator
ventana trasera	**15**	rear window	indicador de aceite/varilla del aceite	**39** dipstick
descongelador/desempañador trasero	**16**	rear defroster	batería	**40** battery
maletero/cajuela	**17**	trunk	bomba de aire	**41** air pump
luz trasera/calavera	**18**	taillight	surtidor/bomba de gasolina	**42** gas pump
luz del freno/indicadora de frenado	**19**	brake light	boca/boquilla	**43** nozzle
luz de retroceso/reverso	**20**	backup light	tapón de gasolina	**44** gas cap
placa/chapa de matrícula/tablilla	**21**	license plate	gasolina	**45** gas
tubo de escape	**22**	tailpipe/exhaust pipe	aceite	**46** oil
silenciador/mofle(r)	**23**	muffler	refrigerante	**47** coolant
transmisión	**24**	transmission	aire	**48** air

bolsa de aire **49** air bag	ventila/rejilla **62** vent	transmisión **76** manual
visera **50** visor	sistema de **63** navigation system	manual transmission
espejo retrovisor **51** rearview mirror	navegación	palanca de **77** stickshift
tablero/panel de **52** dashboard/	radio **64** radio	cambios
instrumentos/ instrument	reproductor de CD **65** CD player	embrague/ **78** clutch
mandos panel	calefacción **66** heater	clutch
indicador de **53** temperature	aire acondicionado **67** air conditioning	seguro **79** door lock
temperatur gauge	descongelador/ **68** defroster	manija/manilla/ **80** door
medidor/ **54** gas gauge/	desempañador	manigueta handle
indicador de gasolina fuel gauge	tomacorriente **69** power outlet	cinturón de **81** shoulder
velocímetro **55** speedometer	guanter a/gavetera **70** glove compartment	seguridad harness
odómetro **56** odometer	freno de emergencia **71** emergency brake	apoyabrazos **82** armrest
señal de alarma/luz **57** warning	freno/pedal de freno **72** brake (pedal)	cabezal/ **83** headrest
(indicadora) de alarma lights	acelerador **73** accelerator/	protector de cabeza
palanca de direccionales **58** turn signal	gas pedal	asiento **84** seat
volante/guía **59** steering wheel	transmisión **74** automatic	cinturón de **85** seat belt
claxon/bocina/pito **60** horn	automática transmission	seguridad
encendido **61** ignition	palanca de cambios **75** gearshift	

[2, 3, 9–16, 24, 35–39, 49–85]
A. What's the matter with your car?
B. The _____(s) is/are broken.

[45–48]
A. Can I help you?
B. { Yes. My car needs ___[45–47]___ .
   { Yes. My tires need ___[48]___ .

[1, 2, 4–15, 17–23, 25]
A. I was just in a car accident!
B. Oh, no! Were you hurt?
A. No. But my _____(s) was/were damaged.

In your opinion, what are the most important features to look for when you buy a car?

Do you own a car? What kind? Tell about any repairs your car has needed.

CARRETERAS/AUTOPISTAS Y CALLES

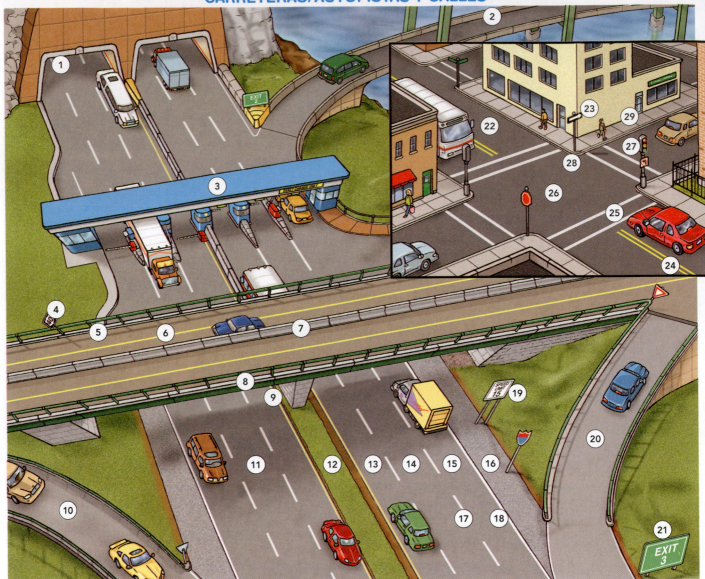

túnel	**1** tunnel	jardín divisor/	**12** median	carril/rampa de salida	**20** exit (ramp)
puente	**2** bridge	vereda/camellón		letrero de salida	**21** exit sign
garita/caseta de peaje	**3** tollbooth	carril izquierdo	**13** left lane	calle	**22** street
letrero/indicador de rutas	**4** route sign	carril central	**14** middle lane/ center lane	calle de un solo sentido	**23** one-way street
autopista	**5** highway	carril derecho	**15** right lane	línea amarilla doble/	**24** double
carretera	**6** road	borde/orilla	**16** shoulder	de "no doblar"	yellow line
muro de contención/ divisor central	**7** divider/ barrier	acotamiento/margen/ de la carretera		vía /paso/ cruce de peatones/	**25** crosswalk
paso elevado/a desnivel	**8** overpass	línea discontinua/ de "se puede pasar"	**17** broken line	línea de seguridad	
paso inferior	**9** underpass	línea continua/	**18** solid line	cruce	**26** intersection
carril/ rampa de entrada	**10** entrance ramp/ on ramp	de "no pasar"		semáforo	**27** traffic light/ traffic signal
autopista interestatal	**11** interstate (highway)	letrero de límite de velocidad	**19** speed limit sign	esquina	**28** corner
				cuadra/manzana	**29** block

[1–28]

A. Where's the accident?

B. It's on/in/at/near the _____.

Describe a highway you travel on.

Describe an intersection near where you live.

In your area, on which highways and streets do most accidents occur? Why are these places dangerous?

PREPOSICIONES PARA DAR DIRECCIONES

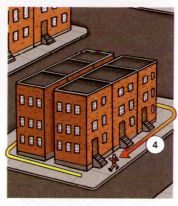

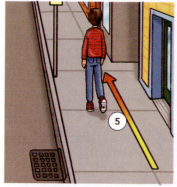

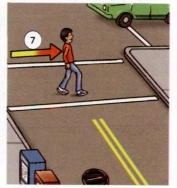

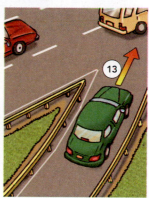

(manejar) sobre/por	**1**	over	(ir) hacia arriba	**5**	up	(subir) al (autobús)	**9**	on
(manejar) por debajo/bajo	**2**	under	(ir) hacia abajo	**6**	down	(bajar) del (autobús)	**10**	off
(manejar) por/a través de	**3**	through	(cruzar) del otro lado	**7**	across	(entrar) a	**11**	into
(caminar) alrededor de	**4**	around	(ir) más allá de	**8**	past	(salir) de	**12**	out of
						(entrar) a/en (la autopista)	**13**	onto

[1–8]
A. Go **over** the bridge.
B. **Over** the bridge?
A. Yes.

[9–13]
A. I can't talk right now. I'm getting **on** a train.
B. You're getting **on** a train?
A. Yes. I'll call you later.

What places do you go past on your way to school?   Tell how to get to different places from your home or your school.

SEÑALES E INDICACIONES/INSTRUCCIONES DE TRÁNSITO

Señales de tránsito	Traffic Signs	unión de carriles	12 merging traffic	Instrucciones para el examen de conducir/manejar	Road Test Instructions
alto/stop	1 stop	ceda el paso	13 yield		
no doble a la izquierda	2 no left turn	desvío	14 detour	Doble a la izquierda.	21 Turn left.
no doble a la derecha	3 no right turn	resbaladizo(a)	15 slippery	Doble a la derecha.	22 Turn right.
no doble en U	4 no U-turn	si está mojado(a)	when wet	Siga derecho/recto.	23 Go straight
doble sólo a la derecha	5 right turn only	estacionamiento para	16 handicapped	Estaciónese paralelo	24 Parallel par
prohibido el paso	6 do not enter	discapacitados(as)	parking only	a la acera.	
un solo sentido	7 one way			Dé un viraje de tres	25 Make a
calle sin salida	8 dead end/no outlet	**Direcciones de la brújula**	**Compass Directions**	puntos.	3-point turr
cruce de peatones	9 pedestrian crossing	norte	17 north	Use señales de mano.	26 Use hand signals.
cruce de rieles/ de ferrocarril	10 railroad crossing	sur	18 south		
cruce escolar	11 school crossing	oeste/poniente	19 west		
		este/oriente	20 east		

[1–16]
A. Careful! That sign says "**stop**"!
B. Oh. Thanks.

[17–20]
A. Which way should I go?
B. Go **north**.

[21–26]
A. Turn **right**.
B. Turn **right**?
A. Yes.

Which of these traffic signs are in your neighborhood? What other traffic signs do you usually see?

Describe any differences between traffic signs in different countries you know.

EL AEROPUERTO

Registro de pasajeros	A Check-In
pasaje/boleto/billete	1 ticket
mostrador de pasajes	2 ticket counter
expendedor(a) de pasajes	3 ticket agent
maleta/valija/petaca	4 suitcase
monitor de llegadas y salidas	5 arrival and departure monitor

Seguridad	B Security
control de seguridad	6 security checkpoint
detector de metales	7 metal detector
guardia de seguridad	8 security officer
máquina de rayos X	9 X-ray machine
equipaje de mano	10 carry-on bag

La puerta/sala (de embarque y desembarque)	C The Gate
mostrador de factura/ registro/chequeo	11 check-in counter
tarjeta de abordaje	12 boarding pass
puerta/sala	13 gate
área de abordaje	14 boarding area

Reclamo/Retiro de equipaje	D Baggage Claim
área de reclamo/retiro de equipaje	15 baggage claim (area)
carrusel de equipaje	16 baggage carousel
equipaje	17 baggage
carreta/carrito para equipaje	18 baggage cart/ luggage cart
carretilla/carrito para equipaje	19 luggage carrier
bolsa para trajes/vestidos/ sacos y abrigos	20 garment bag
etiqueta/boleto de factura del equipaje	21 baggage claim check

Inmigración y aduana	E Customs and Immigration
aduana	22 customs
empleado(a) de aduana	23 customs officer
tarjeta/formulario de declaración de aduana	24 customs declaration form
inmigración	25 immigration
oficial de inmigración	26 immigration officer
pasaporte	27 passport
visa	28 visa

[2, 3, 5–9, 11, 13–16, 22, 23, 25, 26]
A. Excuse me. Where's the _____?*
B. Right over there.

* With 22 and 25 use: Excuse me. Where's _____?

[1, 4, 10, 12, 17–21, 24, 27, 28]
A. Oh, no! I think I've lost my _____!
B. I'll help you look for it.

Describe an airport you are familiar with. Tell about the check-in area, the security area, the gates, and the baggage claim area.

Have you ever gone through Customs and Immigration? Tell about your experience.

EL VIAJE EN AVIÓN

Spanish	#	English	Spanish	#	English
cabina (de mando)	1	cockpit	chaleco salvavidas	19	life vest/life jacket
piloto/capitán	2	pilot/captain	pista	20	runway
copiloto	3	co-pilot	terminal (edificio)	21	terminal (building)
baño	4	lavatory/bathroom	torre de control	22	control tower
aeromozo(a)/azafata/sobrecargo	5	flight attendant	avión/jet	23	airplane/plane/jet
compartimiento superior	6	overhead compartment			
pasillo	7	aisle	quítese los zapatos	A	take off your shoes
asiento con ventanilla	8	window seat	vacíese los bolsillos	B	empty your pockets
asiento central	9	middle seat	ponga el equipaje en la cinta/banda transportadora	C	put your bag on the conveyor belt
asiento de pasillo	10	aisle seat	ponga la computadora en una bandeja	D	put your computer in a tray
señal de "abrocharse los cinturones"	11	Fasten Seat Belt sign	camine a través del detector de metales	E	walk through the metal detector
señal de "no fumar"	12	No Smoking sign	preséntese en la entrada	F	check in at the gate
botón de llamada para servicio	13	call button	obtenga su tarjeta de abordaje	G	get your boarding pass
mascarilla de oxígeno	14	oxygen mask	aborde el avión	H	board the plane
puerta de emergencia	15	emergency exit	guarde su equipaje de mano	I	stow your carry-on bag
mesa abatible	16	tray (table)	encuentre su asiento	J	find your seat
tarjeta de instrucciones de emergencia	17	emergency instruction card	abróchese el cinturón de seguridad	K	fasten your seat belt
bolsa para mareos	18	air sickness bag			

[1–23]
A. Where's the _____?
B. In/On/Next to/Behind/In front of/ Above/Below the _____.

[A–K]
A. Please _____.
B. All right. Certainly.

Have you ever flown in an airplane? Tell about a flight you took.

Be an airport security officer! Give passengers instructions as they go through the security area. Now, be a flight attendant! Give passengers instructions before take-off.

EL HOTEL

portero(a)	**1**	doorman	recepcionista	**9**	desk clerk	elevador/ascensor	**18** elevator
servicio de estacionamiento	**2**	valet	huésped(a)	**10**	guest	máquina	**19** ice machine
a cargo del hotel		parking	escritorio del	**11**	concierge	de hacer hielo	
encargado(a) de	**3**	parking	conserje		desk	pasillo/corredor	**20** hall/hallway
estacionamiento/		attendant	conserje	**12**	concierge	llave	**21** room key
guardacoches			restaurante	**13**	restaurant	carrito de camarero(a)/	**22** housekeeping
botones	**4**	bellhop	sala para	**14**	meeting	recamarero(a)	cart
carreta/carrito para	**5**	luggage	reuniones		room	camarero(a)/	**23** housekeeper
equipaje		cart	tienda para regalos	**15**	gift shop	recamarero(a)	
supervisor de botones	**6**	bell captain	piscina/alberca	**16**	pool	habitación	**24** guest room
vestíbulo/lobby	**7**	lobby	gimnasio	**17**	exercise	servicio de restaurante	**25** room service
recepción	**8**	front desk			room	a la habitación	

A. Where do you work?
B. I work at the *Grand* Hotel.
A. What do you do there?
B. I'm a/an _____ [1, 3, 4, 6, 9, 12, 23] _____.

A. Excuse me. Where's
the _____ [1–19, 22, 23] _____?
B. Right over there.
A. Thanks.

Tell about a hotel you are familiar with. Describe the place and the people.

In your opinion, which hotel employee has the most interesting job? the most difficult job? Why?

ACTIVIDADES MANUALES, PASATIEMPOS Y JUEGOS

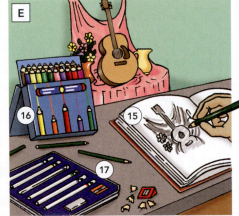
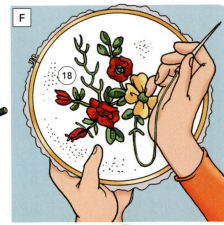

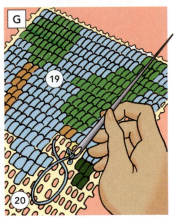

coser	**A**	**sew**
máquina de coser	**1**	sewing machine
alfiler	**2**	pin
alfiletero	**3**	pin cushion
(carrete de) hilo	**4**	(spool of) thread
aguja (de coser)	**5**	(sewing) needle
dedal	**6**	thimble
imperdible/ alfiler de gancho	**7**	safety pin
tejer	**B**	**knit**
aguja de tejer	**8**	knitting needle
estambre/ hilo para tejer	**9**	yarn
tejer a ganchillo/ gancho/crochet	**C**	**crochet**
aguja de gancho/ gancho para tejer	**10**	crochet hook

pintar	**D**	**paint**
pincel	**11**	paintbrush
caballete	**12**	easel
lienzo	**13**	canvas
pintura	**14**	paint
óleo		**a** oil paint
acuarela		**b** watercolor
dibujar	**E**	**draw**
cuaderno de bocetos	**15**	sketch book
(juego de) lápices de colores	**16**	(set of) colored pencils
lápiz de dibujo	**17**	drawing pencil
bordar	**F**	**do embroidery**
bordado	**18**	embroidery

bordar sobre cañamazo	**G**	**do needlepoint**
bordado sobre cañamazo	**19**	needlepoint
patrón	**20**	pattern
tallar madera	**H**	**do woodworking**
juego para tallar madera	**21**	woodworking kit
hacer origami	**I**	**do origami**
papel de origami	**22**	origami paper
hacer alfarería/ cerámica	**J**	**make pottery**
arcilla/barro	**23**	clay
torno (de alfarero)	**24**	potter's wheel

  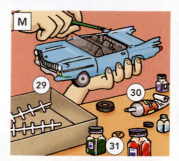 

coleccionar estampillas/ sellos/timbres	**K collect stamps**	observar pájaros	**N go bird-watching**	chaquete/tablas reales/negritas	**37** backgammon

coleccionar estampillas/sellos/timbres **K collect stamps**
álbum para estampillas/sellos/timbres **25** stamp album
lupa **26** magnifying glass

coleccionar monedas **L collect coins**
catálogo de monedas **27** coin catalog
colección de monedas **28** coin collection

armar modelos **M build models**
juego de modelo **29** model kit
goma para armar modelos/pegamento **30** glue
pintura acrílica **31** acrylic paint

observar pájaros **N go bird-watching**
binoculares **32** binoculars
guía **33** field guide

jugar a los naipes/las barajas/cartas **O play cards**
juego de naipes/barajas/cartas **34** (deck of) cards
trébol **a** club
diamante **b** diamond
corazón **c** heart
espada **d** spade

jugar a juegos de tablero **P play board games**
ajedrez **35** chess
damas/tablero **36** checkers

chaquete/tablas reales/negritas **37** backgammon
monopolio **38** Monopoly
dado **a** dice
sopa de letras/scrabble **39** Scrabble

navegar la red/usar el/la Internet **Q go online/browse the Web/"surf" the net**
navegador de Internet **40** web browser
dirección en Internet/URL **41** web address/URL

fotografía **R photography**
cámara **42** camera

astronomía **S astronomy**
telescopio **43** telescope

A. What do you like to do in your free time?
B. I like to _____[A–Q]_____.
I enjoy _____[R, S]_____.

A. May I help you?
B. Yes, please. I'd like to buy (a/an) _____[1–34, 42, 43]_____.

A. What do you want to do?
B. Let's play _____[35–39]_____.
A. Good idea!

Do you like to do any of these activities in your free time? Which ones?

What games are popular in your country? Describe how to play one.

LUGARES DE DIVERSIÓN

museo **1** museum	feria de artesanías **8** craft fair	acuario **14** aquarium
galería de arte **2** art gallery	venta de patio **9** yard sale	jardín botánico **15** botanical gardens
concierto **3** concert	mercado de pulgas/ **10** swap meet/	planetario **16** planetarium
obra de teatro **4** play	mercadillo/tianguis flea market	zoológico **17** zoo
parque de **5** amusement	parque **11** park	cine **18** movies
diversiones park	playa **12** beach	feria ambulante **19** carnival
sitio histórico **6** historic site	montañas **13** mountains	exposición/feria **20** fair
parque nacional **7** national park		

A. What do you want to do today?

B. Let's go to { a/an ___[1–9]___.
                 the ___[10–20]___ .

A. What did you do over the weekend?

B. I went to { a/an ___[1–9]___.
               the ___[10–20]___ .

A. What are you going to do on your day off?

B. I'm going to go to { a/an ___[1–9]___.
                        the ___[10–20]___ .

What are some of your favorite places to go? Where are they? What do you do there?

EL PARQUE Y EL ÁREA DE JUEGOS PARA NIÑOS(AS)

Spanish		English		Spanish		English
pista/camino para bicicletas/ciclovía	**1**	bicycle path/bike path/bikeway	banca	**9**	bench	
estanque para patos	**2**	duck pond	cancha de tenis	**10**	tennis court	
merendero/área para comer al aire libre/de picnic	**3**	picnic area	campo de béisbol	**11**	ballfield	
basurero/zafacón	**4**	trash can	fuente/bebedero	**12**	fountain	
parrilla	**5**	grill	soporte para bicicletas	**13**	bike rack	
mesa para merendar	**6**	picnic table	caballitos	**14**	merry-go-round/carousel	
fuente para beber agua	**7**	water fountain	rampa para patinetas	**15**	skateboard ramp	
pista para trotar/correr	**8**	jogging path	área de juegos para niños(as)	**16**	playground	

pared para alpinismo	**17**	climbing wall
columpios	**18**	swings
trepador	**19**	climber
deslizadero/resbaladero/tobogán	**20**	slide
balancín/sube y baja/tintibajo	**21**	seesaw
caja de arena	**22**	sandbox
arena	**23**	sand

[1–22]
A. Excuse me. Does this park have (a) _____?
B. Yes. Right over there.

[17–23]
A. { Be careful on the _____[17–21]_____!
{ Be careful in the _____[22, 23]_____!
B. I will, Dad/Mom.

Describe a park and playground you are familiar with.

LA PLAYA

salvavidas	**1**	lifeguard	sombrilla de playa/	**11**	beach	concha	**19**	seashell/shell
silla de salvavidas	**2**	lifeguard stand	parasol		umbrella	piedra	**20**	rock
salvavidas/flotador	**3**	life preserver	castillo de arena	**12**	sand castle	hielera/	**21**	cooler
puesto de	**4**	snack bar/	tabla/balsa para	**13**	boogie	nevera de playa		
refrescos		refreshment	girar con la ola		board	sombrero de sol	**22**	sun hat
		stand	amante de asolearse/	**14**	sunbather	loción protectora	**23**	sunscreen/
vendedor(a)	**5**	vendor	broncearse			contra el sol/		sunblock/
nadador(a)/bañista	**6**	swimmer	lentes/gafas de sol	**15**	sunglasses	bronceadora		suntan lotion
ola	**7**	wave	toalla de playa	**16**	(beach) towel	manta/	**24**	(beach)
surfista	**8**	surfer	pelota/balón/	**17**	beach ball	frisa		blanket
cometa/papalote/	**9**	kite	bola de playa			palita	**25**	shovel
chiringa			tabla de surf/deslizador/	**18**	surfboard	cubito	**26**	pail
silla de playa	**10**	beach chair	tabla hawaiana					

[1–26]
A. What a nice beach!
B. It is. Look at all the _____s!

[9–11, 13, 15–18, 21–26]
A. Are you ready for the beach?
B. Almost. I just have to get my _____.

Do you like to go to the beach? Describe your favorite beach. What do you take when you go there?

ACTIVIDADES AL AIRE LIBRE

acampar	**A camping**	**ir de excursión**	**B hiking**	**hacer ciclismo**	**D mountain**

acampar **A camping**
tienda de **1** tent
campaña/carpa
bolsa/saco **2** sleeping bag
de dormir
estacas **3** tent stakes
lámpara de gas **4** lantern
hacha **5** hatchet
hornillo/hornillar **6** camping stove
navaja tipo **7** Swiss army
ejército suizo knife
repelente **8** insect
de insectos repellent
cerillas(os)/fósforos **9** matches

ir de excursión B hiking
mochila de excursión **10** backpack
cantimplora **11** canteen
brújula/compás **12** compass
mapa **13** trail map
aparato de GPS **14** GPS device
(Sistema de Posición Global)
botas de excursión **15** hiking boots

escalar rocas C rock climbing/
technical climbing
aparejo/arnés **16** harness
cuerda (de nudos **17** rope
para trepar)

hacer ciclismo D mountain
de montaña biking
bicicleta de **18** mountain
montaña bike
casco **19** (bike) helmet

merendar/comer E picnic
al aire libre/
ir de picnic
manta/ **20** (picnic)
frisa blanket
termo **21** thermos
canasta/ **22** picnic basket
cesto de picnic

A. Let's go ___[A–E]___ * this weekend.
B. Good idea! We haven't gone
___[A–E]___ * in a long time.

*With E, say: on a picnic.

A. Did you bring
the ___[1–9, 11–14, 16, 17, 20–22]___ ?
your ___[10, 15, 18, 19]___ ?
B. Yes, I did.
A. Oh, good.

Have you ever gone camping, hiking, rock climbing, or mountain biking? Tell about it: What did you do? Where? What equipment did you use?

Do you like to go on picnics? Where?
What picnic supplies and food do you take with you?

DEPORTES Y ACTIVIDADES INDIVIDUALES

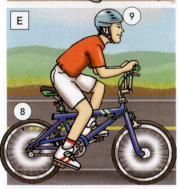

footing/correr al trote/trotar	**A**	**jogging**
traje para correr/chándal	**1**	jogging suit
zapatillas para correr	**2**	jogging shoes
correr	**B**	**running**
shorts para correr	**3**	running shorts
zapatillas para correr	**4**	running shoes
caminar	**C**	**walking**
zapatillas para caminar	**5**	walking shoes
patinaje/patinar	**D**	**inline skating/rollerblading**
patines	**6**	inline skates/rollerblades
rodilleras	**7**	knee pads
ciclismo	**E**	**cycling/biking**
bicicleta	**8**	bicycle/bike
casco	**9**	(bicycle/bike) helmet
andar en patineta/ monopatín	**F**	**skateboarding**
patineta/monopatín/patín	**10**	skateboard
coderas/codales	**11**	elbow pads
jugar a los bolos/al boliche	**G**	**bowling**
bola para jugar a los bolos/ de bolera/boliche	**12**	bowling ball
zapatos para jugar a los bolos	**13**	bowling shoes

montar a caballo	**H**	**horseback riding**
silla de montar/montura	**14**	saddle
riendas	**15**	reins
estribos	**16**	stirrups
tenis	**I**	**tennis**
raqueta de tenis	**17**	tennis racket
pelota/bola de tenis	**18**	tennis ball
shorts para tenis	**19**	tennis shorts
bádminton	**J**	**badminton**
raqueta de bádminton	**20**	badminton racket
gallito de bádminton	**21**	birdie/shuttlecock
pelota vasca/ frontón con raqueta	**K**	**racquetball**
gafas/lentes protectores(as)	**22**	safety goggles
pelota	**23**	racquetball
raqueta	**24**	racquet
tenis de mesa/pimpón/ ping-pong	**L**	**table tennis/ ping pong**
raqueta/paleta	**25**	paddle
mesa para jugar pimpón/ping-pong	**26**	ping pong table
malla/red	**27**	net
pelota/bola de pimpón/ping-pong	**28**	ping pong ball

golf	**M**	**golf**				
palos de golf	**29**	golf clubs				
pelota/bola de golf	**30**	golf ball				

golf   M golf
palos de golf   **29** golf clubs
pelota/bola   **30** golf ball
de golf

**lanzar el disco/   N Frisbee
platillo volador/
Frisbee**
disco/platillo   **31** Frisbee/
volador/Frisbee   flying disc

billar   O billiards/pool
mesa de billar   **32** pool table
taco/palo de billar   **33** pool stick
bolas de billar   **34** billiard balls

artes marciales   P martial arts
cinta/cinturón   **35** black belt
negro(a)

gimnasia   Q gymnastics
potro   **36** horse
barras paralelas   **37** parallel bars
colchoneta/estera   **38** mat
barra/viga de   **39** balance
equilibrio/   beam
balance
trampolín   **40** trampoline

levantar pesas   R weightlifting
barra con pesas   **41** barbell
pesas/   **42** weights
mancuernas

arco   S archery
arco y   **43** bow and
flecha   arrow
diana/blanco   **44** target

boxear   T box
guantes de boxeo   **45** boxing gloves
shorts de boxeo   **46** (boxing) trunks

practicar lucha libre   U wrestle
uniforme de lucha libre   **47** wrestling uniform
lona/estera/   **48** (wrestling) mat
cuadrilátero

hacer ejercicio(s)   V work out/exercise
caminadora   **49** treadmill
estacionaria
remadora   **50** rowing machine
estacionaria
bicicleta estacionaria   **51** exercise bike
equipo de ejercicios   **52** universal/
para estar en forma/   exercise
máquina universal   equipment

[A–V]
A. What do you like to do in your free time?
B. {
I like to go _____[A–H]_____.
I like to play _____[I–O]_____.
I like to do _____[P–S]_____.
I like to _____[T–V]_____.
}

[1–52]
A. I really like this/these new _____.
B. It's/They're very nice.

Do you do any of these activities? Which ones? Which are popular in your country?

DEPORTES EN EQUIPO

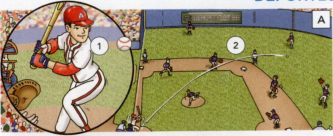

béisbol	**A**	**baseball**
jugador(a) de béisbol	1	baseball player
campo de juego/ diamante de béisbol	2	baseball field/ ballfield
softball/sófbol	**B**	**softball**
jugador(a) de sófbol	3	softball player
campo de sófbol	4	ballfield
fútbol americano	**C**	**football**
jugador(a) de fútbol americano	5	football player
campo de fútbol americano	6	football field

lacrosse/cross	**D**	**lacrosse**
jugador(a) de lacrosse	7	lacrosse player
campo de lacrosse	8	lacrosse field
hockey sobre hielo	**E**	**(ice) hockey**
jugador(a) de hockey	9	hockey player
pista de hielo	10	hockey rink
baloncesto/básquetbol	**F**	**basketball**
jugador(a) de baloncesto/básquetbol	11	basketball player
cancha/pista de baloncesto/básquetbol	12	basketball court

voleibol/ balonvolea	**G**	**volleyball**
jugador(a) de voleibol	13	volleyball player
cancha de voleibol	14	volleyball court
fútbol/ balompié/ sóquer	**H**	**soccer**
jugador(a) de fútbol	15	soccer player
campo de fútbol	16	soccer field

[A–H]
A. Do you like to play **baseball**?
B. Yes. **Baseball** is one of my favorite sports.

A. .... plays __[A–H]__ very well.
B. You're right. I think he's/she's one of the best _____s* on the team.

*Use 1, 3, 5, 7, 9, 11, 13, 15.

A. Now listen, team! I want all of you to go out on that _____† and play the best game of __[A–H]__ you've ever played!
B. All right, Coach!

† Use 2, 4, 6, 8, 10, 12, 14, 16.

Which sports in this lesson do you like to play? Which do you like to watch?

What are your favorite teams?

Name some famous players of these sports.

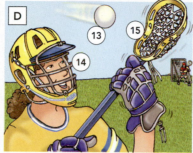

béisbol	**A**	**baseball**		
pelota de béisbol	1	baseball		
bate	2	bat		
casco de béisbol	3	batting helmet		
uniforme	4	(baseball) uniform		
máscara/protector	5	catcher's mask		
guante	6	(baseball) glove		
guante de receptor	7	catcher's mitt		
softball/sófbol	**B**	**softball**		
pelota de sófbol	8	softball		
guante	9	softball glove		
fútbol americano	**C**	**football**		
pelota de fútbol americano	10	football		
casco protector	11	football helmet		
protector de hombros	12	shoulder pads		

lacrosse/cross	**D**	**lacrosse**
pelota de lacrosse	13	lacrosse ball
careta/máscara	14	face guard
raqueta de lacrosse	15	lacrosse stick
hockey sobre hielo	**E**	**(ice) hockey**
disco	16	hockey puck
palo/bastón de hockey	17	hockey stick
máscara/careta	18	hockey mask
guante de hockey	19	hockey glove
patines de hockey	20	hockey skates

básquetbol/baloncesto	**F**	**basketball**
balón de básquetbol/baloncesto	21	basketball
tablero	22	backboard
canasta	23	basketball hoop
voleibol/balonvolea	**G**	**volleyball**
balón de voleibol	24	volleyball
red	25	volleyball net
fútbol/sóquer/balompié	**H**	**soccer**
balón de fútbol	26	soccer ball
espinillera/polaina	27	shinguards

[1–27]
A. I can't find my **baseball**!
B. Look in the closet.*

*closet, basement, garage

[In a store]
A. Excuse me. I'm looking for (a) ___[1–27]___ .
B. All our ___[A–H]___ equipment is over there.
A. Thanks.

[At home]
A. I'm going to play ___[A–H]___ after school today.
B. Don't forget your ___[1–21, 24, 26, 27]___ !

Which sports in this lesson are popular in your country? Which sports do students play in high school?

ACTIVIDADES Y DEPORTES DE INVIERNO

esquiar/practicar esquí alpino	**A (downhill) skiing**	**practicar patinaje artístico**	**D figure skating**
esquís	**1** skis	patines de hielo	**9** figure skates
botas de esquí/esquiar	**2** ski boots	**practicar snowboarding**	**E snowboarding**
ataduras/cogederas	**3** bindings	tabla de snowboard/para nieve	**10** snowboard
bastones/palos de esquí	**4** (ski) poles	**deslizarse en trineo/plato**	**F sledding**
practicar esquí de campo traviesa/fondo	**B cross-country skiing**	trineo	**11** sled
esquís de campo traviesa/fondo	**5** cross-country skis	plato	**12** sledding dish/ saucer
patinar sobre hielo	**C (ice) skating**	**practicar el bobsleigh/ bambolearse sobre hielo**	**G bobsledding**
patines de hielo	**6** (ice) skates	bobsleigh/bobsled/bamboleador	**13** bobsled
cuchilla	**7** blade	**ir de travesía/en moto de nieve**	**H snowmobiling**
protector de la cuchilla	**8** skate guard	moto de nieve	**14** snowmobile

[A–H]
A. What's your favorite winter sport?
B. **Skiing.**

[A–H]
[At work or at school on Friday]
A. What are you going to do this weekend?
B. I'm going to go _____.

[1–14]
[On the telephone]
A. Hello. *Sally's* Sporting Goods.
B. Hello. Do you sell _____(s)?
A. Yes, we do. / No, we don't.

Have you ever done any of these activities? Which ones?

Have you ever watched the Winter Olympics? Which event do you think is the most exciting? the most dangerous?

ACTIVIDADES Y DEPORTES ACUÁTICOS

ir de vela/velear	**A**	**sailing**
velero/bote/barco de vela	1	sailboat
chaleco salvavidas/flotador	2	life jacket/life vest
navegar en canoa	**B**	**canoeing**
canoa	3	canoe
pala/remo	4	paddles
remar	**C**	**rowing**
bote de remos	5	rowboat
remos	6	oars
navegar en kayak	**D**	**kayaking**
kayak	7	kayak
pala/remo	8	paddles
descender en balsa	**E**	**(white-water) rafting**
balsa	9	raft
chaleco salvavidas/flotador	10	life jacket/life vest
nadar	**F**	**swimming**
traje/vestido de baño/bañador	11	swimsuit/bathing suit
gafas/gafas saltonas/gogles	12	goggles
gorra de baño	13	bathing cap
nadar con tubo de respiración/	**G**	**snorkeling**
con esnórquel		
visor/máscara	14	mask
tubo de respiración/esnórquel	15	snorkel

aletas/chapaletas	16	fins
bucear	**H**	**scuba diving**
traje de buceo	17	wet suit
tanque de aire	18	(air) tank
visor/máscara	19	(diving) mask
practicar surf/surfear	**I**	**surfing**
tabla de surf/	20	surfboard
tabla hawaiana/		
deslizador		
practicar windsurfing/	**J**	**windsurfing**
surfear con vela		
tabla de vela	21	sailboard
vela	22	sail
practicar esquí acuático	**K**	**waterskiing**
esquís acuáticos	23	water skis
cable/cuerda de remolque	24	towrope
pescar	**L**	**fishing**
caña de pescar	25	(fishing) rod/
		pole
carrete/bobina	26	reel
sedal/cuerda	27	(fishing) line
red	28	(fishing) net
cebo/carnada	29	bait

[A–L]
A. Would you like to go **sailing** tomorrow?
B. Sure. I'd love to.

A. Have you ever
gone __[A–L]__ ?
B. Yes, I have. /
No, I haven't.

A. Do you have everything you need to go
__[A–L]__ ?
B. Yes. I have my __[1–29]__ (and my __[1–29]__).
A. Have a good time!

Which sports in this lesson have you tried?
Which sports would you like to try?

Are any of these sports popular in your
country? Which ones?

SPORT AND EXERCISE ACTIONS

ACCIONES AL HACER DEPORTES Y EJERCICIOS

pégue(n)le	1	hit		dóble(n)se/	12	bend		zambúlla(n)se/tíre(n)se de	22	dive
lance(n)	2	pitch		haga(n) flexiones				cabeza/haga(n) clavados	23	shoot
tire(n)	3	throw		camine(n)	13	walk		dispare(n)	23	shoot
coja(n)/agarre(n)	4	catch		corra(n)	14	run		pechadas/flexiones/lagartijas	24	push-up
pase(n)	5	pass		salte(n) con un pie	15	hop		abdominales	25	sit-up
patee(n)	6	kick		dé(n) saltos	16	skip		sentadillas	26	deep knee bend
sirva(n)	7	serve		brinque(n)/salte(n)	17	jump		saltos de buscapié	27	jumping jack
rebote(n)	8	bounce		alcance(n)	18	reach		volteretas/vueltas de	28	somersault
haga(n) una finta	9	dribble		balancée(n)se	19	swing		carnero/maromas		
dispare(n)/tire(n)	10	shoot		levante(n)	20	lift		volteretas laterales/mediaslunas	29	cartwheel
estíre(n)se	11	stretch		nade(n)	21	swim		pinos/paradas de cabeza	30	handstand

[1–10]
A. _____ the ball!
B. Okay, Coach!

[11–23]
A. Now _____!
B. Like this?
A. Yes.

[24–30]
A. Okay, everybody. I want you to do twenty _____s!
B. Twenty _____s?!
A. That's right.

Do you exercise regularly?
Which exercises do you do?

Be an exercise instructor! Lead your friends in an exercise routine using the actions in this lesson.

DIVERSIONES

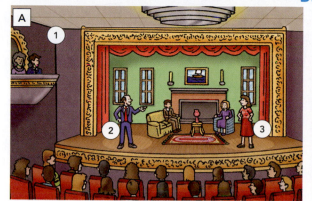

obra de teatro	**A**	**play**	**banda/conjunto musical**	**8**	band	
teatro	1	theater	**ópera**	**C**	**opera**	
actor	2	actor	cantante de ópera	9	opera singer	
actriz	3	actress	**ballet**	**D**	**ballet**	
concierto	**B**	**concert**	bailarín de ballet	10	ballet dancer	
sala de conciertos/	4	concert hall	bailarina de ballet	11	ballerina	
auditorio			**club nocturno/cabaré**	**E**	**music club**	
orquesta	5	orchestra	**con música viva**			
músico	6	musician	cantante	12	singer	
director(a) de orquesta	7	conductor				

películas	**F**	**movies**
sala de cine/cine	13	(movie) theater
pantalla	14	(movie) screen
actriz	15	actress
actor	16	actor
club nocturno/	**G**	**comedy**
cabaré con programa		**club**
de cómicos		
cómico(a)/humorista	17	comedian

[A–G]
A. What are you doing this evening?
B. I'm going to { a _____ [A, B, E, G].
                  the _____ [C, D, F]. }

[1–17]
A. What a magnificent _____!
B. I agree.

What kinds of entertainment in this lesson do you like?
What kinds of entertainment are popular in your country?

Who are some of your favorite actors? actresses?
musicians? singers? comedians?

TIPOS DE DIVERSIÓN

A

B

tipos de música	**A**	**music**
música clásica	**1**	classical music
música popular	**2**	popular music
música country	**3**	country music
música rock	**4**	rock music
música folklórica	**5**	folk music
música rap (de denuncia)	**6**	rap music
gospel	**7**	gospel music
jazz	**8**	jazz
blues	**9**	blues

bluegrass	**10**	bluegrass
hip hop	**11**	hip hop
reggae/regue/reguetón	**12**	reggae
tipos de obras de teatro	**B**	**plays**
dramas	**13**	drama
comedias	**14**	comedy
tragedias	**15**	tragedy
comedias musicales	**16**	musical (comedy)

tipos de películas	**C**	**movies/films**	películas de ciencia ficción	**27**	science fiction movie	programas sobre la vida real/reality show	**33**	reality show
dramas	**17**	drama	películas extranjeras	**28**	foreign film	telenovelas	**34**	soap opera
comedias	**18**	comedy				caricaturas/dibujos/	**35**	cartoon
películas del oeste	**19**	western	**tipos de**	**D**	**TV programs**	viñetas animadas(os)		
películas de misterio	**20**	mystery	**programas de**			programas	**36**	children's
comedias musicales	**21**	musical	**televisión**			infantiles		program
dibujos/viñetas/	**22**	cartoon	dramas	**29**	drama	noticieros/	**37**	news program
caricaturas			comedias	**30**	(situation)	telediarios		
animados(as)					comedy/sitcom	teledeportes	**38**	sports program
documentales	**23**	documentary	programas de	**31**	talk show	programas sobre	**39**	nature program
películas de	**24**	action movie/	entrevistas/			la naturaleza		
aventuras/		adventure	opinión			tevemall/	**40**	shopping
de acción		movie	programas	**32**	game show/	programas de ventas		program
películas de guerra	**25**	war movie	concurso/		quiz show			
películas de horror	**26**	horror movie	de juegos					

A. What kind of ___[A–D]___ do you like?
B. { I like ___[1–12]___.
{ I like ___[13–40]___s.

What's your favorite type of music? | What kind of movies do you like? | What kind of TV programs do you like?
Who is your favorite singer? musician? | Who are your favorite movie stars? | What are your favorite shows?
musical group? | What are the titles of your favorite movies?

INSTRUMENTOS MUSICALES

Instrumentos de cuerda	Strings		Instrumentos de viento	Woodwinds		Instrumentos de percusión	Percussion	
violín	**1**	violin	flautín/píccolo	**9**	piccolo	tambores	**20**	drums
viola	**2**	viola	flauta	**10**	flute	platillos	**a**	cymbals
violonchelo/ chelo	**3**	cello	clarinete	**11**	clarinet	pandereta/pandero	**21**	tambourine
bajo/ contrabajo/ violón	**4**	bass	oboe	**12**	oboe	xilófono	**22**	xylophone
guitarra (acústica)	**5**	(acoustic) guitar	flauta dulce	**13**	recorder	**Instrumentos de teclado**	**Keyboard Instruments**	
guitarra eléctrica	**6**	electric guitar	saxofón	**14**	saxophone	piano	**23**	piano
banjo	**7**	banjo	fagot	**15**	bassoon	teclado eléctrico	**24**	electric keyboard
arpa	**8**	harp	**Los metales**	**Brass**		órgano	**25**	organ
			trompeta	**16**	trumpet	**Otros instrumentos**	**Other Instruments**	
			trombón	**17**	trombone	acordeón	**26**	accordion
			corno francés/trompa	**18**	French horn	armónica	**27**	harmonica
			tuba	**19**	tuba			

A. Do you play a musical instrument?
B. Yes. I play the **violin**.

A. You play the **trumpet** very well.
B. Thank you.

A. What's that noise?!
B. That's my son/daughter practicing the **drums**.

Do you play a musical instrument? Which one?

Which instruments are usually in an orchestra? a marching band? a rock group?

Name and describe typical musical instruments in your country.

LA GRANJA Y LOS ANIMALES DOMÉSTICOS

Spanish	#	English		Spanish	#	English		Spanish	#	English
finca/casa	1	farmhouse		gallo	14	rooster		vaca	26	cow
granjero(a)/ agricultor(a)	2	farmer		pocilga/chiquero/ porqueriza	15	pig pen		carnero/oveja/ borrego	27	sheep
huerta/huerto	3	(vegetable) garden		cerdo/puerco/ marrano/cochino	16	pig		huerto de árboles frutales	28	orchard
espantapájaros	4	scarecrow		gallinero	17	chicken coop		árbol de fruta	29	fruit tree
heno	5	hay		gallina	18	chicken		labrador(a)/ mozo(a) de labranza	30	farm worker
peón	6	hired hand		gallinero	19	hen house		alfalfa	31	alfalfa
granero	7	barn		gallina ponedora	20	hen		maíz	32	corn
establo	8	stable		campo de cultivos	21	crop		algodón	33	cotton
caballo	9	horse		sistema de irrigación	22	irrigation system		arroz	34	rice
corral	10	barnyard		tractor	23	tractor		soja/soya	35	soybeans
pavo/guajolote	11	turkey		campo	24	field		trigo	36	wheat
cabra/chivo	12	goat		dehesa/pasto/potrero	25	pasture				
cordero	13	lamb								

[1–30]
A. Where's the _____?
B. In/Next to the _____.

A. The _[9, 11–14, 16, 18, 20, 26]_ s / __[27]__ are loose again!
B. Oh, no! Where are they?
A. They're in the _[1, 3, 7, 8, 10, 15, 17, 19, 24, 25, 28]_ .

[31–36]
A. Do you grow _____ on your farm?
B. No. We grow _____.

Tell about farms in your country. What crops and animals are common on these farms?

ANIMALES Y MASCOTAS

alce	**1**	moose
cuerno/asta	**a**	antler
oso polar	**2**	polar bear
venado/ciervo	**3**	deer
pezuña-pezuñas	**a**	hoof-hooves
lobo-lobos	**4**	wolf-wolves
pelaje	**a**	coat/fur
oso negro	**5**	(black) bear
garra	**a**	claw
puma	**6**	mountain lion
oso pardo	**7**	(grizzly) bear
búfalo/bisonte	**8**	buffalo/bison
coyote	**9**	coyote
zorro	**10**	fox
mofeta/zorrillo	**11**	skunk
puercoespín	**12**	porcupine
púa	**a**	quill
conejo	**13**	rabbit

castor	**14**	beaver
mapache	**15**	raccoon
zarigüeya/ tlacuache	**16**	possum/ opossum
caballo	**17**	horse
cola	**a**	tail
poni	**18**	pony
burro	**19**	donkey
armadillo	**20**	armadillo
murciélago	**21**	bat
lombriz	**22**	worm
babosa	**23**	slug
mono	**24**	monkey
oso hormiguero	**25**	anteater
llama	**26**	llama
jaguar	**27**	jaguar
manchas	**a**	spots
ratón-ratones	**28**	mouse-mice

rata	**29**	rat
ardilla listada/rayada	**30**	chipmunk
ardilla	**31**	squirrel
topo/ardilla de tierra/ taltuza/tuza	**32**	gopher
perrito de las praderas	**33**	prairie dog
gato	**34**	cat
bigotes	**a**	whiskers
gatito	**35**	kitten
perro	**36**	dog
perrito/cachorro	**37**	puppy
hámster	**38**	hamster
jerbo	**39**	gerbil
conejillo de indias/ cuis/cobayo	**40**	guinea pig
carpa dorada	**41**	goldfish
canario	**42**	canary
perico	**43**	parakeet

antílope	**44**	antelope	tigre	**51**	tiger	hiena	**54** hyena

antílope **44** antelope
mandril **45** baboon
rinoceronte **46** rhinoceros
cuerno **a** horn
panda **47** panda
orangután **48** orangutan
pantera **49** panther
gibón **50** gibbon

tigre **51** tiger
garra **a** paw
camello **52** camel
joroba **a** hump
elefante **53** elephant
colmillo **a** tusk
trompa **b** trunk

hiena **54** hyena
león **55** lion
melena **a** mane
jirafa **56** giraffe
zebra **57** zebra
rayas **a** stripes
chimpancé **58** chimpanzee

hipopótamo **59** hippopotamus
leopardo **60** leopard
gorila **61** gorilla
canguro **62** kangaroo
bolsa **a** pouch
koala **63** koala (bear)
ornitorrinco **64** platypus

[1–33, 44–64]
A. Look at that _____!
B. Wow! That's the biggest
_____ I've ever seen!

[34–43]
A. Do you have a pet?
B. Yes. I have a _____.
A. What's your _____'s name?
B. ....

What animals are there where you live?

Is there a zoo near where you live? What animals does it have?

What are some common pets in your country?

If you could be an animal, which animal would you like to be? Why?

Does your culture have any popular folk tales or children's stories about animals? Tell a story you know.

BIRDS AND INSECTS
PÁJAROS E INSECTOS

Pájaros	Birds								
petirrojo/ pechirrojo	**1** robin	halcón/falcón	**9** hawk	avestruz	**23** ostrich	araña	**33** spider
nido	**a** nest	águila	**10** eagle			telaraña	**a** web
huevo	**b** egg	garra	**a** claw	**Insectos**	**Insects**	mantis/ mariapalito/ santateresa religiosa	**34** praying mantis
urraca azul/ arrendajo	**2** blue jay	cisne	**11** swan	mosca	**24** fly		
ala	**a** wing	colibrí/visitaflor/ picaflor	**12** hummingbird	mariquita/ catarina/ catarinita	**25** ladybug	avispa	**35** wasp
cola	**b** tail	pato	**13** duck	luciérnaga/ cocuyo/cucuyo/ cucubano	**26** firefly/ lightning bug	abeja	**36** bee
pluma	**c** feather	pico	**a** bill			panal	**a** beehive
cardenal	**3** cardinal	gorrión/ tierrerita	**14** sparrow	polilla	**27** moth	saltamontes/ grillo/ chapulín	**37** grasshopper
cuervo	**4** crow	ganso- gansos	**15** goose- geese	oruga	**28** caterpillar		
gaviota	**5** seagull	pingüino	**16** penguin	capullo	**a** cocoon	escarabajo/ cocorrón	**38** beetle
pájaro carpintero	**6** woodpecker	flamenco	**17** flamingo	mariposa	**29** butterfly		
pico	**a** beak	grulla	**18** crane	garrapata	**30** tick	escorpión/ alacrán	**39** scorpion
paloma/ pichón/ tórtola	**7** pigeon	cigüeña	**19** stork	mosquito	**31** mosquito	ciempiés	**40** centipede
		pelícano	**20** pelican	libélula/ caballito del diablo/caballito de San Pedro	**32** dragonfly	grillo/ cigarra/ chicharra	**41** cricket
búho/lechuza	**8** owl	pavo real	**21** peacock				
		papagayo/ loro/cotorra	**22** parrot				

[1–41]
A. Is that a/an _____?
B. No. I think it's a/an _____.

[24–41]
A. Hold still! There's a _____ on your shirt!
B. Oh! Can you get it off me?
A. There! It's gone!

What birds and insects are there where you live?

Does your culture have any popular folk tales or children's stories about birds or insects? Tell a story you know.

PECES, ANIMALES MARINOS Y REPTILES

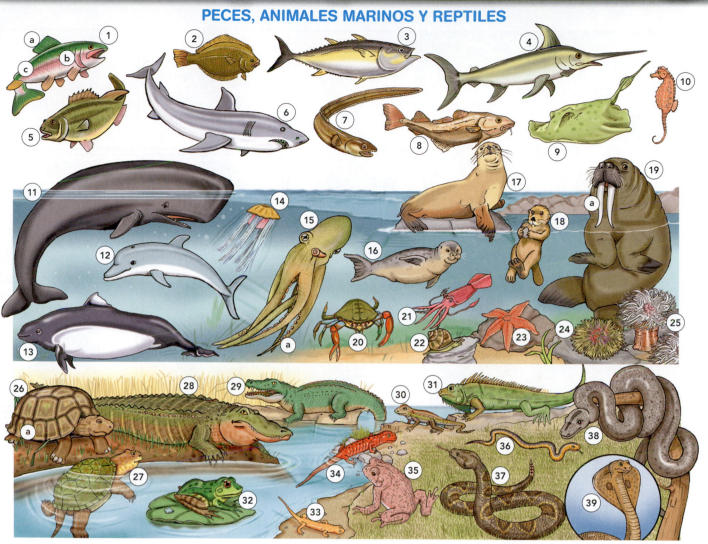

Peces	Fish				
trucha	**1** trout	marsopa/marsopla	**13** porpoise	**Anfibios y reptiles**	**Amphibians and Reptiles**
aleta	**a** fin	aguamala/	**14** jellyfish		
agalla/branquia	**b** gill	medusa/aguaviva		tortuga	**26** tortoise
escamas	**c** scales	pulpo	**15** octopus	caparazón/carapacho	**a** shell
lenguado	**2** flounder	tentáculo	**a** tentacle	tortuga de mar	**27** turtle
atún	**3** tuna	foca	**16** seal	caimán/lagarto	**28** alligator
pez espada	**4** swordfish	león marino/	**17** sea lion	cocodrilo	**29** crocodile
róbalo	**5** bass	vaquita de mar		lagartija	**30** lizard
tiburón	**6** shark	nutria	**18** otter	iguana	**31** iguana
anguila	**7** eel	morsa	**19** walrus	rana	**32** frog
bacalao	**8** cod	colmillo	**a** tusk	tritón	**33** newt
raya/mantarraya	**9** ray/stingray	cangrejo	**20** crab	salamandra	**34** salamander
caballito de mar	**10** sea horse	calamar	**21** squid	sapo	**35** toad
		caracol	**22** snail	culebra/serpiente	**36** snake
Animales marinos	**Sea Animals**	estrella de mar	**23** starfish	serpiente/víbora de cascabel	**37** rattlesnake
ballena	**11** whale	erizo de mar	**24** sea urchin	boa	**38** boa constrictor
delfín	**12** dolphin	anémona de mar	**25** sea anemone	cobra/serpiente de anteojos	**39** cobra

[1–39]
A. Is that a/an _____?
B. No. I think it's a/an _____.

[26–39]
A. Are there any _____s around here?
B. No. But there are lots of _____!

What fish, sea animals, and reptiles can be found in your country?
Which ones are endangered and need to be protected? Why?

In your opinion, which ones are the most interesting?
the most beautiful? the most dangerous?

TREES, PLANTS, AND FLOWERS

ÁRBOLES, PLANTAS Y FLORES

árbol	**1**	tree	cono/piña	**10**	pine cone
hoja-hojas	**2**	leaf-leaves	cornejo/	**11**	dogwood
ramita/	**3**	twig	sanguiñuelo		
bejuco			aquifolio/	**12**	holly
rama	**4**	branch	acebo (árbol)		
brazo	**5**	limb	magnolia	**13**	magnolia
tronco	**6**	trunk	olmo	**14**	elm
corteza	**7**	bark	cerezo	**15**	cherry
raíz	**8**	root	palmera/palma	**16**	palm
aguja/hoja	**9**	needle	abedul	**17**	birch

arce	**18**	maple	bayas/cerecitas	**25**	berries
roble	**19**	oak	arbusto	**26**	shrub
pino	**20**	pine	helecho	**27**	fern
secuoya/secoya	**21**	redwood	mata/planta	**28**	plant
sauce llorón	**22**	(weeping)	cactus	**29**	cactus-cacti
		willow	enredadera	**30**	vine
arbusto	**23**	bush	ortiga/hiedra/	**31**	poison
acebo/flor del	**24**	holly	yedra venenosa		ivy
amor/laurel de			zumaque venenoso	**32**	poison sumac
Navidad			roble venenoso	**33**	poison oak

flor **34** flower	caléndula/maravilla/ **43** marigold	rosa **51** rose
pétalo **35** petal	cempasúchil	girasol **52** sunflower
tallo **36** stem	clavel **44** carnation	azafrán **53** crocus
botón/capullo **37** bud	gardenia **45** gardenia	tulipán **54** tulip
espina **38** thorn	lirio **46** lily	geranio **55** geranium
bulbo/cebolleta **39** bulb	azucena **47** iris	violeta **56** violet
crisantemo **40** chrysanthemum	pensamiento **48** pansy	flor de Navidad/Nochebuena **57** poinsettia
narciso **41** daffodil	petunia **49** petunia	jazmín **58** jasmine
margarita **42** daisy	orquídea **50** orchid	hibisco/papo **59** hibiscus

[11–22]
A. What kind of tree is that?
B. I think it's a/an _____ tree.

[31–33]
A. Watch out for the _____ over there!
B. Oh. Thanks for the warning.

[40–57]
A. Look at all the _____s!*
B. They're beautiful!

*With 58 and 59, use: Look at all the __!

Describe your favorite tree and your favorite flower.

What kinds of trees and flowers grow where you live?

In your country, what flowers do you see at weddings? at funerals? during holidays? in hospital rooms? Tell which flowers people use for different occasions.

LA ENERGÍA, EL MEDIO AMBIENTE Y LA PROTECCIÓN DE LOS RECURSOS NATURALES

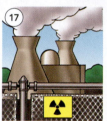

Fuentes de energía	**Sources of Energy**	**Protección de recursos naturales**	**Conservation**	**Problemas ambientales**	**Environmental Problems**
petróleo	**1** oil/petroleum	reciclar/reutilizar	**9** recycle	contaminación del aire	**13** air pollution
gas	**2** (natural) gas	ahorrar energía	**10** save energy/ conserve energy	contaminación del agua	**14** water pollution
carbón	**3** coal			residuos tóxicos	**15** hazardous waste/ toxic waste
energía nuclear	**4** nuclear energy	ahorrar agua	**11** save water/ conserve water	lluvia ácida	**16** acid rain
energía solar	**5** solar energy			radiación	**17** radiation
energía hidroeléctrica	**6** hydroelectric power	compartir el automóvil	**12** carpool	calentamiento de la Tierra	**18** global warming
viento	**7** wind				
energía geotérmica	**8** geothermal energy				

[1–8]
A. In my opinion, _____ will be our best source of energy in the future.
B. I disagree. I think our best source of energy will be _____.

[9–12]
A. Do you _____?
B. Yes. I'm very concerned about the environment.

[13–18]
A. Do you worry about the environment?
B. Yes. I'm very concerned about _____.

What kind of energy do you use to heat your home? to cook? In your opinion, which will be the best source of energy in the future?

Do you practice conservation? What do you do to help the environment?

In your opinion, what is the most serious environmental problem in the world today? Why?

DESASTRES NATURALES

terremoto/temblor **1** earthquake	inundación **6** flood	avalancha/ **11** landslide
huracán **2** hurricane	maremoto/tsunami **7** tsunami	derrumbe de tierra
tifón **3** typhoon	sequía **8** drought	avalancha de lodo **12** mudslide
ventisca/ **4** blizzard	incendio forestal **9** forest fire	alud/avalancha **13** avalanche
tormenta de nieve	fuego arrasador **10** wildfire	erupción volcánica **14** volcanic eruption
tornado/torbellino **5** tornado		

A. Did you hear about the _____ in ......(country)......?
B. Yes, I did. I saw it on the news.

Have you or someone you know ever experienced a natural disaster? Tell about it.

Which natural disasters sometimes happen where you live? How do people prepare for them?

FORMAS PARA IDENTIFICARSE

1

Florida *The Sunshine State*
DRIVER LICENSE CLASS D
D200-555-44-111-0
Dawn Erics
220 Palisades Way
Miami, FL 33017-0000
DOB: 05-20-65   SEX: F   HGT: 5-07
ISSUED: 05-19-05
EXPIRES: 05-20-11
REST: BF   "DORSE
Dawn Erics
ORGAN DONOR   SAFE DRIVER
Q123456789000   SAFE DRIVER
Operation of a motor vehicle constitutes consent to any sobriety test required by law.

2

SOCIAL SECURITY
142-84-5194
THIS NUMBER HAS BEEN ESTABLISHED FOR
PATRICK MICHAEL GAFFNEY
Patrick Michael Gaffney
SIGNATURE

3

International *Student* Identity Card
Carte d'étudiant internationale / Carné internacional de estudiante
S T U D E N T
Studies at / Étudiant / Est. de Enseñanza
School of Audio Engineering
Name / Nom / Nombre
Robert Oliver
Born /Né(e) le / Nacido/a el
19 FEB 1986
Validity / Validité / Validez
09/2005 - 12/2006
ISIC
S 044 201 440 365

4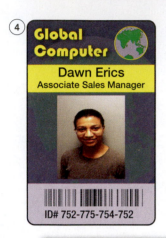

Global Computer
Dawn Erics
Associate Sales Manager
ID# 752-775-754-752

5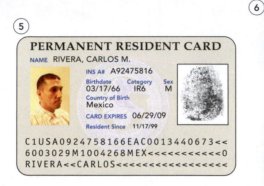

PERMANENT RESIDENT CARD
NAME RIVERA, CARLOS M.
INS A# A92475816
Birthdate 03/17/66   Category IR6   Sex M
Country of Birth Mexico
CARD EXPIRES 06/29/09
Resident Since 11/17/99
C1USA0924758166EAC0013440673<<
6003029M1004268MEX<<<<<<<<<<0
RIVERA<<CARLOS<<<<<<<<<<<<<<<

6

PASSPORT
United States of America

7

VISA   VISA
MONGOLIAN VISA
No 02670
(L) V I S A
2005-10-14

8

WORK PERMIT

INDIVIDUAL WORK PERMIT:
1. Employer completes and signs
2. Parent or guardian completes and signs
3. Employer submits work permit and LEGIBLE copy of minor's proof of age to the Wage and Hour office.
4. When the approved work permit is returned, the minor may begin work.

GENERAL DUTIES WORK PERMIT:
1. Employer completes and signs
2. Employer submits work permit to Wage and Hour office.
3. The approved duties are returned to the employer. After employer obtains the signature of the minor's parent or guardian then the minor may begin work.
4. Employer must return a copy of the work permit signed by the parent or legal guardian and LEGIBLE copy of proof of age to the Wage and Hour office within seven (7) calendar days of minor beginning work.

☐ INDIVIDUAL WORK PERMIT
☐ GENERAL DUTIES WORK PERMIT APPROVED FOR:
☐ 16 & 17 YEAR OLDS; OR
☐ 14 - 17 YEAR OLDS
☐ APPROVED AS AMENDED
☐ DISAPPROVED
By: _____
Date: _____

Return permit to employer's FAX number:
_____

Section (A) to be completed by EMPLOYER
Name of Employer: DBA/
Employer's Local Mailing Address: City: Zip

9

⚡ Voltage Electric Bill

Voltage Electric
20 Spring Street
Paramus, NJ

Service At:
Robert Smith
33 Catherine Rd
Paramus, NJ

Customer Account Number
123456789
Due Date: January 15, 2005   Amount Due: $35.00

Previous Charges

	Account Balance	Amount Due
Total Amount of Last Bill Payment 12/15/04	$ 35.00 $ 35.00	
Previous Balance	$ .00	$ .00

Current Charges
Customer Charge $ 4.75
Delivery Charge $ 12.80

10

CERTIFICATE OF BIRTH
(In the Clerks office of the County Commission of Randolf County)

I, MARK PALMER, Clerk of the County Commision in the County and State aforesaid, it being an office of record, and having a seal, do hereby certify that the records in my office show that
_____ Sex ___
Was born at _____ in Bergen County and the State of New Jersey on the ____ day of _____ and that the parents names are as follows:
Father's name _____
Mother's maiden name _____
are recorded in Birth Record No. _____ at page ____ . Date filed: ____
In testimony whereof, I have hereunto affixed my signature and official seal at Bergen County, NJ
this ____ day of _____, 20____.
_____, Clerk

licencia para manejar/conducir	**1** driver's license	tarjeta de identificación de empleado(a)	**4** employee I.D. badge
tarjeta de seguro social	**2** social security card	tarjeta de residente permanente	**5** permanent resident card
carné/credencial de estudiante	**3** student I.D. card	pasaporte	**6** passport

visa	**7** visa
permiso de trabajo	**8** work permit
comprobante de residencia	**9** proof of residence
certificado de nacimiento	**10** birth certificate

A. May I see your _____?
B. Yes. Here you are.

A. Oh, no! I can't find my _____!
B. I'll help you look for it.
A. Thanks.

Which forms of identification do you have? When do you need to show them?

LA ORGANIZACIÓN DEL GOBIERNO DE LOS ESTADOS UNIDOS

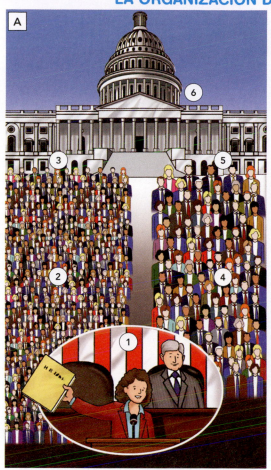

El poder legislativo		A legislative branch
hace las leyes	**1**	makes the laws
representantes/ congresistas	**2**	representatives/ congressmen and congresswomen
Cámara de Representantes	**3**	house of representatives
senadores	**4**	senators
senado	**5**	senate
Edificio del Capitolio	**6**	Capitol Building

El poder ejecutivo		B executive branch
hace cumplir las leyes	**7**	enforces the laws
presidente(a)	**8**	president
vicepresidente(a)	**9**	vice-president
gabinete (cuerpo de ministros(as))	**10**	cabinet
Casa Blanca	**11**	White House

El poder judicial		C judicial branch
explica las leyes	**12**	explains the laws
jueces/juezas de la Corte Suprema de Justicia	**13**	Supreme Court justices
Presidente(a) de la Corte Suprema de Justicia	**14**	chief justice
Corte Suprema de Justicia	**15**	Supreme Court
Edificio de la Corte Suprema de Justicia	**16**	Supreme Court Building

A. Which branch of government ___[1, 7, 12]___ ?
B. The ___[A, B, C]___ .

A. Who works in the ___[A, B, C]___ of the government?
B. The ___[2, 4, 8–10, 13, 14]___ .

A. Where do/does the ___[2, 4, 8–10, 13, 14]___ work?
B. In the ___[6, 11, 16]___ .

A. In which branch of the government is the ___[3, 5, 10, 15]___ ?
B. In the ___[A, B, C]___ .

Compare the governments of different countries you are familiar with. What are the branches of government? Who works there? What do they do?

LA CONSTITUCIÓN Y LA DECLARACIÓN DE DERECHOS

A ①

B ③

C ④  ⑤ ⑥  ⑦

D ⑧ 13th  ⑨ 15th  ⑩ 16th  ⑪ 19th ⑫ 26th

La Constitución	**A**	**The Constitution**	
la Carta Magna	**1**	"the supreme law of the land"	
el Preámbulo	**2**	the Preamble	
La Declaración de Derechos	**B**	**The Bill of Rights**	
las primeras diez enmiendas a la Constitución	**3**	the first 10 amendments to the Constitution	
La primera enmienda	**C**	**The 1st Amendment**	
libertad de expresión	**4**	freedom of speech	
libertad de prensa	**5**	freedom of the press	
libertad de credo	**6**	freedom of religion	

derecho a participar en asambleas **7** freedom of assembly

Otras enmiendas **D** **Other Amendments**

pusieron fin a la esclavitud **8** ended slavery

otorgaron el derecho a votar a los/las afroamericanos(as) **9** gave African-Americans the right to vote

establecieron impuestos sobre los ingresos **10** established income taxes

otorgaron el derecho a votar a las mujeres **11** gave women the right to vote

otorgaron el derecho a votar a los/las ciudadanos(as) mayores de dieciocho años **12** gave citizens eighteen years and older the right to vote

---

A. What is ___[A ,B]___ ?
B. ___[1 ,3]___ .

A. Which amendment guarantees people ___[4–7]___ ?
B. The 1st Amendment.

A. Which amendment ___[8–12]___ ?
B. The _____ Amendment.

A. What did the _____ Amendment do?
B. It ___[8–12]___ .

Describe how people in your community exercise their 1st Amendment rights. What are some examples of freedom of speech? the press? religion? assembly?

Do you have an idea for a new amendment? Tell about it and why you think it's important.

HECHOS IMPORTANTES EN LA HISTORIA DE LOS ESTADOS UNIDOS

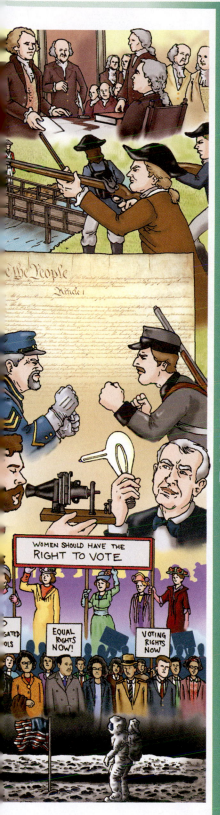

TIMELINE

1607	Colonists come to Jamestown, Virginia. *Los colonos llegan a Jamestown, Virginia.*
1620	Pilgrims come to the Plymouth Colony. *Los primeros colonizadores llegan a la colonia de Plymouth.*
1775	The Revolutionary War begins. *Se inicia la Guerra de Independencia.*
1776	The colonies declare their independence. *Las colonias declaran su independencia.*
1783	The Revolutionary War ends. *Termina la Guerra de Independencia.*
1787	Representatives write the United States Constitution. *Los representantes redactan la Constitución de los Estados Unidos.*
1789	George Washington becomes the first president. *George Washington es nombrado primer presidente de los Estados Unidos.*
1791	The Bill of Rights is added to the Constitution. *Se añade la Declaración de Derechos a la Constitución.*
1861	The Civil War begins. *Comienza la Guerra Civil.*
1863	President Lincoln signs the Emancipation Proclamation. *El Presidente Lincoln firma la Proclamación de Emancipación.*
1865	The Civil War ends. *Termina la Guerra Civil.*
1876	Alexander Graham Bell invents the telephone. *Alexander Graham Bell inventa el teléfono.*
1879	Thomas Edison invents the lightbulb. *Thomas Edison inventa el foco/bombilla(o) incandescente.*
1914	World War I (One) begins. *Comienza la Primera Guerra Mundial.*
1918	World War I (One) ends. *Termina la Primera Guerra Mundial.*
1920	Women get the right to vote. *Las mujeres obtienen el derecho al voto.*
1929	The stock market crashes, and the Great Depression begins. *La bolsa de valores se viene abajo y se inicia la Gran Depresión.*
1939	World War II (Two) begins. *Comienza la Segunda Guerra Mundial.*
1945	World War II (Two) ends. *Termina la Segunda Guerra Mundial.*
1950	The Korean War begins. *Comienza la Guerra de Corea.*
1953	The Korean War ends. *Termina la Guerra de Corea.*
1954	The civil rights movement begins. *Comienza el movimiento de los derechos civiles.*
1963	The March on Washington takes place. *Tiene lugar la Marcha sobre Washington.*
1964	The Vietnam War begins. *Comienza la Guerra de Vietnam.*
1969	Astronaut Neil Armstrong lands on the moon. *El astronauta Neil Armstrong llega a la luna.*
1973	The Vietnam War ends. *Termina la Guerra de Vietnam.*
1991	The Persian Gulf War occurs. *Tiene lugar la Guerra del Golfo Pérsico.*
2001	The United States is attacked by terrorists. *Terroristas atacan los Estados Unidos.*

A. What happened in ___(year)___?
B. ___(Event)___ ed.

A. When did ___(event)___?
B. In ___(year)___.

In your opinion, which event in this lesson is the most important? Why?

Tell about important events in the history of your country.

DÍAS DE FIESTA

Año Nuevo	**1** New Year's Day	Día de los Veteranos(as)	**7** Veterans Day
Día de Martin Luther King, Jr.	**2** Martin Luther King, Jr.* Day	Día de Acción de Gracias	**8** Thanksgiving
Día de San Valentín	**3** Valentine's Day	Navidad	**9** Christmas
Día del/de la Soldado(a)	**4** Memorial Day	Ramadán	**10** Ramadan
Día de la Independencia/ el Cuatro de Julio	**5** Independence Day/ the Fourth of July	Kwanzaa	**11** Kwanzaa
Halloween/Día de las brujas	**6** Halloween	Hanuka/Fiesta de las Luces	**12** Hanukkah

* Jr. = Junior

A. When is _____[1, 3, 5, 6, 7, 9]_____ ?
B. It's on ......(date)....... .

A. When is _____[2, 4, 8]_____ ?
B. It's in ......(month)....... .

A. When does _____[10–12]_____ begin this year?
B. It begins on ......(date)....... .

Which of these holidays do you celebrate? How?

What holidays do people celebrate in your country?

EL SISTEMA JUDICIAL

You have the right to remain silent.

$10,000

 Not Guilty!

 Guilty!

 5 years! $100,000

Spanish		English			Spanish		English
ser arrestado(a)	**A**	be arrested		sospechoso(a)	**1**	suspect	taquígrafo(a) de **14** court
ser fichado(a) en la estación de policía	**B**	be booked at the police station		policía	**2**	police officer	actas/estenógrafo(a) reporter
contratar a un(a) abogado(a)	**C**	hire a lawyer/ hire an attorney		esposas	**3**	handcuffs	abogado(a) **15** defense
				derechos Miranda/ derechos civiles	**4**	Miranda rights	defensor(a) attorney
comparecer en el tribunal/ante el tribunal	**D**	appear in court		huellas digitales	**5**	fingerprints	evidencia **16** evidence
				fotografía policíaca	**6**	mug shot/ police photo	alguacil **17** bailiff
someterse a un juicio	**E**	stand* trial		abogado(a)	**7**	lawyer/attorney	jurado **18** jury
quedar absuelto(a)/ exonerado(a)	**F**	be acquitted		juez(a)	**8**	judge	fallo/veredicto **19** verdict
ser condenado(a)	**G**	be convicted		acusado(a)	**9**	defendant	inocente **20** innocent/ not guilty
ser sentenciado(a)	**H**	be sentenced		fianza	**10**	bail	culpable **21** guilty
ir a la cárcel/prisión	**I**	go to jail/prison		tribunal/juzgado	**11**	courtroom	sentencia/condena **22** sentence
ser puesto(a) en libertad	**J**	be released		fiscal	**12**	prosecuting attorney	multa **23** fine
				testigo	**13**	witness	guardia **24** prison guard
		*stand-stood					convicto(a)/ **25** convict/ prisionero(a)/reo(a) prisoner/ inmate

[A–J]
A. Did you hear about .... (name) ....?
B. No, I didn't.
A. He/She _____ed.
B. Really? I didn't know that.

[A–J]
A. What happened in the last episode?
B. ....(name of character)........ _____ed.

[1, 2, 7–9, 12–15, 17, 24, 25]
A. Are you the _____?
B. No. I'm the _____.

Tell about the legal system in your country.
Describe what happens after a person is arrested.

Do you watch any crime shows on TV? Which ones?
Tell about an episode you remember.

LA CIUDADANÍA

Branches of government
legislative
executive
judicial

I hereby declare . . .

Los derechos y las obligaciones de los/las ciudadanos(as) — Citizens' Rights and Responsibilities

Spanish	#	English
votar	1	vote
obedecer las leyes	2	obey laws
pagar los impuestos	3	pay taxes
servir en un jurado judicial	4	serve on a jury
participar en la vida de la comunidad	5	be part of community life
seguir las noticias para estar al tanto de los acontecimientos del día	6	follow the news to know about current events
inscribirse en el Sistema militar de servicio selectivo*	7	register with the Selective Service System*

* All males in the United States ages 18 to 26 must register with the Selective Service System.

Proceso para obtener la ciudadanía — The Path to Citizenship

Spanish	#	English
solicitar la ciudadanía	8	apply for citizenship
aprender acerca del gobierno de los Estados Unidos y su historia	9	learn about U.S. government and history
presentar el examen de ciudadanía	10	take a citizenship test
tener una entrevista con funcionarios(as) de naturalización	11	have a naturalization interview
asistir a la ceremonia de naturalización	12	attend a naturalization ceremony
prestar el Juramento de Lealtad (a la patria)	13	recite the Oath of Allegiance

A. Can you name one responsibility of United States citizens?
B. Yes. Citizens should ____[1–7]____.

A. How is your citizenship application coming along?
B. Very well. I ____[8–11]____ed, and now I'm preparing to ____[9–13]____.
A. Good luck!

In your opinion, what are the most important rights and responsibilities of all people in their communities?

In your opinion, should non-citizens have all the same rights as citizens? Why or why not?

LOS ESTADOS UNIDOS Y EL CANADÁ

RUSSIA

ARCTIC OCEAN

Chukchi Sea

Bering Sea

Beaufort Sea

Norwegian Sea

GREENLAND

ICELAND

Alaska (US)

Gulf of Alaska

Yukon Territory

Northwest Territories

Nunavut

Baffin Bay

CANADA

Hudson Bay

Newfoundland and Labrador

British Columbia

Alberta

Saskatchewan

Manitoba

Ontario

Québec

Prince Edward Island

New Brunswick

Nova Scotia

PACIFIC OCEAN

Washington

Montana

North Dakota

Minnesota

Maine

Ottawa ★

Oregon

Idaho

Wyoming

South Dakota

Wisconsin Michigan

New York

Vermont
New Hampshire
Massachusetts
Rhode Island
Connecticut
New Jersey
Delaware
Maryland

Nevada

Utah

Nebraska

Iowa

Illinois Indiana Ohio

Pennsylvania

California

Colorado

Kansas

Missouri

West Virginia ★

Virginia

Washington, DC

Hawaii (US)

UNITED STATES of AMERICA

Kentucky

Arizona

New Mexico

Oklahoma

Arkansas

Tennessee

North Carolina

South Carolina

ATLANTIC OCEAN

BERMUDA

Alabama Georgia

Texas

Mississippi

Louisiana

Florida

N
W   E
S

Gulf of Mexico

THE BAHAMAS

MEXICO

CUBA

PUERTO RICO

0   1000 Miles
0   1000 KM

JAMAICA

HAITI

DOMINICAN REPUBLIC

MÉXICO, CENTROAMÉRICA Y EL CARIBE

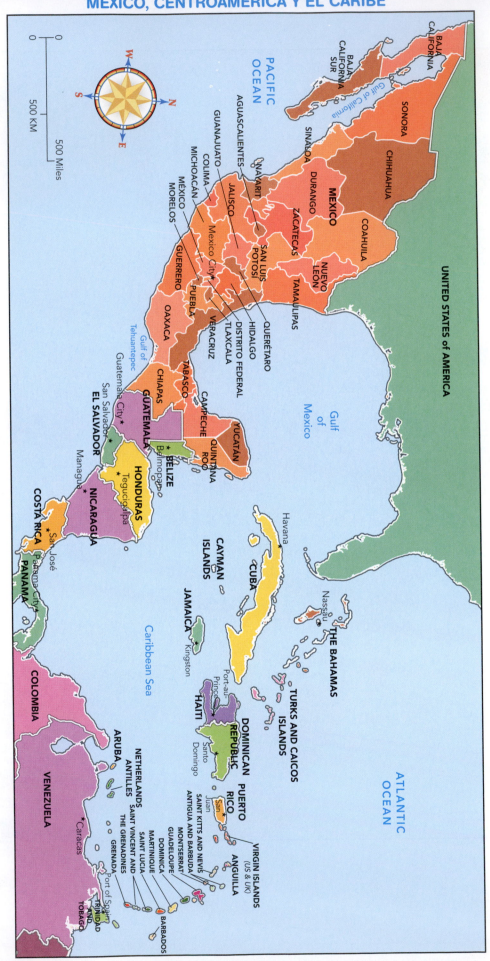

SUDAMÉRICA

Caribbean Sea

Barranquilla
Cartagena
Maracaibo
Valencia
Barquisimeto
Caracas

ATLANTIC OCEAN

VENEZUELA

Medellín

Georgetown
Paramaribo
Cayenne

GUYANA

★ Bogotá

SURINAME **FRENCH GUIANA**

Cali

COLOMBIA

Equator
Quito
Equator

ECUADOR

Belém

Gulf of Guayaquil
Guayaquil

Manaus

Fortaleza

Teresina

PERU

Recife

BRAZIL

★ Lima

Salvador

★ La Paz
★ Brasília

Goiânia

BOLIVIA

Sucre

Belo Horizonte

Rio de Janeiro

PARAGUAY

Campinas

São Paulo

CHILE

Asuncion ★

Curitiba

PACIFIC OCEAN

ARGENTINA

Pôrto Alegre

Córdoba

Rosario

URUGUAY

Santiago ★

Buenos Aires ★
Montevideo

Gulf of San Matías

ATLANTIC OCEAN

N
W — E
S

Gulf of San Jorge

FALKLAND ISLANDS

500 Miles

Strait of Magellan
Port Stanley

SOUTH GEORGIA ISLAND

500 KM

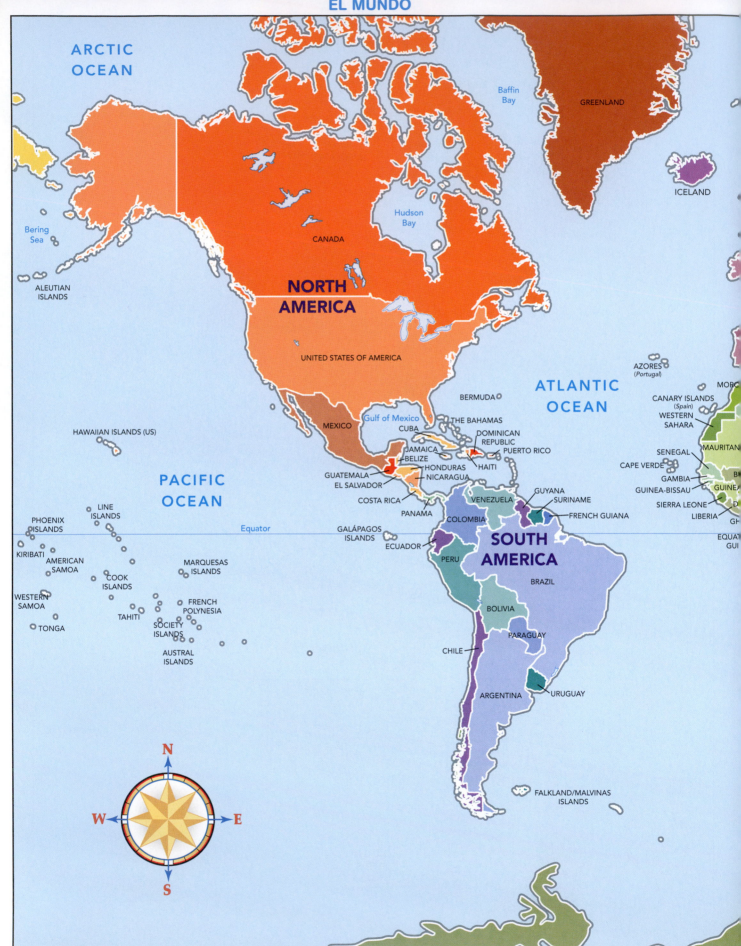

ARCTIC
OCEAN

GREENLAND

Baffin
Bay

ICELAND

CANADA

Hudson
Bay

Bering
Sea

NORTH
AMERICA

ALEUTIAN
ISLANDS

ATLANTIC
OCEAN

UNITED STATES OF AMERICA

AZORES
(Portugal)

MORO

BERMUDA

CANARY ISLANDS
(Spain)

WESTERN
SAHARA

HAWAIIAN ISLANDS (US)

MEXICO

Gulf of Mexico

THE BAHAMAS

CUBA

SENEGAL

DOMINICAN
REPUBLIC

PACIFIC
OCEAN

CAPE VERDE

MAURITAN

JAMAICA

PUERTO RICO

BELIZE

HONDURAS

HAITI

GAMBIA

GUINEA-BISSAU

GUINE

GUATEMALA

NICARAGUA

SIERRA LEONE

EL SALVADOR

GUYANA

LIBERIA

GH

COSTA RICA

VENEZUELA

SURINAME

PHOENIX
ISLANDS

LINE
ISLANDS

PANAMA

COLOMBIA

FRENCH GUIANA

Equator

GALÁPAGOS
ISLANDS

EQUAT

GUI

KIRIBATI

ECUADOR

SOUTH
AMERICA

AMERICAN
SAMOA

MARQUESAS
ISLANDS

PERU

BRAZIL

WESTERN
SAMOA

COOK
ISLANDS

FRENCH
POLYNESIA

BOLIVIA

TAHITI

TONGA

SOCIETY
ISLANDS

PARAGUAY

CHILE

AUSTRAL
ISLANDS

ARGENTINA

URUGUAY

N

W E

S

FALKLAND/MALVINAS
ISLANDS

ARCTIC OCEAN

ARCTIC OCEAN

Barents Sea

Bering Sea

RUSSIA

ASIA

Sea of Okhotsk

EUROPE

KAZAKHSTAN

MONGOLIA

Black Sea

GEORGIA

Caspian Sea

UZBEKISTAN

KYRGYZSTAN

NORTH KOREA

Sea of Japan

ARMENIA   AZERBAIJAN

TURKEY

TURKMENISTAN

TAJIKISTAN

SOUTH KOREA

JAPAN

PACIFIC OCEAN

Mediterranean Sea

CYPRUS

SYRIA

LEBANON

ISRAEL

IRAQ

IRAN

AFGHANISTAN

CHINA

East China Sea

JORDAN

KUWAIT

LIBYA

EGYPT

QATAR

SAUDI ARABIA

UNITED ARAB EMIRATES

OMAN

PAKISTAN

NEPAL

BHUTAN

INDIA

MYANMAR

TAIWAN

DAITO ISLANDS (Japan)

VOLCANO ISLANDS (Japan)

NORTHERN MARIANA ISLANDS

WAKE ISLAND (US)

AFRICA

NIGER

CHAD

SUDAN

ERITREA

YEMEN

DJIBOUTI

SOCOTRA

Arabian Sea

BANGLADESH

LAOS

THAILAND

VIETNAM

South China Sea

CAMBODIA

PHILIPPINES

PARECE VELA (Japan)

GUAM

YAP

PALAU

MARSHALL ISLANDS

FEDERATED STATES OF MICRONESIA

CENTRAL AFRICAN REPUBLIC

CAMEROON

ETHIOPIA

SOMALIA

SRI LANKA

BRUNEI

MALAYSIA

GABON

CONGO

DEMOCRATIC REPUBLIC OF CONGO

UGANDA

KENYA

RWANDA

BURUNDI

SEYCHELLES

TANZANIA

SINGAPORE

Equator

NAURU

SOLOMON ISLANDS

TUVALU

SOME and CIPE

ANGOLA

MALAWI

COMOROS

INDONESIA

EAST TIMOR

PAPUA NEW GUINEA

NAMIBIA

ZAMBIA

ZIMBABWE

MADAGASCAR

MAURITIUS

INDIAN OCEAN

Coral Sea

VANUATU

FIJI

BOTSWANA

MOZAMBIQUE

SWAZILAND

SOUTH AFRICA

LESOTHO

AUSTRALIA

NEW CALEDONIA

TASMANIA (Australia)

NEW ZEALAND

ATLANTIC OCEAN

NORWAY

FINLAND

SWEDEN

ESTONIA

RUSSIA

IRELAND

North Sea

DENMARK

LATVIA

Baltic Sea

LITHUANIA

UNITED KINGDOM

BELARUS

NETHERLANDS

POLAND

BELGIUM

GERMANY

LUXEMBOURG

CZECH REPUBLIC

UKRAINE

FRANCE

AUSTRIA

SLOVAKIA

SWITZERLAND

SLOVENIA

HUNGARY

MOLDOVA

PORTUGAL

ANDORRA

MONACO

ITALY

CROATIA

SERBIA and MONTENEGRO

ROMANIA

Black Sea

SPAIN

BOSNIA and HERZEGOVINA

BULGARIA

MACEDONIA

TURKEY

ALBANIA

GREECE

Mediterranean Sea

MALTA

ANTARCTICA

TIME ZONES
HUSOS HORARIOS

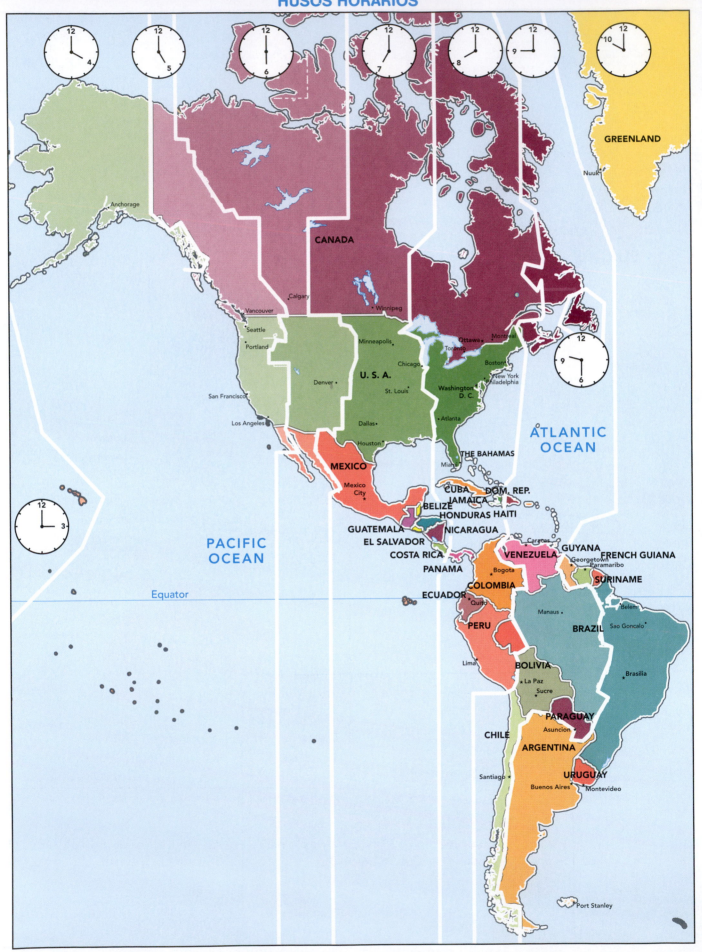

PAÍSES, NACIONALIDADES E IDIOMAS

Country	Nationality	Language
Afghanistan	Afghan	Afghan
Argentina	Argentine	Spanish
Australia	Australian	English
Bolivia	Bolivian	Spanish
Brazil	Brazilian	Portuguese
Bulgaria	Bulgarian	Bulgarian
Cambodia	Cambodian	Cambodian
Canada	Canadian	English/French
Chile	Chilean	Spanish
China	Chinese	Chinese
Colombia	Colombian	Spanish
Costa Rica	Costa Rican	Spanish
Cuba	Cuban	Spanish
(The) Czech Republic	Czech	Czech
Denmark	Danish	Danish
(The) Dominican Republic	Dominican	Spanish
Ecuador	Ecuadorian	Spanish
Egypt	Egyptian	Arabic
El Salvador	Salvadorean	Spanish
England	English	English
Estonia	Estonian	Estonian
Ethiopia	Ethiopian	Amharic
Finland	Finnish	Finnish
France	French	French
Germany	German	German
Greece	Greek	Greek
Guatemala	Guatemalan	Spanish
Haiti	Haitian	Haitian Kreyol
Honduras	Honduran	Spanish
Hungary	Hungarian	Hungarian
India	Indian	Hindi
Indonesia	Indonesian	Indonesian
Israel	Israeli	Hebrew

Country	Nationality	Language
Italy	Italian	Italian
Japan	Japanese	Japanese
Jordan	Jordanian	Arabic
Korea	Korean	Korean
Laos	Laotian	Laotian
Latvia	Latvian	Latvian
Lebanon	Lebanese	Arabic
Lithuania	Lithuanian	Lithuanian
Malaysia	Malaysian	Malay
Mexico	Mexican	Spanish
New Zealand	New Zealander	English
Nicaragua	Nicaraguan	Spanish
Norway	Norwegian	Norwegian
Pakistan	Pakistani	Urdu
Panama	Panamanian	Spanish
Peru	Peruvian	Spanish
(The) Philippines	Filipino	Tagalog
Poland	Polish	Polish
Portugal	Portuguese	Portuguese
Puerto Rico	Puerto Rican	Spanish
Romania	Romanian	Romanian
Russia	Russian	Russian
Saudi Arabia	Saudi	Arabic
Slovakia	Slovak	Slovak
Spain	Spanish	Spanish
Sweden	Swedish	Swedish
Switzerland	Swiss	German/French/Italian
Taiwan	Taiwanese	Chinese
Thailand	Thai	Thai
Turkey	Turkish	Turkish
Ukraine	Ukrainian	Ukrainian
(The) United States	American	English
Venezuela	Venezuelan	Spanish
Vietnam	Vietnamese	Vietnamese

A. Where are you from?
B. I'm from **Mexico**.

A. What's your nationality?
B. I'm **Mexican**.

A. What language do you speak?
B. I speak **Spanish**.

Tell about yourself: Where are you from? What's your nationality? What languages do you speak?

Now interview and tell about a friend.

LISTAS DE VERBOS

Verbos regulares

Los verbos regulares tienen cuatro patrones de deletreo diferentes para el pasado y el participio.

1 Hay que añadir **–ed** al final del verbo. Por ejemplo:

act → act**ed**

act	cook	grill	pass	simmer
add	correct	guard	peel	sort
answer	cough	hand (in)	plant	spell
appear	cover	help	play	sprain
ask	crash	insert	polish	steam
assist	cross (out)	invent	pour	stow
attack	deliver	iron	print	stretch
attend	deposit	kick	reach	surf
bank	design	land	record	swallow
board	discuss	leak	register	talk
boil	dress	learn	relax	turn
box	drill	lengthen	repair	twist
brainstorm	dust	lift	repeat	unload
broil	edit	listen	request	vacuum
brush	end	load	respond	vomit
burn	enter	look	rest	walk
burp	establish	lower	return	wash
carpool	explain	mark	roast	watch
cash	faint	match	rock	wax
check	fasten	mix	saute	weed
clean	fix	mow	scratch	whiten
clear	floss	obey	seat	work
collect	fold	open	select	
comb	follow	paint	shorten	
construct	form	park	sign	

2 Hay que añadir **–d** al verbo que acaba en **–e**. Por ejemplo:

assemble → assemble**d**

assemble	declare	grate	pronounce	shave
bake	describe	hire	prune	slice
balance	dislocate	manage	raise	sneeze
barbecue	dive	measure	rake	state
bathe	dribble	microwave	recite	style
bounce	enforce	move	recycle	supervise
browse	erase	nurse	remove	translate
bruise	examine	operate	revise	type
bubble	exchange	organize	rinse	underline
change	exercise	overdose	save	unscramble
circle	experience	practice	scrape	use
close	file	prepare	serve	vote
combine	gargle	produce	share	wheeze

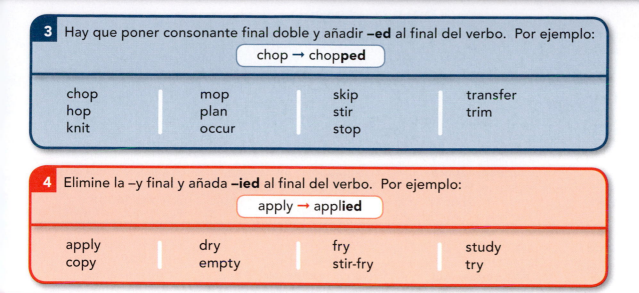

3 Hay que poner consonante final doble y añadir **–ed** al final del verbo. Por ejemplo:

chop → chop**ped**

chop	mop	skip	transfer
hop	plan	stir	trim
knit	occur	stop	

4 Elimine la –y final y añada **–ied** al final del verbo. Por ejemplo:

apply → appl**ied**

| apply | dry | fry | study |
| copy | empty | stir-fry | try |

Verbos irregulares

Los siguientes verbos tienen tiempo pasado y/o participio irregular.

be	was/were	been		know	knew	known
beat	beat	beaten		leave	left	left
become	became	become		let	let	let
bend	bent	bent		make	made	made
begin	began	begun		meet	met	met
bleed	bled	bled		pay	paid	paid
break	broke	broken		put	put	put
bring	brought	brought		read	read	read
build	built	built		rewrite	rewrote	rewritten
buy	bought	bought		run	ran	run
catch	caught	caught		ring	rang	rung
choose	chose	chosen		say	said	said
come	came	come		see	saw	seen
cut	cut	cut		sell	sold	sold
do	did	done		set	set	set
draw	drew	drawn		shoot	shot	shot
drink	drank	drunk		sing	sang	sung
drive	drove	driven		sit	sat	sat
eat	ate	eaten		sleep	slept	slept
fall	fell	fallen		speak	spoke	spoken
feed	fed	fed		stand	stood	stood
fly	flew	flown		sweep	swept	swept
get	got	gotten		swim	swam	swum
give	gave	given		swing	swung	swung
go	went	gone		take	took	taken
grow	grew	grown		teach	taught	taught
hang	hung	hung		throw	threw	thrown
have	had	had		understand	understood	understood
hit	hit	hit		withdraw	withdrew	withdrawn
hold	held	held		write	wrote	written
hurt	hurt	hurt				

GLOSARIO (ESPAÑOL)

El número en negrillas indica la(s) página(s) en donde aparece la palabra. El número que sigue indica la ubicación de la palabra en la ilustración y en la lista de palabras en la página. Por ejemplo, "address **1**-5" indica que la palabra "address" está en la página 1 y es el artículo número 5.

a (entrar) **129**-11
a (la autopista) **129**-13
a la derecha de **8**-9
a la izquierda de **8**-8
a través de **129**-3
a.m. (de la mañana) **16**
abadejo **50**-24
abajo **8**-2
abajo (hacia) **129**-6
abarrotería **37**-28
abdomen **86**-25
abdominales **146**-25
abedul **156**-17
abeja **30**-11d, **154**-36
abierto(a) **45**-57
abogado(a) **114**-2, **165**-7
abogado(a)
   defensor(a) **165**-15
abono **35**-9
abordar el avión **132**-H
abrebotellas **59**-3
abrelatas **59**-2
abrelatas eléctrico **24**-18
abreviaturas en
   los anuncios de
   empleo **118**
abrigo **67**-1,2
abrigo de invierno **67**-25
abrigo de plumas de
   ganso/acolchonado
   67-23
abrigo de punto **67**-6
abrigo para esquiar **67**-20
abrigo tejido **67**-6
abril **18**-16
abrir **31**-19
abrir el libro **6**-11
abrir una cuenta **80**-E
abrocharse el cinturón de
   seguridad **132**-K
absuelto(a) **165**-F
abuela **2**-10
abuelo(s) **2**, **2**-11
aburrido(a) (estar) **47**-28
acampar **139**-A
accesorios para la
   aspiradora **32**-6
accidente (de tránsito/
   tráfico) **85**-1
acción (películas de)
   149-24
acebo **156**-24
acebo (árbol) **156**-12
aceite **53**-25, **126**-46
aceite de oliva **53**-26
aceite para cocinar **53**-25
aceite tres en uno **33**-15
aceitunas **53**-19
acelerador **127**-73
acera **40**-13

acetona **99**-32
acomodar las letras de la
   palabra **7**-58
acomodar las palabras
   7-59
acondicionador **98**-10
acordeón **150**-26
acostarse **9**-13
acotamiento de la
   carretera **128**-16
actividades al aire
   libre **139**
actividades
   extracurriculares **104**
actividades manuales **134**
actor **112**-2, **147**-2,16
actriz **112**-3, **147**-3,15
actuar **116**-1
acuarela **134**-14b
acuario **136**-14
acupuntor(a) **96**-15
acupuntura (recibir
   tratamiento de) **94**-8
acupunturista **96**-15
acusado(a) **165**-9
adaptador **77**-13
aderezo para ensaladas
   53-29, **60**-27
adjetivo **107**-5
administración **102**-A
administrador(a) **114**-5
administrar **116**-16
adolescente **42**-6
aduana **131**-22
adulto **42**-7
adverbio **107**-7
aerograma **82**-3
aeromozo(a) **132**-5
aeropuerto **131**
aerosol para matar
   insectos **33**-18
afanador(a) **102**-11,
   112-20
afección del corazón
   91-22
afeitando (*me estoy*) **99**-L
afeitar (maquinilla de)
   99-21
afeitarse **9**-4
afeitarse (crema para)
   99-20
afilado(a) **45**-67
afueras **20**-14
agalla **155**-1b
agarrador de ollas **24**-22
agarrador **27**-22
agarrar **146**-4
agencia de carros **36**-7
agencia de viajes **39**-27
agenda **120**-6

agenda personal **120**-12
agenda rotatoria **120**-4
agente de ventas por
   teléfono **115**-31
agente de viajes **115**-33
agosto **18**-20
agotado(a) **89**-32
agotado(a) (estar) **46**-3
agradecimiento (una nota
   de) **118**-L
agricultor(a) **113**-27,
   151-2
agua **45**, **62**-B, **158**-11
agua (cuenta del) **81**-12
agua embotellada **51**-25
agua nieve (caer) **14**-13
agua oxigenada **90**-6
aguacate **48**-14
aguamala **155**-14
aguarrás **33**-22
aguaviva **155**-14
agudo (ángulo) **106**-20a
águila **154**-10
aguja **92**-4
aguja (de coser) **134**-5
aguja de gancho **134**-10
aguja de tejer **134**-8
agujetas (de zapatos)
   99-49
ahorrar agua **158**-11
ahorrar energía **158**-10
aire **126**-48
aire acondicionado
   28-28, **31**-21, **127**-67
ajedrez **135**-35
ajedrez (club de) **104**-16
ajo **49**-15
ajos (triturador/
   machacador de) **59**-16
al (autobús, subir) **129**-9
ala **154**-2a
alacena **22**-11
alacrán **154**-39
alambre **34**-24, **122**-26
alargar **72**-22
alarma (luz de) **127**-57
alarma (señal de) **127**-57
alarma contra
   incendios **29**-39, **40**-8
alas de pollo/gallina
   50-18
albañil **112**-10
albaricoque **48**-7
alberca **28**-25, **84**-14,
   133-16
alberca infantil inflable
   79-38
albergue para
   desamparados **20**-9
albornoz **68**-4

álbum para estampillas/
   sellos/timbres **135**-25
alcachofa **49**-27
alcalde **84**-9
alcaldía **40**-7, **84**-D
alcantarilla **40**-10
alcantarilla (boca de la)
   41-38
alcanzar **146**-18
alce **152**-1
alcohol **93**-10
alérgica (reacción) **91**-7
alergista **96**-5
alergólogo(a) **96**-5
aleta(s) **145**-16, **155**-1a
alfalfa **151**-31
alfarería (hacer) **134**-J
alfiler **134**-2
alfiler de gancho **100**-9,
   134-7
alfiler de seguridad
   100-9, **134**-7
alfiletero **134**-3
alfombra **21**-23, **23**-12
alfombra de baño **26**-35
alfombrilla **21**-23
alfombrilla de baño
   26-35
alfombrilla de goma
   26-32
álgebra **105**
algodón **71**-17, **151**-33
alguacil **165**-17
alhajero **23**-21
alicates **34**-16
aliño para ensaladas
   53-29, **60**-27
alisadora de pelo/
   cabello **98**-14
alisar con la plancha **10**-4
alitas de pollo/gallina
   50-18, **64**-4
almacén **37**-18, **121**-11
almacén de música **38**-13
almacén de ropa de
   maternidad **38**-10
almacenaje (estante/
   armario de) **119**-25
almádena **122**-1
almejas **50**-32
almidón en aerosol **73**-20
almocafre **35**-20
almohada **23**-3
almohadilla de tinta
   120-28
almohadilla eléctrica
   94-9
almohadilla estéril **90**-5

erupción volcánica **159**-14

es igual a **105**

esbelto(a) **42**-19

escalar rocas **139**-C

escalera **29**-33, **122**-7

escalera (de mano) **33**-7

escalera automática **74**-4

escalera de emergencia **28**-19, **29**-38

escalera eléctrica **74**-4

escalera mecánica **74**-4

escalinatas **27**-4

escalofrío **88**-21

escalones **31**-18

escalonia **49**-37

escamas **155**-1c

escandaloso(a) **44**-45

escáner **78**-17

escape de gas **85**-14

escarabajo **154**-38

escarda **35**-20

escardilla(o) **35**-20

escayola **93**-19

esclavitud **162**-8

escoba **32**-1

escobilla **32**-3

escojan la respuesta correcta **7**-51

escorpión **154**-39

escribir **117**-36

escribir en la pizarra/el pizarrón/el tablero **6**-8

escribir en una hoja aparte **7**-60

escribir la copia final **107**-21

escribir su nombre **6**-4

escribir un borrador **107**-18

escribir un cheque **81**-17

escribir una carta **11**-15, **119**-f

escribir una nota de agradecimiento **118**-L

escritorio **4**-4, **120**-1

escritorio de la maestra/ del maestro **4**-18

escritorio del/de la conserje **133**-11

escuchar el/la radio **11**-2

escuchar la pregunta **6**-18

escuchar la respuesta **6**-20

escuchar música **11**-2

escucharle el corazón **92**-G

escuela **39**-21

escuela (ir a la/al) **10**-10

escuela de artes y oficios **101**-6

escuela de postgrado/ posgrado **101**-10

escuela para adultos **101**-5

escuela primaria **101**-2

escuela vocacional **101**-6

escurridor **26**-33

escurridor de platos **24**-16

esfera **106**-25

esmalte de uñas **99**-31

esmoquin **66**-27

esnórquel **145**-15

esófago **87**-54

espacio **7**-53

espacio para estacionarse **28**-24

espada **135**-34d

espaguetis **53**-6

espaguetis con albóndigas **64**-16

espalda **86**-27

español **103**-12

espantapájaros **151**-4

esparadrapo **90**-9, **93**-13

espárrago **49**-7

espátula **34**-12, **59**-13

especialista **94**-7

especialista (médico) **96**-8

especialista (ver a un) **94**-7

especialista en dietética **97**-13

especias **53**, **53**-22

especiero **24**-17

espejo **23**-20, **26**-9

espejo lateral **126**-11

espejo retrovisor **127**-51

espejo retrovisor exterior **126**-11

espina **157**-38

espina dorsal **87**-72

espinaca **49**-5

espinilla **86**-37

espinillera **143**-27

esponja **26**-34, **32**-21

esposa **2**-2

esposas **165**-3

esposo **2**-1

esquí acuático **145**-K

esquí alpino (practicar) **144**-A

esquí de campo traviesa (practicar) **144**-B

esquí de fondo (practicar) **144**-B

esquiar **144**-A

esquina **128**-28

esquinera **21**-26

esquís **144**-1

esquís acuáticos **145**-23

esquís de campo traviesa **144**-5

esquís de fondo **144**-5

establo **151**-8

estacas **139**-3

estación de autobuses **124**-7

estación de bomberos **41**-31, **84**-B

estación de computadora **119**-20

estación de enfermeros(as) **97**-B

estación de gasolina **37**-27

estación de policía **40**-11, **84**-A

estación de trabajo **121**-6

estación de trenes **39**-26

estación del metro **40**-21, **124**-19

estación del tren **124**-11

estación espacial **111**-29

estacionamiento **27**-14, **28**-23, **40**-16

estacionamiento con techo **28**-20

estacionamiento de niveles **41**-30

estacionamiento para discapacitados(as) **130**-16

estacionarse paralelo(a) a la acera **130**-24

estaciones **19**

estacionómetro **40**-18

estadística **105**

estado **1**-10

estado de cuenta mensual **81**-21

Estados Unidos **163**

estambre para tejer **134**-9

estampado(a) **71**-29

estampas **79**-24

estampilla(s) **82**-10,11,12,13,23

estanque **109**-10

estanque para patos **137**-2

estante(s) **24**-5, **83**-7, **119**-25

estante de almacenaje **119**-25

estante de artículos de oficina **119**-24

estante para libros **4**-17, **21**-1

estatura **42**

estatura mediana **42**-15

estatura promedio **42**-15

este **130**-20

estenógrafo(a) **165**-14

estera **141**-38,48

estera de goma **26**-32

estéreo **21**-17

estetoscopio **92**-8

estibador(a) **113**-24

estirarse **146**-11

estómago **87**-59

estornudo **89**-34

estrecho(a) **44**-22,30, **72**-3

estrella **111**-2

estrella de mar **155**-23

estrella fugaz **111**-9,10

estribos **140**-16

estuche de la cámara **77**-22

estudiante **4**-3

estudiantes (asociación de) **104**-7

estudiar **10**-8

estudiar la página diez **6**-13

estufa **30**-9

estufa (para cocinar) **24**-24

estupefacto(a) (estar) **47**-22

etiqueta **75**-2

etiqueta con el precio **75**-3

etiqueta de factura del equipaje **131**-21

etiqueta postal **120**-24

evidencia **165**-16

examen de ciudadanía **166**-10

exámenes **7**-47,50

exámenes médicos **94**-16

examinarle los dientes **93**-E

examinarle los ojos, oídos, nariz y garganta **92**-F

excelente **118**-13

exclamación (signo de) **107**-10

exclamativo **107**-D

excursión (ir de) **139**-B

excusado **26**-26, **30**-4

exonerado(a) **165**-F

expendedor(a) de pasajes **131**-3

experiencia **118**-11

experiencia laboral **118**-I

explica las leyes **161**-12

exploración espacial **111**

explosión **85**-3

exposición **136**-20

expresión **162**-4

expreso **82**-7

extensión (alargador) **33**-5

extinguidor de incendios **123**-23

extintor de aspersión contra incendios **29**-40

extintor de incendios **123**-23

extra grande **71**-37

extra pequeño(a) **71**-33

garrapata **154**-30
gas (cuenta del) **81**-10
gas (natural) **158**-2
gasa **90**-8, **93**-12
gaseosa **51**-23, **60**-17
gases (tener) **89**-30
gasolina **126**-45
gasolinera **37**-27
gastroenterólogo(a) **96**-13
gatito **152**-35
gato **10**-6, **152**-34
gato (de vehículo) **126**-26
gaveta **73**-24
gavetera **127**-70
gavetero **23**-13, **25**-3
gaviota **154**-5
gel para el pelo/ cabello **98**-16
gelatina **64**-27
gemelos **70**-13
geografía **103**-4, 109
geometría **105**
geométricas (formas) **106**
geranio **157**-55
gerente **55**-21, **114**-5, **119**-23
geriatra **96**-4
gibón **153**-50
gimnasia **141**-Q
gimnasio **38**-3, **84**-11, **102**-H, **133**-17
ginecólogo(a) **96**-2, **97**-19
giradiscos **76**-21
girasol **157**-52
giro **82**-14
giro postal/telegráfico **81**-4, **82**-14
gis **5**-32
globo del mundo **4**-16
globo terráqueo **4**-16
gobierno **103**-5, **166**-9
gobierno de los Estados Unidos **161**
gofres **61**-10
gogles **145**-12
golf **141**-M
golf (bola de) **141**-30
golf (palos de) **141**-29
golf (pelota de) **141**-30
Golfo Pérsico (Guerra del) **163**
goma **120**-13,30
goma (de llanta) **126**-6
goma (neumático) **126**-6
goma de borrar **5**-22
goma de masticar **55**-9
goma de pegar **33**-16
goma para armar modelos **135**-30
goma sintética **120**-31
gordo(a) **42**-17, **44**-13
gorila **153**-61

gorra **67**-8
gorra de baño **145**-13
gorra de béisbol **67**-10
gorra de esquiar **67**-19
gorra(o) de baño **98**-8
gorrión **154**-14
gorro de esquiar **67**-19
gospel **148**-7
gotas para los ojos **95**-10
gotear **30**-1
gotera **27**-26, **30**-5
gotero **110**-15
GPS (Sistema de Posición Global, aparato de) **139**-14
grabadora de cintas magnetofónicas **76**-17
gradas **102**-Ia
gradería **102**-Ia
grama **35**-A
Gran Depresión **163**
grande **44**-9, **71**-36, **72**-5
granero **151**-7
granizar **14**-12
granja **20**-10
granjero(a) **113**-27, **151**-2
grapa **120**-15
grapadora **120**-2
grifo **24**-11, **26**-7
grifo (cabello/pelo) **43**-29
grillo **154**-37,41
gripe **91**-12
gris **43**-34, **65**-16
grúa **122**-15
grúa (camión) **125**-13
grúa (con plataforma movible) **122**-16
grueso(a) **44**-23, **72**-11
grulla **154**-18
grupo **7**-38
guagua **41**-33, **124**-A
guajolote **50**-20, **52**-20, **151**-11
guante (de béisbol) **143**-6
guante de hockey **143**-19
guante de receptor **143**-7
guante de sófbol **143**-9
guantera **127**-70
guantes **67**-21, **93**-23
guantes de boxeo **141**-45
guantes de jardín **33**-17
guantes de látex **123**-11
guantes enteros **67**-24
guapo(a) **45**-53
guardabarros **126**-5
guardafango **126**-5
guardapolvo **66**-19
guardar cama **94**-1
guardar el libro **6**-15
guardar la ropa (limpia) **73**-I
guardar su equipaje de mano **132**-I

guardería infantil **36**-9, **84**-18,G, **100**-19
guardería infantil (auxiliar de) **112**-17
guardia **165**-24
guardia de seguridad **80**-11, **102**-7, **115**-23, **131**-8
guarnición **64**
güero **43**-32
guerra (películas de) **149**-25
Guerra Civil **163**
Guerra de Corea **163**
Guerra de Independencia **163**
Guerra de Vietnam **163**
Guerra del Golfo Pérsico **163**
Guerra Mundial (Primera) **163**
Guerra Mundial (Segunda) **163**
guía **74**-1, **135**-33
guía (volante) **127**-59
guillotina **119**-16
guineo **48**-4
güira(o) **49**-14
guisante **49**-16
guisar **58**-20
guitarra **11**-9
guitarra (acústica) **150**-5
guitarra eléctrica **150**-6

haba **49**-18
habichuelas coloradas **49**-20
habichuelas tiernas **49**-17
habilidades **118**-H
habitación **45**, **133**-24
hablar **117**-27
hablar sobre su experiencia laboral **118**-I
hablar sobre sus aptitudes y habilidades **118**-H
hace cumplir las leyes **161**-7
hace las leyes **161**-1
hacendado(a) **113**-27
hacer **116**-5
hacer banca en línea **81**-18
hacer ejercicio **11**-11, **94**-5
hacer el almuerzo **9**-16
hacer el balance de las cuentas **81**-16
hacer el desayuno **9**-15
hacer gárgaras **94**-3
hacer inventario **117**-30
hacer la cama **9**-10
hacer la cena **9**-17
hacer su depósito **81**-25

hacer su tarea **6**-21
hacer sus deberes **6**-21
hacer un cheque **81**-17
hacer un depósito **80**-A
hacer un retiro **80**-B
hacer una pregunta **6**-17
hacer una presentación **119**-b
hacerle algunas preguntas sobre su salud **92**-E
hacha **34**-3, **139**-5
hacia abajo **129**-6
hacia arriba **129**-5
hacienda **20**-10
halcón **154**-9
Halloween **164**-6
hambre (tener) **46**-7
hamburguesa **60**-1
hamburguesa con queso **60**-2
hámster **152**-38
Hanuka **164**-12
hardware (de computadora) **78**
harina **53**-35
harina preparada para bizcocho **53**-37
harto(a) (estar) **47**-19
hatchback **125**-2
hebilla de cabello **70**-12
hebilla para el pelo/ cabello **98**-18
Heimlich (la maniobra de) **90**-17
helada (caer una) **14**-13
heladería **38**-6
helado **52**-18, **60**-14, **64**-26
helado de yogur **60**-15
helar **14**-26
helecho **156**-27
hemorragia nasal **88**-16
heno **151**-5
herido(a) **91**-1, **93**-B
hermana **2**-8, **45**
hermano **2**-9
hermanos(as) **2**
herramientas (caja de) **34**-17
hervidor **24**-23
hervir **58**-16
hibisco **157**-59
hidrante **40**-5
hiedra venenosa **156**-31
hielera **138**-21
hielo (bolsa de) **93**-16
hielo (máquina de hacer) **133**-19
hielo (pista de) **142**-10
hiena **153**-54
hígado **50**-9, **87**-57
higiene **103**-10
higienista dental **93**-21
higo **48**-12

El número en negrillas indica la(s) página(s) en donde aparece la palabra. El número que sigue indica la ubicación de la palabra en la ilustración y en la lista de palabras en la página. Por ejemplo, "address 1-5" indica que la palabra "address" está en la página 1 y es el artículo número 5.

NÚMEROS, DÍAS DE LA SEMANA, MESES DEL AÑO

Cardinal Numbers

1	one
2	two
3	three
4	four
5	five
6	six
7	seven
8	eight
9	nine
10	ten
11	eleven
12	twelve
13	thirteen
14	fourteen
15	fifteen
16	sixteen
17	seventeen
18	eighteen
19	nineteen
20	twenty
21	twenty-one
22	twenty-two
30	thirty
40	forty
50	fifty
60	sixty
70	seventy
80	eighty
90	ninety
100	one hundred
101	one hundred (and) one
102	one hundred (and) two
1,000	one thousand
10,000	ten thousand
100,000	one hundred thousand
1,000,000	one million
1,000,000,000	one billion

Ordinal Numbers

1st	first
2nd	second
3rd	third
4th	fourth
5th	fifth
6th	sixth
7th	seventh
8th	eighth
9th	ninth
10th	tenth
11th	eleventh
12th	twelfth
13th	thirteenth
14th	fourteenth
15th	fifteenth
16th	sixteenth
17th	seventeenth
18th	eighteenth
19th	nineteenth
20th	twentieth
21st	twenty-first
22nd	twenty-second
30th	thirtieth
40th	fortieth
50th	fiftieth
60th	sixtieth
70th	seventieth
80th	eightieth
90th	ninetieth
100th	one hundredth
101st	one hundred (and) first
102nd	one hundred (and) second
1,000th	one thousandth
10,000th	ten thousandth
100,000th	one hundred thousandth
1,000,000th	one millionth
1,000,000,000th	one billionth

Days of the Week

Sunday
Monday
Tuesday
Wednesday
Thursday
Friday
Saturday

Months of the Year

January	July
February	August
March	September
April	October
May	November
June	December